UNEXPLAINED FACTS

The Olde, Old, very Olde Man or Thomas Par, the
Sonne of Iohn Parr of Winnington in the Parish of Alberbury:
In the County of Shropshire who was Borne in 1483 in
The Raigne of King Edward the 4ᵗʰ and is now liuing in
The Strand, being aged 152 yeares and odd Monethes 1635
He dyed Nouember the 15ᵗʰ And is now buryed in Westminster 1635

THOMAS PARR

NOTE.—This is reproduced from a copper-plate engraving published, as a broadside, two days before Parr's death. It will be noticed that the engraver has
added the date of this subsequently

UNEXPLAINED FACTS
Enigmas and Curiosities

By RUPERT T. GOULD

Originally entitled *Enigmas: Another Book of Unexplained Facts*

BELL PUBLISHING COMPANY
NEW YORK

Library of Congress Catalog Card Number: 79-28078
This edition is published by Bell Publishing Company,
a division of Crown Publishers, Inc.,
by arrangement with University Books, Inc.
  b c d e f g h
BELL 1980 EDITION

Manufactured in the United States of America

Library of Congress Cataloging in Publication Data

Gould, Rupert Thomas, 1890-1948.
    Unexplained facts.
    Reprint of the 1965 printing of the 2d ed. published
by University Books, New Hyde Park, N. Y., under title:
Enigmas.
    Includes bibliographical references and index.
    1. Curiosities and wonders. I. Title.
[AG243.G64 1980]   031'.02   79-28078
ISBN 0-517-31081-3

PREFACE

TO THE READER, PLEADING EXTENUATING CIRCUMSTANCES

I do not think that I can explain the intention of this book more clearly than by quoting from the Preface to its predecessor, *Oddities:*

"The essays contained in this book, although apparently disconnected, were written at one time and with one object — to collect and digest the facts relating to a number of incidents which have not, at present, been satisfactorily explained.

"In order to present these facts as clearly as possible, I have quoted rather extensively from the original sources. As most of these are not very accessible, I hope that I may be spared the reproach that the book has mainly been put together with scissors and paste."

This book differs slightly from *Oddities* in scope, but the method pursued has been the same: to present the facts, wherever possible, in the form of quotations from the original sources, and to supply enough references to enable any one who will to go into them more deeply.

With one exception, the present essays have not previously been published. "The Landfall of Columbus" was read before the Royal Geographical Society in February 1927, and appeared in the *Geographical Journal* for the following May. I have to thank the Council of the Royal Geographical Society for permission to reprint it here. I should like also to express my thanks to the authorities of the Royal Society, the Royal Astronomical Society, and the Admiralty Library for much information freely placed at my disposal; and to many friends and correspondents, particularly Mr. E. Heron Allen, F.R.S., the Rev. T.E.R. Philllips, and Mr. R. Humphrey Eggar.

RUPERT T. GOULD

ASHTEAD, 1929

PREFACE
TO SECOND EDITION

In revising this book for re-issue I have done my best to incorporate — either as text, footnote, or postscript — the bulk of the information which, in consequence of much correspondence and a certain amount of research, has come my way since the book was first published sixteen years ago.

I have omitted, as of insufficient general interest, two of the geographical essays — "The Strait of Anian" and "New South Greenland" — replacing them by "The *Victoria* Tragedy" and "Abraham Thornton offers Battle". Neither of these has been published before: though the latter embodies the substance of a talk which I gave to the Sette of Odd Volumes on May 26, 1936 — the 119th anniversary of the dance which led to Mary Ashford's tragic death.

A third essay, "The Landfall of Columbus", has been extensively recast, my views having been modified in consequence of a re-examination of the subject, stimulated by the work of the late Mr. L. R. Crawshay. In making this, I was greatly helped by information received from Sir Harold Spencer Jones, F.R.S. (H.M. Astronomer Royal) and from Mr. G. R. Hayes.

My grateful thanks are also owing to all those correspondents, known or unknown, whose collaboration has lightened the work of revision.

My acknowledgments are due to the Controller, H.M. Stationery Office, for the quotations from the Command Paper relating to the loss of the *Victoria*.

RUPERT T. GOULD

BARFORD ST. MARTIN, 1945

CONTENTS

ILLUSTRATIONS

PLATES

FIGURES

UNEXPLAINED FACTS

THERE WERE GIANTS
IN THOSE DAYS

In the year 1577 a skeleton of enormous size was discovered at Willisau, in the canton of Lucerne, Switzerland. The local authorities, undecided as to the nature of the remains, which were incomplete, and doubtful whether (as in the famous case of the Peruvian mummy left unclaimed in the parcels-office of a London station*) they ought not to hold an inquest and/or give them Christian burial, consulted the famous Dr. Felix Plater, of Basle, the most expert anatomist (strange though it may seem) of his day. Plater gave it as his opinion that the bones were undoubtedly human, and forwarded to Lucerne an anatomical drawing of their original owner, who must (according to this) have stood some nineteen feet high.† The "Giant of Lucerne" lay in state at the town hall of Lucerne until, in an evil hour, he was visited by a still more competent anatomist than Plater—one J. F. Blumenbach (1752–1840), of Göttingen, a savant possessed in full or even brimming measure of that irritating turn of mind which takes nothing for granted. One glance at the bones was enough for him—but it was no easy matter to convince the good citizens of Lucerne, who had adopted the Giant as one of the supporters of their city arms, that he was only a mammoth.

Giants of this kind had a habit of turning up, during the Middle Ages and even later, in all parts of Europe. For example, in 1613 the learned world was astounded to hear of a giant found by some workmen in a sandpit near the castle of Chaumont, not far from St. Antoine. At a depth of 18 feet they discovered a brick tomb 30 feet long, 12 feet wide, and 8 feet high. In this lay an entire human skeleton, over 25 feet in length, 10 feet across the shoulders,‡ and 5 feet deep from the breast to the back. Further-

---

* This inquest was actually held, and the very reasonable verdict returned that the deceased had come by his death so long ago that the cause of it could not be ascertained. As the law then stood (it has since been altered), the holding of an inquest, even in such ridiculous circumstances, was imperative.

† See Fig. 1.

‡ This, in itself, was suspicious. The breadth of the shoulders in man is generally not much more than a quarter of the height.

more, an inscription in Gothic characters on the lid of the tomb read
"Teutobochtus Rex", and demonstrated, in conjunction with medals,
coins, etc., found near by, that the body was that of Teutobochtus, the
giant king of the Cimbri, who was defeated and captured by Marius near
Aix, in Provence; and whose head, as he walked behind his conqueror's

FIG. 1 —The Giant of Lucerne. Re-drawn from an engraving in J. L.
Cysat's *Beschreibung dess berühmbten Lucerner* . . . (Lucerne, 1661)

NOTE —The engraving represents a painting by Johann Bock (after a
drawing by Felix Plater) presented to the Senate of Lucerne in July,
1584

triumphal car, is recorded by Florus* to have overtopped the trophies carried on the Roman spears (as well it might). The details of this truly
amazing find were vouched for by one Dr. Mazurier,† a surgeon, who
shortly afterwards issued a pamphlet about them—the first shot of a long
battle.

The genuineness of Mazurier's account was violently attacked;
notably by one Jean Riolan, a celebrated naturalist of the period, in two
tracts with the snappy little titles of *Gigantomachia* and *Gigantologie*. In all,
over a dozen pamphlets were hurled to and fro. Finally, it was made clear
that Mazurier had bought from the workmen various enormous bones
which they had found in the pit, and had supplied the rest of the details
himself. Teutobochtus, restored to his original configuration—that of a
mastodon—is now in the Musée de Paléontologie, Paris.

* In his *Epitome de Gestis Romanorum*.

† He seems to have used the pseudonym "Nicholas Habicot". Can Voltaire have
confused him with his ". . . *coquin d'Habacuc, capable de tout*"?

In the time of James I, certain "big, outlandish bones" were discovered at Gloucester, and Lord Herbert of Cherbury was appointed to find out what he could about them. He was assisted (or, perhaps, impeded) by several pundits, some of whom advised the re-interment of the bones with Christian rites; while others, including the great William Harvey, declared them to belong to "some exceeding great beast, as an elephant". One of them, Bishop Hakewell, remarks:

"His Lordship showed me some bones, which he had collected; which were a huckle-bone,* part of the shoulder-blade, some parts of a tooth, and the bridge of a nose—all of a huge bigness. . . . The bridge of the nose was what confirmed his lordship's and my opinion, that it could not be that of a man, for it did seem to be a bone very apt to bear up the long snout of an elephant. One of the teeth of this pretended giant, by the special favour of my lord of Gloucester, was examined by me. I found it to be a stony substance, both for hardness and weight; and it should seem, by his lordship's letter to me, that he himself was not confident that it was the tooth of a man."

As Greenwood† has pointed out, in those days simple arithmetic seems to have been as unknown a science as comparative anatomy. The tooth in question, if that of an elephant (which, no doubt, it was) would have weighed some ten pounds. Human teeth scale about 160 to the pound; and in the same proportion the owner of the tooth, if he were human, would have weighed about a hundred tons.

But, while such blunders seem almost incredible to-day, there are two potent factors to be borne in mind. Until the very end of the eighteenth century it was generally believed that the fauna of a given locality must have persisted, unchanged, since the Creation; and when, for example, Cuvier first announced the discovery of elephant, hippopotamus, and rhinoceros remains in the upper European strata, he was gravely informed that these must belong to the elephants brought from India by Pyrrhus.

And, secondly, a general belief in the existence of various giant races of men seems to be almost as old as humanity. The mythologies of all races and all creeds are full of giants—their existence is one of the most widely spread of all beliefs. To our forefathers, it was an immeasurably more natural thing to discover the bones of a giant than those of an elephant. Sometimes, indeed, one comes across a reputed giant who could scarcely have been an elephant—witness the following:

* I.e. hip-bone.
† Wild Sports of the World, J. Greenwood, London, 1862.

"A True Report of Hugh Hodson, of Thorneway, in Cumberland, to
Sʳ. Robert Cewell, of a gyant found at S. Bees, in Cumb'land.

"The said gyant was buried 4 yards deep in the ground, wᶜʰ is now a
corn feild (sic). He was 4 yards and a half long, and was in complete
armour: his sword and battle-axe lying by him. His sword was two spans
broad, and more than 2 yards long. The head of his battle-axe a yard long,
and the shaft of it all of iron, as thick as man's thigh, and more than 2
yards long.

"His teeth were 6 inches long, and 2 inches broad; his forehead was
more than 2 spans and a half broad. His chine bone could contain 3 pecks
of oatmeale. His armour, sword, and battle-axe are at Mr. Sand's, of
Redington, and at Mr. Wyber's, at St. Bees."*

It would have simplified matters if only the bones, or only the armour,
had been found. The bones would naturally have been those of an elephant, while it was not unknown for chiefs in bygone days to have some
of their personal property made of exaggerated size, so as to give a false
idea of their strength and stature.† As this "True Report" stands, one can
only conclude that Hugh Hodson, of Thorneway, in Cumberland, had
the makings of a very expert witness.

The Patagonian Giants

But the mediæval believers in a giant race were not satisfied by merely
finding relics of it, however large. They argued that such a race must still
exist; and it so happened that while Magellan was showing the way round
the world he incidentally provided the credulous with a legend—that of
the gigantic natives of Patagonia—which exercised men's minds for fully
three centuries. These may be divided, roughly, into a century of
credulity, a century of incredulity, and a century during which it
became apparent that the story of the Patagonian giants had a real, if
slender, basis of truth. Here is a short outline of the events of these three
periods.

The First Period

The discovery of Patagonia‡ is due to Magellan, who coasted its

---

* Quoted from Jefferson's *History and Antiquities of Allerdale above Derwent*, and
stated to be taken from the Machel MSS. (Carlisle), vol. vi.

† Plutarch records this of Alexander the Great.

‡ Patagonia, as the geographical name of a region, covers all land between the Rio
Negro (in approximately 39° S.) and Magellan Strait; and hence includes the southern
portions of Argentina and Chile. The region supposed to be inhabited by giants was in
the near vicinity of the Strait.

PLATE II

COMMODORE BYRON AND THE GIANTS

From Hawkesworth's "Voyages of Byron, Wallis, Carteret, and Cook"

Facing page 16

eastern shores, and passed through Magellan Strait, which divides it from
Tierra del Fuego, in 1520.*

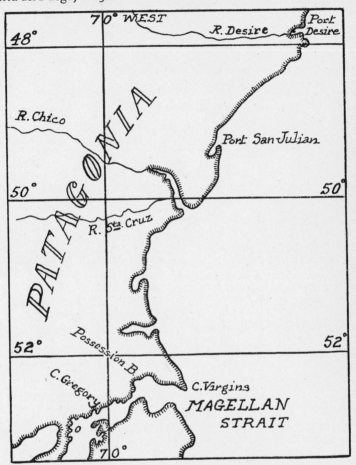

FIG. 2 —Sketch-map, showing various localities in which the "Patagonian
Giants" have been encountered

While Magellan's fleet was lying in Port San Julian† in June 1520, a
gigantic native appeared on the beach near the ships. "This man", says
Pigafetta, a companion of Magellan, "was so tall that our heads scarcely

* Here, and later, I have generally used the epitomes of the early voyages compiled
by such writers as Hawkesworth and Burney.

† 49¼°S., 68°W.—on the Argentine coast. It was here that Magellan strangled
Quesada, one of his mutinous captains; and here also that Drake beheaded Thomas
Doughty. See Fig. 2.

came up to his waist, and his voice was like that of a bull." He was well treated, and other natives soon appeared, of whom Herrera,* less hyperbolic than Pigafetta, remarks only that the smallest of them was taller and bulkier than any of the Spaniards.† Magellan gave them the name of "Patagones" ("Pata" being Spanish for "hoof"), from the guanaco-skin moccasins which they wore. By a stratagem he managed to put two of them in irons,‡ intending to take them to Europe. Both died before crossing the Line. Pigafetta managed to compile a short glossary of their principal words, in which it is interesting to find the name "Setebos" used (as, later, in *The Tempest*) for their principal deity.

Drake, who anchored in Port San Julian in June 1578, also saw "men of large stature", and had an affray with them, losing two of his crew. They are described as standing a little under 7 feet 6 inches.

Pedro Sarmiento, in February 1580, saw "people of large stature" in Magellan Strait, but their height is not stated; while Tomé Hernandez, who had spent about a year in the Strait in 1584, could say nothing about the stature of the natives, except that they were "very corpulent". As he nearly died of starvation there, he probably felt strongly on the subject.

Anthony Knyvet, who accompanied Cavendish in his disastrous second voyage and traversed the Strait in April 1592, speaks§ of having seen Patagonians 14 to 16 spans (i.e. 10½ to 12 feet) in height; and also of having measured several dead bodies of the same size at Port Desire.

Sebald de Weert, who visited the Strait in 1598, speaks of the natives as being 10 or 11 feet high; and Joris Spilbergen, on April 3, 1615, saw "a man of extraordinary tall stature" watching his ships from the south side of the eastern entrance. On an island near by his men found the dead bodies of two natives, half-buried. One was of ordinary stature, but the other 2½ feet taller.

Jacob Le Maire and Wilhelm Schouten are said, but on doubtful authority, to have found skeletons 10 or 11 feet long at Port Desire in December 1615. Aris Clatz, Le Maire's "Commissary" (supercargo), is supposed to have made the discovery, but it is not mentioned in the earliest account of the voyage.||

* Official historian of the Spanish voyages to the New World. He did not take part in any.

† According to Max. Transylvanus, the tallest Patagonian seen stood 7 feet 6 inches.

‡ Two others were, with difficulty, overpowered by nine of the Spaniards and bound; one, however, broke loose, and the other got away later.

§ In his *Relation* . . ., for which see Purchas. Burney speaks of it as " . . . a Relation by Anthony Knyvet, which contains many things not credible."

|| *Journal of the Voyage of Wilhelm Schouten* (Amsterdam, 1617). Clatz's story appeared in the second (1619) edition.

The Second Period

It might be thought that, by this time, the existence of men much above the common height in Patagonia was fairly well established. But such was not the case. The voyagers of the late sixteenth century, as a class, seem to have gone out of their way to point out that they had seen no gigantic Patagonians (which was no doubt true); and, as a natural deduction, that none existed (which was unwarrantable). For example, Sir John Narborough, who spent ten months on the Patagonian coast in 1670, expressly denied that the Patagonians were any taller or bigger than other men. He attested that he had often measured the skulls and footprints of the savages whom he met in Magellan Strait, and found these to be of ordinary size; and that the same was the case with the numerous natives whom he had seen at Port St. Julian. It was recalled that John Winter, Drake's disaffected second-in-command, had stated on his return to England that he had seen no giants in the Strait, and that their existence was a fable invented by the Spaniards; and de Gennes, who followed Narborough in 1696, supported his views. On the other hand, Captains Harrington and Carman, commanding two French ships,* saw giants repeatedly in Possession Bay; six on one occasion, seven on another, and yet again "about four hundred men, part of whom were gigantic and part of the common stature". And Frezier was informed by the Spanish authorities at Valdivia, Chile, in 1712, that a tribe of gigantic natives, averaging 9 to 10 feet in height, existed in the interior of southern Patagonia. Oliver van Noort, in 1599, had heard the same story from natives (of the ordinary size) whom he took on board in Magellan Strait and, somewhat barbarously, instructed in the Dutch tongue.

The Third Period

The visit of Commodore Byron to Magellan Strait in 1764 was long regarded as having definitely established the existence of the Patagonian giants. Even before his time, however, it had come to be recognized that Patagonia was a large place; that its interior was unknown; that it was apparently inhabited by various nomadic tribes differing widely in many ways; and that no inference drawn from the stature of the natives encountered at a particular place could be relied upon to indicate what would be met with elsewhere by the same voyager, or at that place by a later one.

Byron, in the *Dolphin*, anchored inside C. Virgins, at the eastern

* One appears to have been the *Jaques* of St. Malo.

entrance to the Strait, on December 21, 1764. As he anchored he caught
sight of a number of natives on horseback,* waving to invite the strangers
on shore. Accordingly, he landed with an armed party, and was at once
confronted by a native who appeared to be a chief. The remainder of the
Patagonians, some five hundred, kept at a little distance. Here is Byron's
(or, rather, Hawkesworth's)† account of the meeting:

"One of them, who afterwards appeared to be a Chief, came towards
me: he was of a gigantic stature, and seemed to realize the tales of mon-
sters in a human shape: he had the skin of some wild beast thrown over his
shoulders. . . . I did not measure him, but if I may judge of his height by
the proportion of his stature to my own, it could not be much less than
seven feet. When this frightful Colossus came up, we muttered somewhat
to each other as a salutation, and I then walked with him towards his companions. . . ." (See Plate II.)

Later, when friendly relations had been established, he is made to
remark:

"Mr. Cumming came up with the tobacco, and I could not but smile
at the astonishment which I saw expressed in his countenance, upon per-
ceiving himself, though six feet two inches high, become at once a pigmy
among giants; for these people may indeed more properly be called giants
than tall men; of the few among us who are full six feet high, scarcely any
are broad and muscular in proportion to their stature, but look rather like
men of the common bulk, run up accidentally to an unusual height; and a
man who should measure only six feet two inches, and equally exceed a
stout well-set man of the common stature in breadth and muscle, would
strike us rather as being of a gigantic race, than as an individual accidentally anomalous; our sensations, therefore, upon seeing five hundred
people, the shortest of whom were at least four inches taller, and bulky in
proportion, may be easily imagined."

The *Annual Register* for 1768 contains an account of the same meeting, written by Mid. C. Clerke,‡ one of Byron's officers. He says:

* Bulkeley, a survivor from the wreck of the *Wager*, speaks of having seen three
mounted Patagonians near C. Virgins on December 12, 1741. This is the earliest recorded instance of their having been seen to use horses.

† Dr. John Hawkesworth (*ob.* 1773) was paid £6,000 by the Admiralty for editing
the journals of Byron, Wallis, Carteret, and Cook (first voyage), which he published in
three ponderous volumes just before his death. He was a disciple of Johnson, and in
consequence emended the plain English of Byron and the others into Johnsonese,
often with absurd results.

‡ Afterwards Cook's second-in-command, 1776–1779.

". . . some of them are certainly nine feet, if they do not exceed it. The commodore, who is very near six feet, could but just reach the top of one of their heads, which he attempted, on tip-toe; and there were several taller than him on whom the experiment was tried. They are prodigious stout, and as well and proportionably made as ever I saw people in my life. . . . The women, I think, bear much the same proportion to the men as our Europeans do; there was hardly a man there less than eight feet, most of them considerably more; the women, I believe, run from $7\frac{1}{2}$ to 8."

These remarks show the writer to have been misled by that curious illusion which makes most people over-estimate the height of any one who is considerably taller than they are. By experiment, it will be found that the man whose head Commodore Byron could barely touch must have stood just about 8 feet—or, if anything, an inch or so less.[*]

Wallis and Carteret, who visited C. Virgins two years later (December 1766), took more accurate measurements of the natives (not necessarily, of course, the tribe seen by Byron). Wallis states:

"As I had two measuring rods with me, we went round and measured those that appeared to be tallest among them. One of these was six feet seven inches high, several more were six feet five and six feet six inches; but the stature of the greater part of them was from five feet ten to six feet."

These measurements were in agreement with some obtained a little earlier (May 1766) by Duclos Guyot, one of Bougainville's captains, at a point in the Strait a little westward of C. Virgins. One of his officers measured the shortest of six natives whom he met, and found his height to be a quarter of an inch under 6 feet. He contented himself with noting that "the others were considerably taller".

Hawkesworth, summing up all the evidence then (1773) available, reached the conclusion that the more settled natives on both sides of the Strait were of ordinary stature, and that the "giants" spent most of their time on the western side of the Andes, and elsewhere in the interior— only visiting the shores of the Strait at rare intervals. He winds up his analysis by remarking triumphantly:

"Upon the whole, it may be reasonably presumed, that the concurrent testimony of late navigators, particularly Commodore Byron, Captain

* I stand 6 feet $4\frac{1}{2}$ inches, and span 6 feet 8 inches from finger-tip to finger-tip: and I find that (standing on tip-toe) I can just touch a point, on a vertical wall, 8 feet 6·3 inches from the ground.

Wallis, and Captain Carteret,* Gentlemen of unquestionable veracity, who are still living, and who not only saw and conversed with these people, but measured them, will put an end to all the doubts that have hitherto been entertained of their existence."

But if these "prave 'orts" gladdened the hearts of Lord Monboddo† and other cranks, they were not confirmed by later explorers. No one has yet obtained definite proof that Hawkesworth's supposed giant race actually exists. On the other hand, there is plenty of testimony to the great average stature of many Patagonians. Darwin‡ says:

"During our previous visit (in January),§ we had an interview at Cape Gregory with the famous so-called gigantic Patagonians, who gave us a cordial reception. Their height appears greater than it really is, from their large guanaco mantles, their long flowing hair, and general figure: on an average their height is about six feet, with some men taller and only a few shorter; and the women are also tall; altogether they are certainly the tallest race which we anywhere saw."

And Bourne, who spent some time among them *circa* 1849, remarks:

"In person they are large; on first sight they appear absolutely gigantic. They are taller than any other race I have seen, though it is impossible to give any accurate description. The only standard of measurement I had was my own height, which is about five feet ten inches. I could stand very easily under the arms of many of them, and all the men were at least a head taller than myself; their average height I should think is nearly six and a half feet, and there were specimens that could have been little less than seven feet high."

Believers in a living race of giants, if they are not satisfied with the Patagonians' average height of 6 feet or a little over (which is considerably above that of any other race) may, if they wish, still believe that the 9-foot men alleged to have been seen by Byron (or, for that matter, Knyvet's

---

* It will be noticed that he makes no mention of Cook. The latter, as we might expect, wasted no time in the Strait, but went round the Horn.

† James Burnet, Lord Monboddo (1714–99), was a Scottish lawyer, chiefly remembered by the pertinacity with which he defended his remarkable theory that all children are born with tails—these, in civilized countries, being surreptitiously removed by the midwives. He was also a strenuous advocate for the existence of the Patagonian giants. In justice to the memory of a much-derided man, it should be pointed out that he was far in advance of his time in maintaining that a close relation existed between the physical structure of man and of the higher apes.

‡ *Voyage of the "Beagle"*, chap. xi.   § 1834.

men of 10 to 12 feet) were stray members of a tribe of colossi still surviving in the heart of Patagonia. It cannot definitely be said that such is an
impossibility. There are enormous areas in southern Patagonia which are
still quite unexplored. It may be remembered that a considerable sensation
was caused in 1897–8 by the discovery, in a cave at Consuelo Cove, Last
Hope Inlet, on the western coast of Patagonia, of what was, apparently,
some quite fresh skin from a Mylodon, or giant sloth—an animal hitherto
supposed to have been extinct since prehistoric times. An expedition,*
sent out to test the supposition that surviving specimens of the Mylodon
might still be found in some remote and unknown regions of Patagonia,
left the question undecided; but it showed conclusively that very much
more exploration would have to be effected before the theory could be
rejected as impossible.

If we do not wish to locate our giant race in South America, we can
fall back on the recent reports of the mysterious "Migues", or "abominable snow-men", of the Himalayan slopes; who are stated (by their native
neighbours) to be from 10 to 12 feet high.† They have never been seen by
a white man, although the Mount Everest expeditions heard some vague
rumours about them. There is also the hairy and gigantic "Wendigo", of
whom the Canadian and Alaskan Indians tell many blood-curdling tales.

But we need not go far to find an actual race of giants—although they
are an artificial product. They are to be found where one would scarcely
think of looking for them—in Japan. The average Japanese wrestler is of
huge size, sometimes exceeding 7 feet, and of more than corresponding
bulk. There is a delightful description of them, and of the incredibly funny
ceremonies attending their contests, in the late Lord Curzon's *Tales of
Travel*—a book which incidentally reveals its author as possessed of a very
keen sense of humour. He compares these vast beings, very justly, to
Daniel Lambert‡—and speaks of their evolution thus:

"I afterwards inquired how it was that this strange and abnormal type
of manhood was produced, and I learned that it was by the practice of
eugenics *in excelsis*. The wrestlers are selected in boyhood from parents of

* Led by the late H. Hesketh Prichard, and financed by the late Sir C. A. Pearson.
It did not succeed in reaching Last Hope Inlet. See *Through the Heart of Patagonia*, by
H. Hesketh Prichard (London, 1902).

† They are also said to be white, hairy, and extremely fond of honey—points which
naturally suggest that they are really snow-bears. It must be remembered, however,
that bears are quite as familiar a sight to the natives as omnibuses to the Londoner.

‡ One of the fattest men who ever lived (1770–1809). He weighed 739 lb.—52
stone 11 lbs. *The Times* of 10.vii.42 chronicles the death, at Johannesburg, of a man
weighing 756 lb., and measuring 6 feet 8 inches round the chest.

unusual size; they are dieted and treated from the earliest years; as they grow up and enter the ring they are attended by a special bodyguard of masseurs, trainers, barbers, clothiers, and cooks; they are encouraged to consume an incredible amount of strength-producing food; and they constitute a separate guild, graded, numbered, and registered according to their capacity."

There is no doubt that careful breeding can accomplish wonders—for example, I believe that the mastiff and the pug (both, of them, alas, breeds which have been ousted from favour by the Chow, the much-maligned Alsatian, and the Pekingese) have been developed from a common strain —but it is difficult of application to human beings. Still, we may yet see

FIG. 3 —*Left*, Commodore Byron and a Patagonian. *Right*, Fedor Machnov

giants bred in small numbers for show purposes—in which case Bishop Berkeley's (alleged) artificial giant* will no longer be unique among white men.

---

* It used to be related that the great and good George Berkeley, Bishop of Cloyne, better known for his idealistic philosophy and his unequalled power of writing dialogue, had succeeded, by a system of dietary (on the lines of Wells' "Food of the Gods"), in making an unfortunate child grow into a giant. The true facts are these. A peasant boy named Cornelius Magrath, suffering from gigantism and half-starved for lack of food, was brought to the notice of Berkeley, who nursed him back to comparative health in his own house, and afterwards befriended him in many ways. Magrath died in 1760, aged 24. His skeleton (7 feet 8 inches) is in Trinity College, Dublin.

But I question whether there is, or ever has been, a race of men averaging, say, 8 feet or more in height. It is true that isolated cases of greater stature have occurred, but they are the results of accidental disease, and not of heredity. The giant of the dime-show and the music-hall is of interest to medical men with an eye to the dissection of his pituitary gland, and in their sight he may be a desirable specimen. But he is a poor specimen of humanity; disproportionate,* feeble, ailing, and with acromegalic hands, jaw, and feet. Machnov (9 feet 3 inches), who was better-made than most of his kind, could never have been taken for a normal man, even in a photograph which gave no indication of scale. Such giants die young;† and if they beget children (which is seldom) these, more fortunate, are usually of normal size.‡

As Domain, maker of robots, remarks:§ "Our planet is too small for giants." There is a structural limit to the useful size of all creatures built of flesh and bone. A man's weight varies, roughly, as the cube of his height; but his strength (which depends on the cross-section of his muscles) as the square of it. If, say, a man of 5 feet 10 inches were to be increased by one-seventh all round, he would become about half as heavy again, but he would only be stronger in the proportion of 64 to 49, so that he would actually be less efficient, physically, than he was before—and, both now and always, the future is to the efficient. The huge beasts and birds of prehistoric times, and some which survived till a quite recent day, died out because, even if Man spared them, Nature would not. And so, even if it be true that "there were giants in the earth in those days",‖ it is probable that their descendants have long since joined the Dodo, the Mammoth, the Moa, and Steller's Sea-cow in whatever limbo is reserved for Nature's discarded experiments.

* Chang Wow Gow (1845–1893) is, I believe, the only case on record of a man 8 feet high and perfectly proportioned. He was a splendid specimen of humanity and extremely intelligent, speaking six languages. At the Prince of Wales' request, he once wrote his name on a wall at the height of over 10 feet from the floor.

† In almost every case, before thirty. Chang died at forty-eight; M. C. Miller (7 feet 10 inches) at sixty. I believe that an American giant, Captain M. V. Bates (who stood about 7 feet 10 inches and his wife 7 feet 9 inches), lived to be over fifty; but I am not certain of this.

‡ With regard to the children of giants, it should be noted that J. R. Forster, who sailed (and squabbled) with Cook on his second voyage round the world, records that the average height of the citizen of Potsdam was unusually great, a fact which he ascribes to their frequent intermarriages with the soldiers of the King of Prussia's "giant regiment".

§ In Kapek's R.U.R.—a strange play which has given a new word to the English language.

‖ Genesis vi. 4.

THREE STRANGE SOUNDS

THE CRY OF MEMNON

Still from his chair of porphyry gaunt Memnon strains his lidless eyes
Across the empty land, and cries each yellow morning unto thee.

If Tennyson, as seems likely, excelled Wilde as a poet, he nevertheless
showed himself inferior to the author of *The Sphinx** in accuracy when
he wrote:

> . . . from her lips, as morn from Memnon, drew
> Rivers of melodies.

The sounds which are recorded as having been emitted by the famous
"vocal statue of Memnon" were neither many nor melodious. Infre-
quently, but always at sunrise, those who stood near it long ago might hear
a thin, strident sound, like the breaking of a harp string. That was all—
an aimless cry heard at rare intervals during a relatively short period of
two hundred years, a period preceded and followed by many centuries of
silence. Yet it was a phenomenon of which hardly any similar case is on
record—and it was not, it should seem, a deception. The statue, which
had been silent for so long, and has again sunk into silence, did once
acquire and exercise some strange inherent power of saluting the sun.

The statue of Memnon—which, incidentally, is not the statue of
Memnon, but of Amenophis III or Amenhotep—was erected about
1500 B.C. Its architect (we can hardly, *pace* Mr. Epstein, call him a
sculptor) was, rather confusingly, also named Amenhotep, son of Hapu.
It forms one member of a pair of twin colossi, still standing, about a mile
from the western bank of the Nile, among the ruins of Thebes.†

Here is their creator's own description of them:‡

"For my Lord the King was created the monument of sandstone.
Thus did I, . . . causing to be made two images of a most noble hard
stone, in his likeness . . . wonderful for their breadth, lofty in their height,
the stature whereof made the gate-tower to look small. Forty cubits was

* The initial quotation is taken from that bizarre poem—one of the few really
original pieces that Wilde ever wrote. It will be noticed that the metre, though not the
form, is that of *In Memoriam*.
† See Fig. 4.
‡ From an inscription on his own statue, now in the Boulak Museum, at Cairo

their measure. In the glorious sandstone mountain* wrought I them, on this side and on that, on the east side and on the west. Furthermore, I caused to be built eight ships, whereon they were carried up. . . ."

Even in their present mutilated and defaced condition, the two colossi are a most impressive sight. Each is some 50 feet high,† and there is about the same distance between them. They sit side by side, looking S.S.E. towards the Nile.

The western figure, a single piece of stone, is featureless, and the breast, legs, and feet are badly damaged. The eastern, which is the celebrated vocal statue, has obviously suffered far more extensive mutilation. From the pedestal to the waist it is a single block, extensively cracked; from the waist

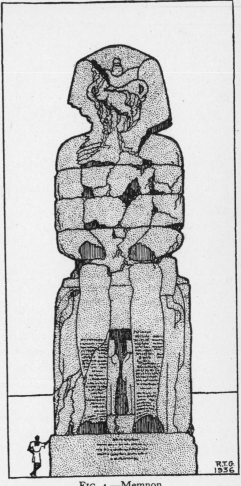

FIG. 4 —Memnon

upwards it is composed of five tiers of lighter stone, as if foreshadowing that puerile monstrosity the 100-foot "statue of Columbus" recently constructed at Palos. As with its fellow, the breast is damaged and the features unrecognizable.

* Obviously, from the context, some quarry down river—possibly that of Toora, near Cairo.

† Wilkinson and Curzon, both writing from personal observation, differ in the heights which they assign. Wilkinson made the western statue, by sextant angles, 47 feet high, and the eastern (the vocal statue) 47 feet 9 inches by actual measurement. Curzon gives 51 feet for each. Both sets of dimensions are exclusive of the pedestal.

The material of the western statue, and of the lower part of the eastern, is stated* to be a "coarse hard gritstone". The upper part of the eastern statue is of sandstone.

As already remarked, the eastern or reconstructed statue is that which is credited with having once emitted sounds. Before discussing this question, however, it may be as well to subjoin a short outline of its history (so far as that is known or conjectured)—a personal selection from the opinions expressed by several experts, often at variance.† The dates are approximate.

1500 B.C. Erection of the statues.

524 B.C. The statues defaced by Cambyses.‡

27 B.C. Upper half of the eastern statue thrown down by an earthquake, which also caused additional damage to the western statue.

20 B.C. Strabo, the historian, visited Thebes, and recorded the fact that, both by report and his own observation, the eastern statue emitted a sound at sunrise.

19 A.D. The sound heard by Germanicus.

90 A.D. The sound heard by Juvenal.

130 A.D. The sound heard by the Emperor Hadrian, and by Pausanias.

196 A.D. Last recorded occasion on which the sound was heard.

(later) Eastern statue reconstructed.

The dates on which the sound was heard, as given above, are only intended to provide a few points of reference. During the period 20 B.C.– A.D. 196 it seems to have occurred quite frequently, if irregularly— certainly not every morning, but probably several times a year at least. The authorities as to the simple fact of it being heard include Strabo, Pliny (not from personal observation), Pausanias, and Juvenal; the last of whom speaks of "dimidio Memnone"—halved Memnon, indicating that

* Wilkinson.

† The literature of the subject is quite extensive. In the short sketch here given I have relied chiefly upon the following:

  La Statue Vocale de Memnon. J. A. Letronne (Paris, 1833).

  Modern Egypt and Thebes. Sir G. Wilkinson (London, 1843).

  The Voice of Memnon. Lord Curzon of Kedleston. This originally appeared in The Edinburgh Review for July 1886, and was reprinted, with slight alterations, in Curzon's Tales of Travel (London, 1923).

‡ Cambyses, King of Persia, subjugated Egypt about 525 B.C., and ruled it for some five years, during which time he is credited with having done an almost incredible amount of wanton damage to its temples and monuments. Possibly, like Cromwell, he may have been a dog with a bad name.

Memnon (right-hand figure)

the statue had not then been restored. But, in addition to these, there is a considerable body of testimony inscribed on the statue itself. Its feet exhibit a series of eighty-seven inscriptions* in Greek and Latin (there are none in Egyptian characters) made by visitors who, like modern trippers, were moved by the desire to carve their name on something, and who took the opportunity of recording that they had, or had not, heard the cry of Memnon. These inscriptions range over a period of about two centuries. The last was made in A.D. 196.

As to the nature of the sound, Strabo speaks of it as resembling the sound of a slight blow. Pausanias states that it can only be compared to the sound made when the string of a lyre breaks. One of the inscriptions describes it as a high-pitched note, like that produced by striking brass.

The inscriptions contain some thirty-nine references to the time of day at which the sound was heard. Tabulated, the results are as follows:

Before sunrise	2
At sunrise	18
Less than an hour after	8
An hour after	6
Less than two hours after	2
Two hours after	3

The months most frequently mentioned are February and March, probably because they were those in which visitors to the statue could most easily ascend the Nile. Several of these heard the sound more than once—on the other hand, two inscriptions record success only at the second visit; and one, not until the third.

It is not absolutely certain, but almost so, that the statue has been silent since about A.D. 200 or so. There is one recorded instance of its having sounded in quite modern times; but this event is attested in so curiously roundabout a fashion that its value as evidence is exceedingly slight. Here is the original authority, *verbatim*. (*Revue Encyclopédique*, Tom. IX, p. 598. Paris, March 1821).

"EGYPTE.—*Antiquité.*—*Statue de Memnon.*—Dans une lettre adressée à l'ambassadeur de Russie à la cour de Rome, sir A. Smith, voyageur anglais, qui est maintenant à Thèbes, dit avoir examiné lui-même, avec sa nombreuse escorte, la célèbre statue de Memnon. A six heures du matin, il a entendu très-distinctement les sons dont il a été parlé si souvent dans l'antiquité. *Memnonis saxea effigies, ubi radiis solis icta est, vocalem sonum*

* These were all copied by Letronne, and are illustrated in his monograph.

reddens. Tac. ann. 2. M. Smith assure que ce bruit mystérieux ne sortait pas de la statue, qui a été renversée par un tremblement de terre, mais du piédestal; il le regarde comme le résultat de la percussion de l'air sur les pierres de ce piédestal, qui, selon lui, sont disposées de manière à produire cet effet."

It is somewhat singular, but apparently true, that the Theban investigations of this distinctively named English traveller, "sir A. Smith", would have been lost to posterity had it not been for this short abstract, in a French periodical, of a letter written by him to a Russian friend resident in Italy. During the past century, Smith's visit has often been cited as proving that the cry of Memnon has been heard in modern times, but no one seems to have discovered any better authority for it than the *Revue Encyclopédique*. For my own part, although I have not been able to spare the ten years or so which would be required to make a really exhaustive search, I have done my limited best to throw more light on the subject—without success. I have not succeeded either in identifying "sir A. Smith" or in finding any further account of his travels in Egypt.

It will be noticed that he is stated to have assured himself that the sound came from the pedestal—which is a squared socle, some 13 feet high,* and in one with the lower half of the statue itself. It is curious that this observation, reported to have been made by the last man who heard the cry, is in close agreement with the account given by Strabo, who was the first. Speaking from his own experience (he visited Memnon in 20 B.C., in company with Aelius Gallus, the Roman governor of Egypt), he relates that he heard a sound, but "could not affirm whether it proceeded from the pedestal or from the statue itself, or even from some of those who stood near its base".† His last suggestion—that the whole thing was a trick—is, in itself, plausible; and it is quite possible that the sound heard (if it was heard) by Smith really emanated from one of his "numerous escort", anxious that he should not be disappointed; but, as will be seen, this hypothesis does not cover the events of the period during which the sound was of frequent occurrence. Wilkinson, who was firmly convinced that the sound was an imposture, makes no mention of Smith's visit at all, although writing twenty years after it had become generally known: he merely remarks, in a footnote, "More than one traveller has repaired to the statue before sunrise in hopes of hearing the sound",‡ leaving it to be inferred that none succeeded in doing so.

---

* About 6 feet of this are above the sand and 7 below.

† Strabo, lib. xvii.

‡ When the first edition of this book was in proof, I found that the printer, very appositely, had omitted the "to" in this quotation.

But, whatever conclusion may be formed as to the reality of the events associated with the mysterious Smith, there can be little doubt that the cry of Memnon was repeatedly heard, by quite a cloud of witnesses, during the first two centuries of the Christian era. I turn to the question of how that sound was produced. Opinion on this subject is as sharply and naturally divided as the original half of the statue itself; in which a fissure, running east and west, extends from the waist to the pedestal. Some hold that the sound was the result of human agency: in plainer language, a pious fraud—others regard it as a rare, but not unknown, phenomenon due to natural causes.

The hypothesis of fraud has, at first sight, a great deal to recommend it. The suggestion of imposture is inevitable. Here is a statue, of a semi-religious character, visited by crowds of superstitious and ignorant persons who have been drawn to it by the belief that it has miraculous powers. Where miracles are expected, miracles can usually be made to occur—witness the punctual and obliging* manner in which the blood of St. Januarius usually liquefies several times a year in Naples cathedral.

So far so good. But three questions remain to be answered, namely:

1. How was it done?
2. Who did it?
3. Why was it done?

To the first question there are several possible replies, some of which are more plausible than others. The sound may have come from some interested person who had stationed himself (possibly, like the more speculative type of bookmaker, with a few "minders" in attendance) near the statue—and it may have been produced by a small pair of cymbals, or an actual lyre, or some device of the kind; which, as any Customs searcher will testify, could easily be concealed in the thaumaturgist's clothing. Such is the simplest explanation. On the other hand, some have imagined that the sound was produced in the interior of the figure. Two French writers, Langlès and Salverte, worked out the details of an elaborate mechanism which, according to them, must have filled quite a large space in Memnon's interior.† Unfortunately, no trace of such mechanism or cavity remains.

* So much so that it found no difficulty in conforming with the alteration of the calendar effected by Pope Gregory XIII in 1582.

† See Salverte's *Des Sciences occultes* . . . (Paris, 1829). He provided for a system of hammers, striking on sonorous stones, and driven by a water-clock. The machinery was let off by the expansion of a metal rod, on which the sun's rays were concentrated by a lens which the figure held between its lips. He does not seem to have thought of adding an aerial and a few loud-speakers.

A statement published by Sir Gardner Wilkinson, F.R.S., in 1843, was long regarded as having demonstrated not only the fact of fraud, but also the way in which this was effected. Here it is:*

"In the lap of the statue is a stone, which, on being struck, emits a metallic sound, that might still be made use of to deceive a visitor who was predisposed to believe its powers; and from its position, and the squared space cut in the block behind, as if to admit a person who might thus lie concealed from the most scrutinous observer in the plain below, it seems to have been used after the restoration of the statue; and another similar recess exists beneath the present site of this stone, which might have been intended for the same purpose when the statue was in its mutilated condition."

As Curzon has pointed out, Wilkinson is at some pains to make his theory of imposture absolutely unassailable. He is not content with finding one suspicious recess; he produces two, one used when only the lower half of the statue remained, the other after the reconstruction. Furthermore, he "proceeds to narrate" that while he had considered, in 1824, that the "metallic sound" produced by striking his stone did not tally with the traditional sound of Memnon, he subsequently (in 1830) came across the inscription† which compared this to the sound made by striking brass. Fortified by this, he stationed some fellahin below, and tapped his "sonorous block" with a small hammer.‡ His audience, on being asked what they heard, replied, "*Ente betídrob e'nahás*": which is, being interpreted, "You are striking brass".

Unfortunately for Wilkinson's reputation, Curzon (who visited the statue in 1886) discovered, with the help of a ladder and a foot-rule, that his "sonorous block" was simply a stone which had fallen from the superstructure (which was not, apparently, in place when the sounds used to be heard) and had jammed in the natural fissure dividing the lower (original) half of the figure. Nor was this all. Wilkinson's "squared space" was simply the gap which was left in the superstructure when the stone fell, and his other "similar recess" was nothing but the fissure itself! Wilkinson had obviously distorted the evidence of his own eyes into conformity with his prejudices.

So far as is known, there is nothing in the structure of the figure which affords any positive evidence of fraud. On the other hand, it is quite

* *Modern Egypt and Thebes*, vol. ii, p. 161.

† On the statue itself, by one Ballilla. See p. 29.

‡ As Wilkinson recalls, Strabo declared the sound to resemble that of a slight blow, or tap.

possible that the sounds could have been made by someone standing near it.

The remaining questions—"who did it" and "why was it done"—can best be discussed jointly, for each involves the other. The obvious answer to them is "The Egyptian priests, to gain prestige and/or money".

Unfortunately, this is contradicted by the facts. There is nothing which would lead us to suppose that the Egyptian priests were any more averse from "working the oracle" than those of all creeds, ages, and nations have generally shown themselves to be. But how comes it that they should have so shamefully neglected their opportunities? During many centuries the statue stood, intact, in front of the splendid temple of King Amenhotep. There is no contemporary inscription—no vestige of evidence at all—that during this period, when the priests and their strange religion held full sway, the cry of Memnon was ever heard.* As was first pointed out by Letronne, there are no Egyptian inscriptions on the statue, and nothing to show that it was ever regarded by the Egyptians as miraculous. This was reserved for its Greek visitors, fifteen centuries after its erection, when Egypt was in Roman hands. The Greeks probably knew the statue as Memnon because, if it sounded at sunrise, they would naturally associate it with the fabled son of the Dawn; but to the Egyptians it was merely Amenhotep—and, it would seem, not an object of worship at all.†

Even if it be supposed that the priests, or any other interested persons (finding that the statue was, or might be, worshipped as Memnon by alien visitors) decided to make it appear to be vocal, one would at least imagine that there would have been some method in their proceedings. One would, for example, have expected that the sound would be heard when, and as often as, best suited the convenience of its visitors. In particular, one would imagine that if it were visited by any exalted person, whom it would be impolitic to offend, the sound which that person had come to hear would most undoubtedly be heard. But the facts are quite otherwise. If we are to judge by the inscriptions, many visitors never heard the cry of Memnon at all; many others must have had to make repeated pilgrimages before they heard it; and, while it is true that the statue apparently

* Juvenal, it is true, is responsible for the statement that "when mutilated by Cambyses, the statue which saluted both the sun and the king afterwards saluted only the sun". But such a statement, made hundreds of years after the event, is not evidence.

† Much ink has been spilt on the question of how the mythical Greek hero Memnon came to be associated with various statues and temples in Egypt. Wilkinson has pointed out that *Miamun* was a title of Rameses II. Either this name or Amenophis might easily have been converted into *Memnon* by credulous Greek immigrants, eager to find support for the Homeric legends.

performed three times* for the Emperor Hadrian, it is equally true that it remained obstinately silent on the first occasion when his consort paid it a visit (a fact which, as is duly recorded on the statue by one of her ladies-in-waiting, enraged her exceedingly)—while the Emperor Septimius Severus never succeeded in hearing the sound at all. It is past all believing that those responsible for the supposed deception could have acted with such wanton disregard of the feelings of the great. Such behaviour presupposes an absolute lack of elementary common sense—it would have been that of fools, not knaves.

There is much more to be said for the opposition theory; indeed, except for the sake of completeness, such a proceeding savours of "blacking the chimney", for this theory is now generally accepted. On the supposition that the sound was a purely natural phenomenon, many of the difficulties connected with it—*e.g.* the varying descriptions of the sound itself and of the time of day when it was heard—become much less formidable. Such a phenomenon would almost certainly be irregular both in its nature and its recurrence.

The sound was only heard at or near sunrise; it varied in note and intensity; and it occurred, at irregular intervals, during a period which apparently began when the upper half of the statue was demolished (and the lower half split) and ended as soon as (but, possibly, before) the upper half was rebuilt. From these data it is difficult to avoid drawing the conclusion that the sound was caused by the sun's rays warming the cleft and truncated lower half of the statue; that it was produced by the unequal expansion of the two portions of this fractured monolith—causing them to move, fractionally, one against the other; and that they no longer had free scope for this interplay when they were compelled to support the great weight of the rebuilt upper portion.†

Although no exactly similar case is known, there is a certain amount of evidence which goes to show that in all probability the cry of Memnon was due to a natural cause. Jomard, Jollois, and Devilliers, three of the scientists who accompanied Napoleon's expedition to Egypt, heard a similar sound, at sunrise, on two occasions—once in the granite quarries at Syene and once in a temple at Karnak. They describe it (exactly in the manner of Pausanias) as resembling the sound made by a breaking string. In their opinion it was caused by air, occluded in the crevices of the stone and expanded by heat, making its way out. Rather singularly, they did not connect their experience with the sounds traditionally accredited to

---

* On separate days. One or two of the inscriptions, however, record that the sound was heard twice on the same morning.

† See Fig. 4.

Memnon. These they regarded as fabulous. Their experience at Karnak was confirmed later by Brugsch, who was there in 1851 and also heard the sound in question.

To my mind, the theory of unequal expansion has more to recommend it than that of occluded air, although the latter was also put forward independently by Humboldt as explaining certain sounds, like the note of an organ, sometimes heard near sunrise at various points on the Orinoco.* If it be the true explanation, it is difficult to understand why such sounds should not be fairly common wherever stone of a suitable kind is exposed to changes of temperature. On such an assumption, for example, most of the other Egyptian statues and buildings should also emit sounds.

On the theory of unequal expansion, it is true, we can only escape from this objection by supposing that the sounds heard at Syene and Karnak came from stones which, like the statue, had also been fractured in a somewhat similar manner. There is no evidence for or against this supposition.

In any event, it seems most likely that the cry of Memnon had its origin in the fissure dividing the truncated monolith, and that if the circumstances of the fracture had been slightly different the sound probably would never have been heard at all; just as it ceased when the self-adjustment of the two portions was disturbed by the superimposed load.† It must be remembered, however, that there is no actual evidence that the reconstruction of the upper portion synchronized with Memnon's renewed silence, since the date of the reconstruction is not known, although tradition associates it with the Emperor Septimius Severus (in whose reign the sound ceased).

Not only is the date of the reconstruction obscure,‡ but also its motive. It was possibly done with a view to propitiating Memnon, in which case it may well have been ordered by Severus (who, as already stated, paid the statue a fruitless visit), particularly since such a piece of work demanded resources of labour and material which only an Emperor could command. The tiers of the Roman work are an eloquent tribute to the engineering ability of Amenhotep, son of Hapu, and his men. In its original monolithic condition, the complete statue must have weighed some 1,200 tons; yet the Egyptians hewed it in the "glorious sandstone mountain", transported it many miles by water, and successfully erected it—all with the crudest of appliances. I do not imagine that many modern engineers

* Humboldt did not hear these sounds himself.
† I regard the "sir A. Smith" incident as "not proven".
‡ The left foot was certainly repaired after the date of Hadrian's visit (c. A.D. 130), for one of the cramps has been let in through the inscription recording this.

would care to prepare an estimate for such a job, and it is no disgrace to the Romans that a similar feat proved beyond their powers. To reconstruct the figure even as it now stands was a very considerable achievement.

A minor point of interest in connection with the statue of Memnon is the fate of the missing upper half. It does not seem to be anywhere in the vicinity of the figure; and, weighing some 500 tons, it was scarcely likely to have been removed in one piece. On the other hand, if it were broken in the fall, or subsequently,* the pieces would seem to have been removed (for some unknown motive) before the reconstruction, or else deliberately rejected—for the new work is of distinctly lighter stone. One is almost tempted to believe that the Roman engineers found it, still whole, near by; and that, unable to replace it, they found means to break it up and remove it, lest it put them to open shame.

PARRY'S CANNON

The cry of Memnon is an example of a strange sound which is known, by name at least, to most people. On the other hand, the remarkable incident which occurred in the course of some experiments on the velocity of sound made by Captain W. E. Parry in 1822 seems to have been almost forgotten.

Parry, who had already made himself famous by reaching Melville Island, half-way to Bering Strait, while searching for the N.W. Passage in 1819,† spent the winter of 1821–22 at Winter Island (66° N., 83° W.). He was not the man to waste his time; and during this period of enforced inactivity he carried out, with the assistance of his officers, a very considerable amount of scientific research. The results fill a quarto volume of 432 pages;‡ and a notion of the diligence with which the work was done may be gathered from the fact that his astronomer, the Rev. George Fisher, took no less than 2,500 "lunar distances" (for determining longitude) in December 1821,§ and an equal number in the following March.

Amongst his other researches, Parry made a series of experiments to determine whether the normal velocity of sound underwent any notice-

---

* If it were deliberately broken up, this must have been an exceedingly difficult task. Wilkinson, however, speaks of a statue in the palace of Rameses II which he took to be Shelley's Ozymandias, and which was so utterly shattered that it almost seemed to have been blown up.

† By so doing he secured the Parliamentary reward of £5,000 offered in 1818 to the first explorer who, sailing westward to the north of the American continent, should pass the meridian of Long. 110° W.

‡ *Appendix to Captain Parry's Journal of a Second Voyage*, London, 1825.

§ It is sad to record that the mean of these, although they were all taken on shore, differed from that of the March observations by no less than 14′.

able alteration at low temperatures. His opportunities for making them were excellent. The temperatures available ranged from about $-45°$ to $+40°$ Fahr., and he was able to use an absolutely ideal testing-ground. Between Winter Island and the mainland of Melville Peninsula, to the south-westward, is an arm of the sea—practically land-locked and (during the winter) frozen hard. Parry named it the Frozen Sea. Here, on eighteen days between December 29, 1821, and June 18, 1822, Parry made his experiments, from which he deduced the expected result that the average velocity of sound decreased slightly as the temperature fell, the amount of alteration being small and uniform. But on one occasion he encountered another deviation from the normal which, it is safe to say, he did not at all expect.

The experiments of February 9, 1822, were made as follows. A base-line slightly over a mile (5,645 feet) long was carefully marked out on the surface of the ice. At one end Parry mounted a six-pounder gun and its crew, with an officer in charge. Together with another observer (Fisher), he stationed himself at the opposite end of the base. The gun was given an elevation of about $10°$, and pointed towards the observers. It is hardly necessary to add that it fired a blank charge. The temperature was $-25°$ Fahr.

The procedure was as follows. The officer at the firing-point, when assured that the observers were ready, gave the order to fire the gun. Each observer noted independently, by a pocket chronometer,* the interval between seeing the flash of the gun and hearing the report. It should be added that on this and every occasion the experiments were made late at night, in order to avoid atmospheric disturbances. Both flash and report therefore, could be noted with very fair accuracy.

Fifteen rounds were fired. The observed times agreed well, and gave a mean velocity of 1,023 feet per second. But Parry and Fisher were perplexed to notice that, on several occasions, the order "Fire", which was plainly audible (although uttered something over a mile away) reached them about half a second *after* the report of the gun. Here is Fisher's own statement, extracted from his official "Abstract of Experiments to determine the Velocity of Sound" (*loc. cit.*, p. 239).

"The experiments on the 9th February, 1822, were attended with a singular circumstance, which was—the officer's word of command 'Fire'

* The pocket chronometer—a watch with the spring-detent or chronometer escapement—is now obsolete, on account of its liability to be stopped in the pocket by a shake or jar. Unlike a lever watch, it will not restart itself. Stop-watches were not in common use until long after Parry's time.

was several times distinctly heard both by Captain Parry and myself about one beat of the chronometer* *after* the report of the gun; from which it would appear, that the velocity of sound depends in some measure upon its intensity. The word 'fire' was never heard during any of the other experiments; upon this occasion the night was calm and clear, the thermometer 25° below zero, the barometer 28·84 inches, which was lower than it had ever been observed before at Winter Island. Upon comparing the intervals between the flash and report of a musket with the gun, upon other occasions, there appears to be no assignable difference."

The exact meaning of the last sentence eludes me; it is not very clearly expressed. Fisher leaves the reader in doubt as to whether, on this particular occasion, comparative tests between gun and musket did show a difference; or whether no such tests were made on that occasion, but that they were made at some later date, and no difference observed. I assume that, whenever the tests may have been made, the object of them was to test Fisher's theory that the velocity of the sound depended on its intensity. That they gave entirely negative results is not altogether surprising; so far as I know, the phenomenon of "Parry's cannon" remains unique, not only in his experience but universally.

It is easy to be wise after the event. In the *Philosophical Transactions* for 1860 there appeared a learned paper on the theory of sound,† written by the Rev. S. Earnshaw. In this he lays down and elaborates the theory that, in certain circumstances, waves of sound have a power of propagating themselves, in advance, along the path which they are travelling. He continues:

"I should expect, therefore, that in circumstances where the human voice can be heard at a sufficiently long distance, the command to fire a gun, if instantly obeyed, and the *report* of the gun might be heard at a long distance in an inverse order; *i.e. first* the report of the gun, and *then* the word 'fire'."

(He next proceeds to lay a pitfall for the inquiring reader by referring, in a footnote, to Parry's singular experience, and citing the wrong authority for it.‡)

This is "all werry capital", but his theory does not square with the

---

* This beat eight times in three seconds; an unusual and inconvenient arrangement. Most pocket chronometers have an "18,000 train", and beat five times in two seconds.

† "On the Mathematical Theory of Sound" (*loc. cit.*, pp. 133–48).

‡ He remarks: "See Suppt. to Appendix of *Parry's Voyage in 1819–20* . . ." This supplement relates solely to natural history. "1819–20" should read "1821–23".

facts. The circumstances which he postulates, allowing the human voice to be heard at long distances, are not at all unusual in the Arctic. During Parry's third voyage, for example, Lieutenant Foster, one of his officers, found that it was perfectly possible to carry on a coversation across the frozen surface of Port Bowen Harbour* between the ship and a shore observatory distant no less than a mile and a quarter. Similar acoustic conditions prevailed during the period of Parry's experiments on the Frozen Sea. Yet on no other occasion did the sound of the gun outrun the order to fire it—nor, as will be noticed, did this invariably occur even during the series made on February 9, 1822.

Sir G. B. Airy, in his treatise on Sound,† suggested that the cause of the anomaly was physiological; that owing to the abnormal cold the observer's power of apprehending sound was affected, and less sensitive for some noises than for others. He suggests, in fact, a sort of delay-action between ear and brain, which affected the order more than the report. But this theory, also, is open to the same objection. The cold was not so great as that experienced in several of the other experiments; for example, those of February 16th (a week later) were made in $-45°$ Fahr—$20°$ colder than it was on the 9th. In fact, the only distinctive circumstance on that date was, as remarked by Fisher, the abnormally low barometer.

(*Postscript*. A correspondent whose opinion I value has pointed out that sound travels faster in warm than in cold air; and that during Parry's experiments the stratum of air lying nearest the surface of the ice was probably the coldest. The order "Fire!" would travel through this stratum, and the sound of the gun—owing to the $10°$ elevation—through one somewhat higher. He admits, however, that the difference in time ought not, theoretically, to be nearly so much as $\frac{3}{8}$ sec. I will add, that the simple supposition that what Parry and his men heard was a faint echo from some object about 200 feet in rear of them is ruled out by the fact that they must then also have heard the echo of the report itself.)

THE BARISAL GUNS

The Barisal guns have no affinity to Parry's cannon—in fact, it is quite certain that they are not guns at all. The term is used to denote certain remarkable sounds resembling gun fire, but certainly not such, which occur in many parts of the world—particularly the Sundarbans, or Sunderbunds, that enormous network of swamps and morasses through

* 73° 13′ N., 88° 52′ W.
† *On Sound, and Atmospheric Vibrations* ... (London and Cambridge, 1868, pp. 134, 135).

which the Ganges finds its way by many channels to the sea. Barisal itself is a village in the Sunderbunds, a little westward of the principal mouth of the Ganges and about 70 miles southward of Dacca.

At Barisal, and many other places in the Ganges delta, the guns are often heard. Here is one observer's account of them:*

"I first heard the Barisal Guns in December 1871, on my way to Assam from Calcutta through the Sundarbans. The weather was calm and clear, no sign of any storms. All day the noises on board the steamer prevented other sounds from being heard; but when all was silent at night, and we were moored in one or other of the narrow channels in the neighbourhood of Barisal, Morelgunge, and upwards, far from any villages or other habitations, with miles and miles of long grass jungle on every side, the only sounds the lap of the water or the splash of earth, falling into the water along the banks, then at intervals, irregularly, would be heard the dull muffled boom as of distant cannon.

"Sometimes a single report, at others two, three, or more in succession; never near, always distant, but not always equally distant. Sometimes the reports would resemble cannon from two rather widely separated opposing forces, at others from different directions but apparently always from the southward, that is seaward. We were not very far from the sea when I first heard them, and on mentioning to an old lady on board that I heard distant cannon, she first told me of the mysterious sounds known as the 'Barisal Guns'."

Colonel H. S. Olcott† speaks of the sound heard by him, at Barisal itself, as being so sharp and loud that he thought it was the evening gun being fired at a cantonment in the village.

Mr. Scott, in the account previously quoted, also speaks of having heard similar sounds at Chilmari, on the Brahmaputra, about 300 miles inland.

"I specially remember spending a quiet Sunday, in the month of May, with a friend at Chilmari, near the river-bank. We had both remarked the reports the night before, and when near the hills previously. About 10 a.m. in the day, weather clear and calm, we were walking quietly up and down the river-bank, discussing the sounds, when we heard the booming distinctly, about as loud as heavy cannon would sound on a quiet day, about ten miles off, down the river. Shortly after we heard a heavy boom very much nearer, still south. Suddenly we heard two quick successive

* A memorandum by Mr. G. B. Scott, quoted in *Nature*, 2. i. 1896.
† The Theosophist. See his letter in *Nature*, 12. xii. 1895.

reports, more like horse-pistol or musket (not rifle) shots close by. I thought they sounded in the air about 150 yards due west of us over the water. My friend thought they sounded north of us. We ran to the bank, and asked our boatmen, moored below, if they heard them, and if so in what direction. They pointed south!"

Similar sounds were heard on several occasions by Colonel Godwin Austen, of the Survey of India, still further inland. In the spring of 1865, while near Buxa, Bhutan, on the southern slopes of the Himalayas, "the report of a heavy gun was heard in the direction of the mountains, clear and distinct, yet a long way off, followed closely and at irregular intervals by two other discharges. . . . These reports were louder and more distinctly like artillery fire than any I afterwards heard in the hills further to the east. These last had the nature of a very, very distant boom, coming from no well-defined direction".* He also speaks of having several times heard noises, like the distant report of heavy guns, in the North Cachar Hills.

Although an Indian village is the eponym of the "Barisal Guns", India has no monopoly of them. Such noises have been heard in the British Isles—on Dartmoor, at several places in Scotland, and, quite frequently, on the shores of Lough Neagh. Here are some notes on the last-named by the Rev. W. S. Smith, of Antrim.†

"For many years after my settlement here as minister from England, I heard at intervals, when near the lake, cannon-like sounds. . . . In time I came to understand that it was not from the opposite shores, but from the lake itself that the sounds proceeded. After questioning many of the local residents, I extended my enquiries to the fishermen, but they could assign no cause. A strange thing about the matter is that the people generally know nothing of the phenomenon, and that it is shrouded in mystery. . . . I have heard the sounds probably twenty times during the present year,‡ the last being on a Sunday afternoon a month since, when I heard two explosions; but with two exceptions they have all seemed to come from many miles away, from different directions at different times. They have come apparently from Toome Bay, from the middle of the lake, and from Langford Lodge Point, about nine miles distant. . . .

"I have as yet spoken to no one who observed any movement of the waters when explosions took place, nor have I spoken to any one who was close to the spot at the time, rather every one seems to have heard them only in the distance, which is strange, as fishermen are on the lake during many months in the year, at all hours of the day and night."

* *Nature*, 16. i. 1896.   † *Ibid.*, 2. i. 1896.   ‡ 1895.

Similar "guns" are often heard off the Belgian coast, where they are locally known as "mist poeffers" (*lit.* "fog-pistols"),* while they have been reported from many parts of Australia. The earliest account of these which I can trace is that given by Sturt when describing his great journey of 1828–9, in which he discovered the Darling and Murray Rivers. Encamped near the Darling, in February 1829, he notes in his journal:

"About 3 p.m. on the 7th, Mr. Hume and I were occupied tracing the chart upon the ground. The day had been remarkably fine, not a cloud was there in the heavens, nor a breath of air to be felt. On a sudden we heard what seemed to be the report of a gun fired at the distance of between five and six miles. It was not the hollow sound of an earthly explosion, or the sharp cracking noise of falling timber, but in every way resembled a discharge of a heavy piece of ordnance. On this all were agreed, but no one was certain whence the sound proceeded.

"Both Mr. Hume and myself had been too attentive to our occupation to form a satisfactory opinion; but we both thought it came from the N.W. I sent one of the men immediately up a tree, but he could observe nothing unusual. The country around him seemed to be equally flat on all sides, and to be thickly wooded: whatever occasioned the report, it made a strong impression on all of us; and to this day, the singularity of such a sound, in such a situation, is a matter of mystery to me."†

Mr. H. L. Richardson, of Hillsprings, Carnarvon, W. Australia, reported hearing three explosions high up in the air, followed by a rushing noise like escaping steam (which lasted for several seconds), on June 26, 1908.‡

It is a far cry from W. Australia to the Rockies; yet here, too, we find the Barisal Guns.

On July 4, 1808, the Lewis and Clark expedition was encamped at Great Falls, Montana, about eighty miles eastward of the main range of the Rockies. The explorers record in their journal:

"Since our arrival at the Falls we have repeatedly heard a strange noise coming from the mountains in a direction a little to the north of west. It is heard at different periods of the day and night, sometimes when

---

* See a series of articles, covering the whole range of the reported phenomena, by E. Van den Broek, of the Natural History Museum at Brussels, in *Ciel et Terre*, 1895–96.

† *Two Expeditions into the Interior of Southern Australia*, 2nd edit., 1834, vol. i. p. 98.

‡ *Nature*, 27. viii. 1908. See also a letter in the same paper, 4. vi. 1908, from Mr. J. Burton Cleland, describing a "dull roar, lasting several seconds", heard by him on August 9, 1907, when encamped on the Strelley River.

the air is perfectly still and without a cloud, and consists of one stroke only, or five or six discharges in quick succession. It is loud, and resembles precisely the sound of a six-pound piece of ordnance at the distance of three miles."

A party equipped by J. J. Astor, the American fur magnate, skirting the Black Hills of Wyoming and Dakota, noted in 1810: "In the most calm and serene weather, and at all times of the day or night, successive reports are now and then heard among these mountains, resembling the discharge of several pieces of artillery. Similar reports were heard by Messrs. Lewis and Clark in the Rocky Mountains." It may be added that in 1854 a Mr. Doty, when near the point of the Rockies from which the sounds heard by Lewis and Clark seemed to come, heard similar noises, and was certain that they emanated from the mountains. On the other hand, later visitors to the locality do not seem to have heard them.[*]

The Barisàl Guns have also been frequently heard in Haiti,[†] where the sound is known as the "gouffre". They have also, though rarely, been known to occur at sea; witness the following entry in the meteorological log of the S.S. *Resolute*, Captain W. Deuchars, for July 30, 1883, 8 p.m. "Six reports like those of guns heard to the westward, supposed to be caused by electricity, as no ships are thought to be in the vicinity." The position given is 71° 09′ N., 12° 28′ W., about sixty miles westward of Jan Mayen Island.[‡] Similar sounds, too, are often heard in the neighbourhood of Lake Bosumtwi, Ashanti.[§]

The guns heard at Barisal, then, appear to be only a leading case of a very widespread phenomenon.[||] Many explanations have been suggested —fireworks, actual gun fire, bamboos bursting in jungle-fires, thunderclaps, the collapsing of banks, globular lightning, landslips, submarine eruptions, and a good many more. So far, none of these has been accepted by those who have heard the sounds in the Sunderbunds; or for that matter, in the other localities.

Mr. H. S. Schurr, writing in 1899,[¶] pointed out that in his experience

[*] *Nature*, 26. iii. 1896.

[†] E.g. in the autumn and winter months of 1912, over the south-western part of the island.

[‡] *Nature*, 30. i. 1896.

[§] *Geographical Journal*, Jan. 1936.

[||] Without extensive investigation, it is impossible to affirm that all the instances quoted are exactly on all fours, and it is not suggested that they are necessarily all due to the same cause: but they have at least a strong family resemblance—and, for all of them, no simple explanation seems adequate.

[¶] *Nature*, 7. xii. 1899.

the "Barisal Guns" always occur in triplets, with a slight echo-like sound immediately after each report, and a subsequent interval of from three to ten seconds before the next, thus: BANG-bang . . . BANG-bang . . . BANG-bang. He rejected, as inadequate, all the explanations offered.

Quite the most fascinating theory as to the origin of the sounds heard in the Ganges delta is that outlined by Lieutenant-Colonel W. P. Drury, of the Royal Marines, in that masterpiece of Marine fiction, *The Peradventures of Private Pagett*.* His hero, who is more of a living character than many real Marines (when these are on duty), is supposed to go adrift in the Sunderbunds in a small dinghy. He is being towed by the steam-cutter, and the painter carries away,† unnoticed by those ahead. He is left paddling about aimlessly like a lost dog, despairing of rescue and fortifying himself against impending death by repeating the only portion of the Prayer Book he can call to mind—which happens to be, *A Man may not marry his Grandmother*.

Round a bend in one of the innumerable channels he catches sight of a large stranded vessel. She proves to be one of H. M. ships, wrecked many years before, but still tenanted by a few greybeards commanded by a senile midshipman, the only surviving officer. All suffer from two fixed ideas—that they must never abandon the ship, and that they must fire guns at intervals to scare away wild beasts. He is shown two small signalling guns, and realizes that these are the famous "Guns of Gungapore"—in other words, the Barisal guns. Parting company with these Rip van Winkles more in anger than sorrow, he makes his way, after many adventures, back to his ship—where, curiously enough, no one will believe his story.

It is a good yarn—and it is meant, I imagine, to be nothing more. Yet part of it, at any rate, might have been founded on fact. When Wallis, on his way round the world, touched at Batavia with the *Dolphin* in December 1767, he found there another King's ship, H.M.S. *Falmouth*, "lying on the mud in a rotten condition". She had been there nearly ten years. She was worn out, and so were her men. Wallis states that the ship was in so decayed a state that she could hardly be expected to survive the next monsoon—only the mud kept her from sinking at her anchors; while her ship's company consisted of no more than a few men, old and broken. There were no executive officers left, and of the remainder the gunner was dead, the boatswain had gone mad, and the carpenter was dying. The survivors entreated Wallis to discharge them from the hulk which they had tended so long, and to let them embark with him for home; offering to forfeit the ten years' pay due to them, "and go home sweepers, rather

* London, 1904. See the story entitled *The Signal Guns of Gungapore*.
† *I.e.* the tow-rope breaks.

than continue the miseries of their present situation". He refused. They had Government stores on their charge, and they must await orders from England as to the disposal of these before they could quit Batavia. Poor fellows, they had never had an order of any kind from England since their arrival ten years earlier. Nothing definite is known of their fate; but Carteret, who was at Batavia in August 1768, incidentally refers to the *Falmouth* as having been condemned.

Despite the assertions of the veracious Pagett, it does not seem likely that the Barisal Guns are due to actual gunfire, or to human agency of any kind. They are probably a natural phenomenon, but whether this should be located in the air, the land, or the sea remains at present an open question. It might very suitably form the subject of an investigation to be conducted by that proposed* triple combination of Forces—the Ministry of Defence.

* So in 1929—since realised, after a fashion.

OLD PARR, AND OTHERS

Life is very sweet, brother—who would wish to die?

Such was the oft-quoted question put to the despondent Borrow by Jasper Petulengro. To the speaker, of course, the answer was a fore-gone conclusion. He had just delivered his opinion (not, curiously enough, quoted nearly so often) about human survival:

". . . When a man dies, he is cast into the earth, and his wife and child sorrow over him. If he has neither wife nor child, then his father and mother, I suppose; and if he is quite alone in the world, why, then, he is cast into the earth, and there is an end of the matter."

Assuredly Jasper Petulengro, in the prime of life, and thinking so, would not wish to die. Yet one wonders whether his wife's mother, "who died at the age of 103 and sleeps in Coggeshall churchyard", was of the same opinion in her last years. Centenarians, so far as one can judge by what one reads about them, are chiefly occupied in boring their atten-dants, or reading without glasses and intelligence, and otherwise demon-strating that their faculties are no worse than they always were. If they put anything on record except a malicious codicil or so, it is usually a testimonial to the virtues of their pet nostrum, or an affidavit certifying that throughout their lives they have always shunned (or, alternatively, eagerly consumed) tobacco and/or alcohol. Very few of them have left us any means of judging what they thought of old age, as a condition—prob-ably they lacked the energy to do so. No doubt they speculated upon it when they were leaving their youth behind them, just as we speculate to-day; and when, if ever, we learn what they have learned we, too, shall dismiss the knowledge as trivial and not worth recording. I have often wondered, for example, what W. K. Clifford, if he were living to-day, would have said to this passage, which he wrote in 1875, when he was a young and ailing man of thirty.

"In those cases of ripe old age not hastened by disease, where the physical structure is actually worn out, having finished its work right honestly and well; where the love of life is worn out also, and the grave appears as a bed of rest to the tired limbs, and death as a mere quiet sleep from thought; there also, in so far as we are able to realize the state of the aged and to put ourselves in his place, death seems to be normal and natural, a thing to be neither sought nor shunned. But such putting of ourselves in the place of one to whom death is no evil must in all cases be imperfect.

"I cannot, in my present life and motion, clearly conceive myself in so parlous a state that no hope of better things should make me shrink from the end of all. However vividly I recall the feelings of pain and weakness, it is the life and energy of my present self that pictures them; and this life and energy cannot help raising at the same time combative instincts of resistance to pain and weakness, whose very nature it is to demand that the sun shall not go down upon Gibeon until they have slain the Amalekites.

"Nor can I really and truly put myself in the place of the worn-out old man whose consciousness may some day have a memory of mine. No force of imagination that I can bring to bear will avail to cast out the youth of that very imagination which endeavours to depict its latter days; no thoughts of final and supreme fatigue can help suggesting refreshment and new rising after sleep.

"If, then, we do not want to die now, nor next year, nor the year after that, nor at any time that we can clearly imagine; what is this but to say that we want to live for ever, in the only meaning of the words that we can at all realize?"*

The centenarian—the *authentic* centenarian, complete with birth certificate and other *pièces justidcatives*—is quite a modern phenomenon. In former times, before the compulsory registration of births, it was often quite impossible to verify any claim of the kind. Nowadays, however, one sees accounts in the Press twice or three times a month of persons who have celebrated their 100th birthday (or who have done so and subsequently died). And there can be little doubt that most of these cases are authentic. Yet it is not so very long ago that the view was roundly asserted, and supported by a formidable body of destructive criticism, that there was no genuine case on record, supported by evidence of a kind which a Court would receive, that any known person had ever reached the age of 100 years. The leading exponent of this attitude was Sir George Cornewall Lewis (1806–63),† aided and abetted by W. J. Thoms and other sceptics,

---

* This passage is quoted from Clifford's review, "The Unseen Universe", which appeared in *The Fortnightly Review*, June 1875. To write it, he sat up all night, at a time when his health was about to break down altogether. He died of consumption at Madeira on March 3, 1879, at the age of thirty-four. He had been Professor of Applied Mathematics at University College, London, at the age of twenty-six, and F.R.S. at twenty-nine.

† See *Notes and Queries*, 1862, *passim.*

one of whom nearly disproved, in his own person, the correctness of his opinion.

It must be admitted that this view, although it went too far, was only a very natural reaction against the slip-shod "curiosities of longevity" current at the time, and earlier. For example, "Rainy-day" Smith, in writing of various deaths which occurred in the year 1772, calmly records the following, without any details whatever:*

"(Age) 125, Rice, a cooper in Southwark; 133, Mrs. Keith, at Newnham, in Gloucestershire; 138, the widow Chum, at Ophurst, near Lichfield."

And Bailey's *Records of Longevity*† display the same uncritical spirit. In his pages the names of old folk who have reached 110 are as common as capital letters. He seems to have compiled his statistics, if one can so term them, on the theory that "if you see it in print, it *is* so". Hence such valuable pieces of information as the following:

"Mackarny, Susan, of Dublin, a mendicant, died 1751, aged 120.
"Moony, Catherine, near the City of Tuam, Ireland, died 1768, aged 136.
"Sharphy, William, Knockall, county of Roscommon, Ireland, died 1757, aged 138."

Nor is this all. Bailey gravely records the legendary case of one Petratsch Zartan, alleged to have been born at Kofrek, four miles from Temesvar, Hungary, in 1539; and to have died in 1724, at the patriarchal age of 185!

In dealing with such collections of rumours and hearsay, the acute and indefatigable W. J. Thoms‡ was like a pike in a carp-pond. Penetrated with Cornewall Lewis' theory that all "centenarians" are liars, he dealt most faithfully with every case he could find, applying to each a minute and searching scrutiny which most of them were entirely unable to withstand.

But even Thoms had to admit defeat. Not only was he confronted with unexceptionable evidence as to the age of J. W. Luning (who was born on May 19, 1767, and died on June 23, 1870), but he could find no conclusive means of disproving a much more remarkable case—that of Robert Bowman, of Irthington in Cumberland, who died on June 23, 1823, and was then believed to be in his 119th year. The matter was raised in *Notes and Queries* (of which Thoms was then editor) by Canon C. G. V. Harcourt in 1870:§ and inquiries specially set on foot by Thoms

* *A Book for a Rainy Day* (London, 1845, p. 19).   † London, 1857.
‡ *The Longevity of Man*, London, 1879.   § *Loc. cit.*, 4th Ser., vi 91.

with the object of exposing a mare's-nest resulted only in showing that, while the evidence of Bowman's great age was not perfectly conclusive, the presumption was in favour of it, and that it could only be set aside if one were to hold, *a priori*, that such a span of life was absolutely impossible.* Such, of course, was Thoms' conviction; and he ". . . said it very loud and clear", as follows:

"(some may) believe it. I do not: and in the absence of direct and more satisfactory evidence to the contrary shall continue to assert that ROBERT BOWMAN WAS NOT 118."†

Needless to say, Thoms would not hear a word in favour of what are generally regarded as the three leading cases of enormously-prolonged human life—those of Old Parr (152?), Henry Jenkins (169 or 160?), and the Countess of Desmond (140?). His criticism, granting his peculiar views, was perfectly fair, and he certainly demonstrated the now-accepted fact that there is no really valid evidence which can be adduced in support of any of them; but for the first and third there is still enough to interest any but the most hardened sceptic—and it must be remembered that the lack of conclusive evidence (often occasioned by adopting an impossibly high standard of such evidence) is not by any means the same thing as conclusive disproof. On the other hand, there is hardly any subject upon which it is easier to create a personal "legend". Let it once be believed that some person has neared or reached the century, and the neighbours, friends, and relations, shining with reflected glory, will make it an article of faith, and justify it by all manner of strange arguments, after the fashion of Smith the weaver.‡

---

* As an example of Thom's rigorous but rather irritating methods, it may be noted that he accepted Luning's marriage certificate (dated August 4, 1796) as referring to Luning (still living, 1869) but not as referring to the child born in May 1767 (which was also Luning). What finally removed his doubts was the fact that Luning had insured his life with the Equitable Co. when he was thirty-six, and had maintained the policy ever since. As Thoms admits " . . . No man ever makes himself older than he is when effecting an insurance, and few live seventy-seven years after it."

† *Loc. cit.*, p. 207.

‡ CADE. . . . The elder of them, being put to nurse,
Was by a beggar-woman stol'n away;
And, ignorant of his birth and parentage,
Became a bricklayer when he came to age:
His son I am; deny it if you can.

DICK. Nay, 'tis too true; therefore he shall be king.

SMITH. Sir, he made a chimney in my father's house, and the bricks are alive at this day to testify it; therefore, deny it not.

King Henry VI, Part II, Act IV, Sc. 2.

I propose to give a short outline of the known facts about Old Parr, the Countess of Desmond, and C. J. Drakenberg (1626–1772). I omit Henry Jenkins, because I cannot think that he stands on the same footing as the other three. There is, literally, not a particle of evidence for his age except his own unsupported and contradictory assertions—made when he was an old man, past work and depending for a living on the charity of the curious. He had an active interest in maintaining the "Jenkins legend", and it is significant that Charles Anthony, vicar of Catterick, who buried Jenkins on December 9, 1670, and who is described as "a strict exact man, and evidently a very careful parish priest", merely entered him in the register (of Bolton-on-Swale) as "a very aged and poore man", and refrained from making any mention of his age. This can scarcely have been an oversight, since Jenkins had given evidence in Anthony's favour in a tithe case at Catterick some years earlier, and had then described himself as being 157.

OLD PARR

In dealing with "Old Parr" it is best to begin the wrong way round. There is no doubt at all as to when he died, but the date of his birth is uncertain.

Thomas Parr died in London on November 14, 1635. Until a couple of months before, he had spent his whole life at Alberbury, near Shrewsbury; being, in effect, a standing proof that the late A. E. Housman's phrase about ". . . the lads who will never grow old" is of limited application, even in Shropshire.

In the spring of 1635 Thomas Howard, Earl of Arundel, then on a visit to his estates near Shrewsbury, happened to hear of Parr as having reached the age of 152. He visited him (Parr was then blind and, not unnaturally, rather feeble), and "the report of this aged man was certified"— by what particulars does not appear. Howard determined to bring him up to London, for the delight of the Court; and did so, in a litter, by easy stages.*

He was presented at Court, where tradition relates that Charles I put to him the rather embarrassing question, "You have lived longer than other men—what have you done more than other men?" and received the blunt

---

* Winnington - Wem - Shifnal - Wolverhampton - Birmingham - Coventry - Daventry - Stony Stratford - Redbourn - London. The *cortege* averaged about eighteen miles a day. Why they went round by Wem to reach Shifnal (where Howard had a seat) is obscure; they could have saved nearly ten miles by going through Shrewsbury. At Coventry Parr was mobbed by the local rubber-necks, which greatly distressed him.

reply, "I did penance (for incontinence) when I was an hundred years old".* For some weeks "the old, old, very old Man", as he came to be called, was exhibited at the Queen's Head in the Strand; where, although in no need, he continued to occupy himself with "twisting of small lines, and Cords . . . and this hee doth with an apprehension that it getteth him money".† But the change of air, diet, and mode of living, together with the constant disturbance and excitement occasioned by curious sightseers, were too much for the old man, and he withered in London like an uprooted tree.

William Harvey, famous as the discoverer of the circulation of the blood, made a complete examination of Parr's body on November 16, 1635, in the presence of several others of the King's physicians. He drew up a very interesting report, which is printed in his *Works*. Apparently he could find no unequivocal indications of great age; in fact, from the wording of his account the body might have been that of a man of between sixty and seventy. There is nothing of general interest in the medical details. Harvey concludes thus:

"All the internal parts, in a word, appeared so healthy, that had nothing happened to interfere with the old man's habits of life, he might perhaps have escaped paying the debt due to nature for some little time longer.

"The cause of death seemed fairly referable to a sudden change in the non-naturals, the chief mischief being connected with the change of air, which through the whole course of life had been inhaled of perfect purity . . . but in this great advantage . . . this city is especially destitute: . . . a city whose grand characteristic is an immense concourse of men and animals, and where ditches abound, and filth and offal lie scattered about, to say nothing of the smoke engendered by the general use of sulphureous coal as fuel, whereby the air is at all times rendered heavy, but much more so in the autumn than at any other season. Such an atmosphere could not have been found otherwise than insalubrious to one coming from the open, sunny and healthy region of Salop; it must have been especially so to one already aged and infirm.

* How this would have delighted Charles II—who, however, was then only five years old.

† Quoted from a broadsheet headed "THE WONDER OF THIS AGE", issued two days before Parr's death, and containing a portrait (see Frontispiece.), a little biographical information, and a good deal of clap-trap. On a copy in the British Museum the engraver has added, in a vacant space at the foot of the portrait, "He dyed November the 15th (sic) And is now buryed in Westminster 1635".

"And then for one hitherto used to live on food unvaried in kind, and very simple in its nature, to be set at a table loaded with variety of viands, and tempted not only to eat more than wont, but to partake of strong drink, it must needs fall out that the functions of all the natural organs would become deranged. . . .

(and so on, in a manner very commendable, and deserving the attention of the New Health Society).

". . . The brain was healthy, very firm and hard to the touch; hence, shortly before his death, although he had been blind for twenty years, he heard extremely well, understood all that was said to him, answered immediately to questions, and had perfect apprehension of any matter in hand; he was also accustomed to walk about, slightly supported between two persons.

"His memory, however, was greatly impaired, so that he scarcely recollected anything of what had happened to him when he was a young man, nothing of public incidents, or of the kings or nobles who had made a figure, or of the wars or troubles of his early life, or of the manners of society, or of the prices of things—in a word, of any of the ordinary incidents which men are wont to retain in their memories. He only recollected the events of the last few years. Nevertheless, he was accustomed, even in his hundred and thirtieth year, to engage lustily in every kind of agricultural labour, whereby he earned his bread, and he had even then the strength required to thrash the corn."

Parr was buried in Westminster Abbey, under a stone recording that he had lived in the reigns of ten monarchs—Edward IV to Charles I, inclusive.*

And now, when was he born?

The only contemporary authority for his life is a pamphlet† by John Taylor, the "water-poet", which must have been "yarked up" in great haste, for it was on sale in London on November 12, 1635, two days before Parr's death. It is dedicated to Charles I, and is partly in prose and

---

* The inscription was recut in 1870. Parr is also commemorated by a brass in his parish church of Alberbury.

There is no record of his burial in the Westminster Abbey registers. Before 1660 these are very imperfect—there are only two interments recorded as having taken place in 1635.

† *The Old, Old, Very Old Man: or the Age and Long Life of Thomas Parr . . .*, by John Taylor, London: printed for Henry Gosson, at his Shop on *London Bridge*, neere to the Gate. 1635.

partly in somewhat pedestrian verse—rhymed couplets, such as the following:

> ". . . He was of old *Pithagoras* opinion
> That greene cheese was most wholsome (with an onion) . . ."

In view of what Harvey says about Parr's impaired memory, one can only imagine that Taylor got his facts—if they are facts—from some of the old man's attendants. They have never been verified, and no new evidence has since come to light.

According to Taylor, Thomas Parr was the son of John Parr, of Winnington,* and was born in 1483. The method used by Taylor in computing his dates was based on particulars of the various leases granted to Parr in respect of a small holding which had passed to him from his father, and which he continued to cultivate throughout his long life. Reduced to prose and tabular form, they are as follows.

Age of Parr	Date	
18	1501	John Parr obtained a twenty-one years' lease of his holding from Lewis Porter.†
35	1518	John Parr died. Thomas Parr, then in service, returned to Winnington to enjoy the remaining four years of the above lease.
39	1522	Parr obtained a second lease of twenty-one years from Lewis Porter.
60	1543	Parr obtained a third lease of twenty-one years from John, son of Lewis Porter.
81	1564	Parr obtained a fourth lease of twenty-one years from Hugh, son of John Porter.
102	1585	Parr obtained a lease for the term of his life from John Porter, son of Hugh Porter above. This he enjoyed for fifty years.
152	1635	Death of Thomas Parr.

In connection with the life-lease, an anecdote of Taylor's will bear re-telling:‡

"One remarkable passage of the old man's policy must not be omitted or forgotten, which is thus; his three leases of sixty-three years being ex-

* A hamlet in the parish of Alberbury, nine miles 280° from Shrewsbury.
† This is inferred.
‡ I have modernized the spelling.

pired, he took his last lease of his landlord, one Master John Porter, for his life; with which lease, he hath lived more than fifty years; . . . but this old man would, for his wife's sake, renew his lease for years,* which his landlord would not consent unto; wherefore old Parr, having been long blind, sitting in his chair by the fire, his wife looked out of the window, and perceived Master Edward Porter, the son of his landlord, to come towards their house, which she told her husband, saying, 'Husband, our young landlord is coming hither'.

"'Is he so?' said old Parr; 'I prithee, wife, lay a pin on the ground near my foot, or at my right toe', which she did; and when young Master Porter (yet forty years old) was come into the house, after salutations between them, the old man said, 'Wife, is not that a pin which lies at my foot?' 'Truly, Husband', quoth she, 'it is a pin indeed'; so she took up the pin, and Master Porter was half in a maze that the old man had recovered his sight again; but it was quickly found to be a witty conceit, thereby to have them to suppose him to be more lively than he was; because he hoped to have his lease renewed for his wife's sake, as aforesaid."

The date of this interview is not stated by Taylor, but it was probably towards the end of Parr's life-lease, for he did not go blind until 1616.† We can scarcely blame John Porter the younger for refusing a further twenty-one years' lease to a tenant of over 130; although as he had already run through three and a bit (as well as thirty years of a life-lease), and had held two of them from Porter's great-grandfather, it would not have been surprising if Edward Porter had considered that Parr was not unlikely to see his father and himself under the ground also.

The wife referred to above was Parr's second venture. Apparently he remained a bachelor until he was eighty; after which, grown reckless, he married Jane Taylor, by whom he had a boy and a girl (both of whom died in infancy). His married life was not entirely uneventful, for in 1588 he is supposed (as he boasted to Charles I) to have done penance, in a white sheet, in Alberbury Church for having begotten a bastard child by one Catherine Milton. In 1595 he buried his first wife, but with unshaken nerve he took a second, Jane Lloyd (or Flood) ten years later—by whom, not unnaturally, he had no offspring:‡ a fact which, as he had no

* Under a lease for his life, and not for a specific term, his wife, at his death, must have relinquished the holding. He had no legal offspring, but if he were a "tenant for years" his wife could have inherited the unexpired portion of the lease, as Parr did from his father.

† Peck, *Collection of Curious Historical Pieces* (London, 1740, p. 51).

‡ In fairness to Parr, however, Harvey's testimony on this point should be quoted: "The organs of generation were healthy . . . (*desunt nonnulla*); so that it seemed not improbable that the common report was true, viz. that he did public penance under a

surviving children by his first wife, somewhat embarrasses the historian
who is compelled to record that an alleged great-grandson, Robert Parr,
died at Mitchelstown in July 1761 (aged 127?), and an equally alleged
great-granddaughter, Catherine Parr, at Skiddy's Almhousess, Cork, in
October 1792 (aged 103).* It may be noted that Ireland shares with
Russia the distinction of having provided the largest number of utterly
baseless reports of extremely long-lived persons.

As already stated, Taylor is practically the sole authority for the dates
of Parr's history, which entirely lacks any definite confirmation. But
there are two points to be noted. Unlike Jenkins, Parr (if we accept
Harvey's account) did not profess to be an authority as to his own age.
Owing to his impaired memory, Taylor, Howard and the rest must have
obtained their information about him from other sources. We have no
right to assume that they made no critical investigation whatever at the
time—and they were certainly (if, perhaps, easily) satisfied. If Parr had
been simply a man of seventy or so, as he appeared to be by Harvey's
examination, it is scarcely credible that his neighbours could have endured
to see him so civilly treated by the quality, provided with a litter and atten-
dants, and carried off to distant London with every circumstance of
respect, and in a state far above that to which his humble circumstances
entitled him—it is scarcely credible, I say, that they could have seen all
this and not have yielded to the temptation to put a spoke in his wheel.
And if, on the other hand, he were at least very much older than his neighbours—say, upwards of a century old—then the physical condition of his
body was certainly abnormal, and his real age may have been equally so.
"Hard cases make bad law."

Admittedly, conclusive evidence as to Parr's century and a half is lacking; on the other hand, that he was generally regarded, in the last years of
his life, as phenomenally old is a fact which admits of no dispute. We may,
if we please, hold that this was occasioned simply by the strong love of the
marvellous which is innate in most of us; or we may merely consider that
the story, intrinsically improbable, is now incapable of conclusive proof or

conviction for incontinence, after he had passed his hundredth year; and his wife,
whom he had married as a widow in his hundred-and-twentieth year, did not deny
that he had intercourse with her after the manner of other husbands with their wives,
nor until about twelve years ago had he ceased to embrace her frequently." In view of
the foregoing, and of his exploit in the Armada year, it would be rash to assert that he
left no surviving descendants. Not improbably those who have claimed to be such took
a pride in their left-handed pedigree: just as Davenant eagerly passed for one of Shakespeare's love-children, and the Maltese boatman tells you with pride that he is
descended from the Knights of Malta—a celibate order.

* See the *Annual Register* for 1792.

disproof, and should be regarded as "not proven". But, in my submission, we cannot call it incredible.

KATHERINE, COUNTESS OF DESMOND

As in the case of Old Parr, it is best to begin the story of "the old Countess of Desmond" at the date of her death. Since she was of Irish lineage, the procedure is peculiarly appropriate.

Katherine Fitzgerald, wife of Thomas, twelfth Earl of Desmond, is believed to have died in 1604 at Inchiquin Castle, near Youghal, Co. Cork.* The cause of her death is uncertain†—in all likelihood it was due to old age, for she was supposed to be about 140.

Although stories as to her very great age had been current for many years before her death, the first more or less definite statement on the subject is that published by Fynes Morison in 1617‡—thirteen years after it. He records that "in our time" she had lived to the age of "about" 140, although she was able, even in her last years, to go on foot to the market-town, three or four miles distant, once a week. There is little doubt that when Morison visited Youghal in 1613 he must have met with many who had personal knowledge of her. Contemporary writers, such as Bacon, Raleigh, and Archbishop Ussher,§ accepted and repeated his statement. Raleigh, in his *History of the World* (published 1614), refers to her as having been living in 1589 "and many years since": a fact to which he could ruefully testify, for in 1588 and 1589 he had to grant certain leases at a reduced rent pending the life of "the ladie Cattelyn, old countess dowager of Desmond", who had a life-interest in the lands. And in Sir John Harrington's *Short View of the State of Ireland*, written in 1605 but not published until 1879, occurs the following remark, apropos of the Irish climate: ". . . . where a man hath lived above 140 year, a woman, and she a countess, above 120, the country is like to be helthy". The man has not been identified; nor can I say with certainty why Harrington considered that countesses, as a class, were generally short-lived.

Unfortunately, the date of the Countess' birth is unknown; and that of her marriage has not yet been definitely established. The facts are these. Her husband, the twelfth Earl of Desmond, had previously been married

---

* The authority for this is a MS. (No. 626) in the Lambeth Library.

† Various apocryphal stories have been told of her dying as the result of a fall from an apple, walnut, or cherry tree.

‡ In his *Itinerary*.

§ Author, *inter alia*, of the long-accepted chronology of Scripture found in most Bibles. He determined the date of the Creation as Sunday, October 23, 4004 B.C. He refers to the "Old Countess" as having been in his time "both living and lively".

to Sheela, daughter of Cormac McCarthy. This lady is known to have been living in 1505, for documentary evidence exists that on June 9th in that year Gerald, eighth Earl of Kildare, granted her* a lease of certain lands for five years. On the other hand the Earl, who died in 1534 at the age of eighty, had a daughter by his second wife, the "old countess", and there is therefore a presumption that his remarriage took place some considerable period before his death.

On the known facts, the age of "the old countess" can never be arrived at with certainty. Any result which one reaches depends entirely upon the view taken as to the relative chances of two events, both *prima facie* improbable. "The case stands thus". To the seventy years (1534–1604) which the countess survived her husband, we must add (*a*) her probable age at the time of her marriage, and (*b*) her daughter's age at the time of her husband's death. An advocate, such as Thoms, actively interested in reducing her age to its lowest possible amount, might assume for (*a*) and (*b*) the values of 16 years and 0 months respectively. In this way he would make the countess 86 at the time of her death. On the other hand a credulous author of the Bailey type might take (*a*) as 45, or even 50, and (*b*) as 28, which would bring her age out at 148.

The truth lies somewhere between these two extremes; where, is a matter of pure assumption. A vigorous husband of eighty is almost as unusual a phenomenon as a Transit of Venus; still, women of 140, or even 120, are not as plentiful as blackberries.

As a matter of fact, Thoms concedes that the Countess "was probably about a hundred . . . at the time of her death". Adopting this opinion of the *advocatus diaboli*, stern fact compels us to add another twenty-three years or so to it—for this reason. He took the date of the grant to Desmond's first wife as being "20 Henry VIII"; *i.e.* 1528. The correct date, however, is "20 Henry VII", or 1505. Since his time the document, on which the date is plainly legible, has been published in facsimile†—moreover (a point which Thoms overlooked) the Earl of Kildare who made the grant in question died in 1513.‡

It is safe to conclude that the Countess of Desmond had long exceeded the century when she died, and that an arguable case could be made out for her having attained the age of 120. There is no conclusive proof that

---

* Under her Irish style of Gilis ny Cormik. At that period the Irish language, not being compulsory, was in common use in Ireland.

† *Journal of the Kilkenny Archæological Society*, new ser., iv. 111. 1864.

‡ As Swift has put it:
"Who killed Kildare? Who dared Kildare to kill?
Death killed Kildare—who dare kill whom he will."

she did not reach the span claimed for her—140—but, equally, there is nothing but hearsay to be cited in support of it. It has, it is true, been stated that "documentary evidence of the Countess of Desmond's age is said to exist"—but I fancy that this statement is based merely on a letter, signed "A Resident in the County of Waterford", which appeared in *The Times* of May 24, 1872. The writer declared that it was in his power to confirm the statement (as to the Countess being 140), for "a landlord in the county of Waterford has in his possession a legal document of the time of James I, wherein it is set forth that certain lands would fall in on the death of the Countess of Desmond, now aged seven score years". The following day, a letter from Thoms appeared, inviting him, in the interests of historical truth, to furnish particulars of this extremely curious document—but none such were forthcoming. In any case, the instrument in question would only provide additional, and superfluous, proof that the Countess was *reputed* to be "seven score years" old at or about the time of her death.*

CHRISTIAN JACOBSEN DRAKENBERG

In the case of C. J. Drakenberg, it is possible to give a straightforward account of his long life, since the dates of his birth and death, and of the principal events of his history, are fairly well known.† But, as will be seen, there is a "veiled period" in his life, and its later years are not free from a suspicion of personation.

Drakenberg was born at Blomsholm, Norway, on November 18, 1626. As a Norseman should, he went to sea; we find him, at the age of eleven, sailing in his Dutch uncle's‡ ship. He continued to follow the sea uninterruptedly until about 1694, making voyages to Greenland, North and South America, and the Mediterranean, as well as serving two terms, one of three and the other of six years, in the Danish Navy during the chronic wars between that country and Sweden.

About 1694, while on a voyage to Cadiz for a cargo of wine and salt,

---

* The case of the Hon. Katherine Plunkett provides a modern and well-authenticated parallel to that of the Countess of Desmond. Born on Nov. 22, 1820 (as a child, she sat on Sir Walter Scott's knee), she died peacefully and suddenly, of sheer old age on Oct. 14, 1932, aged nearly 112.

† Drakenberg seems to have escaped the notice of most writers on the subject of longevity. I have found short notices of him here and there, in various books; but the best which I have come across is an article by Miss C. Fox-Smith, which appeared in *The Blue Peter* for March 1927, and which I have used as the basis of my account of him. I am bound to say, however, that it contains some internal contradictions in matters of chronology.

‡ The uncle seems to have lived up to the disciplinary traditions of his species, for after three years Drakenberg transferred to another Dutch skipper's vessel.

his ship was captured by Algerine pirates, then and for more than a century afterwards the scourge of the Mediterranean. As was the custom, the captured crew were sold into slavery, and Drakenberg remained in this condition, serving various masters, for some sixteen years. In 1710 he was at Aleppo, in the household of a rich Jew, and it was then that, having made a friend at Court, he scented an opportunity to escape. The friend in question was a Swede named Stephen Johansen Ert, apparently a renegade ex-slave, who had obtained a measure of liberty (and freedom to trade) as the price of his "conversion", and who had turned his opportunities to such useful account that he had been able to remit considerable sums to Sweden. He had recently obtained leave to go there (pledging his honour, for what it may have been worth, that he would return) and had booked a passage on board an English ship lying at Iskanderun.

Drakenberg, and five of his fellow-captives, won Ert over, and with him the English skipper. The details were soon arranged. Drakenberg's master, who was on friendly terms with Ert, came on board to see him off, accompanied by Drakenberg and two other slaves. The captain and Ert plied the unfortunate Jew so hard with farewell toasts that he was soon under the table. A boat, armed and provisioned, was standing by; a signal was made to the other three prisoners; and in a short time the refugees were heading seaward. Coasting the shore by night, and sheltering from pursuit as best they could in the daytime, they made their way to Malta, losing one of their number en route through privation and exposure. From Malta, Drakenberg made his way to Bordeaux, where he joined a ship bound to Arendal, in Norway.

Although now eighty-five, Drakenberg continued to follow the sea. He made a voyage to Spain, and then enlisted in the Norwegian Navy. The story is told, that while so engaged he had a narrow escape of being hanged. He met Norway's greatest naval hero—the almost legendary Tordenskjold, then a lieutenant—in the streets of Oslo, and neglected to salute him. Tordenskjold, in true Zabern style, struck him with the flat of his sword, whereupon the fiery old sailor, who was always notorious both for his strength and his fits of berserk rage, whipped it out of his hand and threw it over the roof of a house. He was promptly laid in irons, but Tordenskjold let him off with a caution.

After some three years with the fleet, he went back to the merchant service, and was wrecked off Husum in the great gale of December 1717. From 1718 to 1720 he was in Holland. Then he visited Sweden, and afterwards made a long stay, as an honoured guest, with one Lieutenant-Colonel Berregaard at the latter's estate of Orsevkloster in Denmark. By this time his age—he was 100 in 1726—was beginning to bring him fame, if not fortune. It won him, for example, an interview with King Christian VI, who is stated to have given him the rank and pay of a naval boatswain and the price of a new suit of clothes.

After reaching his hundredth year, he "swallowed the anchor", and the sea knew him no more. He found a patron, one Count Danneskiold Samsoe, who provided him with a house at Aarhus, and benefited him in many ways. As some slight return, Drakenberg made a journey to his birthplace, Blomsholm—no light undertaking, even for a much younger man—in 1732–3, and brought back with him, for the satisfaction of one of Samsoe's guests, documentary evidence of his remarkable age; to wit, a baptismal certificate signed by the parish priest.

In 1736, being then in his 111th year, he married a mere child of sixty, whom he survived many years. With all a sailor's recklessness, he did his best to find a second consort—but his luck held to the end.

He died at Aarhus in October 1772, aged 145 years and eleven months, and was buried in Aarhus Cathedral. As Lenin does now, he lay in state, in an open coffin, for many years—until 1840.

Such is the story of Christian Jacobsen Drakenberg, that ancient mariner. At first sight, it seems a first-class "news-feature". The tale is supported by quite a lot of evidence, and the dates of birth and death will stand detailed scrutiny. But the natural question arises—were there two, or even more, Drakenbergs? Was the Drakenberg who died in 1772 the same man who saw the light in 1626?

There may have been two of him. Clearly, the weakest link in the chain is the period of Drakenberg's sixteen years' captivity in Algiers. He was already sixty-eight or so when captured, and would have been eighty-four when he escaped. Did he die in the bagnio, and did someone else assume his identity?

Miss C. Fox-Smith has suggested that such may have been the case. She has even identified the supplanter as the merchant S. J. Ert (or, should we, in view of his somewhat mysterious character, read this as "Ert, S. J."?). Here is her presentation of the case:

". . . He (Ert) fills the bill in more ways than one. He was something of a linguist, and we are told that Drakenberg in his old age spoke several languages well. He desired to revisit Sweden, which country Drakenberg actually did visit very soon after his escape. The fact of his having been amassing money in Sweden explains his anxiety to regain his liberty, while his promise to the Sultan to return provides a sufficient reason for getting rid of his own identity. He must, moreover, have had ample opportunity to familiarize himself with the main points of Drakenberg's early career. Men thrown together in captivity soon become intimate; and we are also told that Ert had been accustomed to act as letter-writer in ordinary to his fellow-prisoners, which would have afforded him ample opportunity to find out personal details about them.

"But—it may be objected—how would it be possible for a man of forty or fifty to step into the shoes of one of ninety? Easily enough, says our sceptic: men age very quickly, as everyone knows, in slavery, and it is, further, specifically stated by those who knew Drakenberg after his return from Asia that he 'might easily have been taken for a man of sixty'."

And she goes on to suggest that Ert or another, finding that Drakenberg's fame as a later Old Parr was a useful asset, kept up the deception (originally meant to be soon discarded) until his death; just as the Tichborne claimant found that every step in his career of imposture led him on to another.

I confess that I cannot follow this argument. I pass over the perfectly delightful specimen of a fallacy to be found in the remark about Drakenberg's linguistic powers; and I need not stress the point that Drakenberg did not, apparently, visit Sweden "very soon after his escape", but some ten years later. The main objections seem to me to be these.

What had Ert to gain by saying he was Drakenberg? So far as I can see, nothing whatever. Drakenberg would have had much more reason for saying that he was Ert. Ert was a man of substance, going home to enjoy large sums which he had remitted to Sweden. What on earth could induce him to do his utmost to forfeit his rights in them by announcing on his arrival that he was not Ert, but a poor seaman named Drakenberg? After his long absence, the slightest suspicion that he was not S. J. Ert, of Aleppo, would have made it very difficult for him to recover his money—and what would be more likely to breed such suspicion than any attempt to personate a man many years older, and of different speech, education, and profession?

Even supposing (which I cannot) that Ert could carry off his impersonation successfully, the question of motive remains unanswered. What had he, in Sweden, to fear from the Turks? And, if the Sultan's arm could have reached him there, how would he better his lot by ceasing to be Ert —a merchant overstaying his leave—and becoming Drakenberg, a runaway slave who had escaped from the Sultan's dominions, probably not without violence?

Lastly, even if we suppose that Ert, for no assignable motive, decided that he would ply the trade of modern Methuselah at the sign of the Drakenberg's Head, the fact remains that there was no money in that trade for a long time after he escaped from Aleppo. Drakenberg—or Ert —was at sea for several years more, and faring by no means sumptuously. If a clever man like Ert, in the prime of life, was content to serve, as Jacob did, seven years on the off-chance that he might later on be able (if he lived) to beg a pittance as a freak—so be it: one cannot argue about the motives of a man who acts in such a way, for he is evidently insane.

It will be gathered that I do not believe that the Drakenberg of 1710–72 was Ert. There is no evidence that he was any other pretender. On the facts, I consider that the balance of evidence is in favour of the view that the Drakenberg of 1626 was the Drakenberg of 1772—the hiatus in his history notwithstanding.

It is curious to reflect that, as a boy, he was contemporary with Parr. Had they ever met, the spectacle would have been unique: a man born in 1483 shaking hands with one who died in 1772—their joint lives spanning a period of nearly three centuries.

Conclusion

Many more cases of abnormal longevity could be cited, but space forbids. I have tried to give an outline of the evidence (such as it is), which goes to show that in one or two very exceptional cases human life may extend longer than is generally thought possible. Lovers of the marvellous, if they are uncritical, can easily find stories much more wonderful. In addition to Petratsch Zartan (185?), already referred to, here is a list, in Bailey's manner, of cases which are periodically given an airing in print by the snippet-journalist. They are all entirely unsubstantiated.

				Obiit.	Ætat.
William Edwards, Cardiff	-	-	-	1668	168
Jonas Warren, Baldoyle	-	-	-	1787	167
Louisa Truxo, Brazil	-	-	-	1780	175
Jean Korin, Hungary	-	-	-	——	172
Thomas Caron, Shoreditch	-	-	-	1588	207

In the last case, that of Caron, it is quite certain that the age originally inscribed on his tombstone was 107, and that this was altered at a later date.

According to the Press,* we can still find people living who are 150 and

* The following misprint, in *The Times* of November 13, 1872, suggests, at first sight, a rather high "expectation of life":

A RESPECTABLE YOUNG PERSON WANTED, age about 81 or 19, as HOUSEMAID, and to wait at table. Apply between 10 and 12 at 40, Queen's Road, Bayswater.

upwards—generally, and not unnaturally, in regions where life-assurance agents find their own lives rather insecure, and the recording of births and deaths is performed, mentally, by the oldest inhabitant. Thus in 1926 we were informed that one Zaro Agha, of Constantinople, aged 150, was undoubtedly the "world's oldest". Not long afterwards, it was reported that the results of a census taken in Angora had revealed the existence of a woman, named Fatma Handum, who was 160.* Nor was the unfortunate Zaro Agha long permitted to enjoy even the lesser distinction of being the oldest man in the world, for a report soon afterwards arrived from Sarajevo—much less unhealthy, apparently, for peasants than for Archdukes —that Tadija Moustafitch, a native of Herzegovina, claimed to be 156.†

Such reports, from their *ex-parte* character and lack of detail, do not inspire much confidence—nor, indeed, is it to be expected that they should. Yet it is scarcely fair to regard them as intrinsically impossible. It is perfectly true that most recorded instances of abnormal longevity are based upon the flimsiest evidence, or none; and that even the few to which this objection does not apply are based upon a mixture of evidence and assumption;‡ but it is one thing to regard them, if we wish, as "not proven"—it is quite another to draw an arbitrary line (whether it be at 100, or 110, or even 120 years) and dogmatically assert that it is, in the nature of things, utterly impossible that human life should ever extend beyond this limit.

As an analogy, consider the case of abnormal height. There is a well-defined average height for most races, just as there is an average duration of life; and, if we look only at averages, there is a well-marked upper limit to both. A man 6 feet 3 inches or so is as much above the average as a man of seventy-five, and one of, say, 6 feet 10 or 11 about as uncommon as a centenarian. Above 7 feet we get into the region of the definitely abnormal, and the percentage of such cases in relation to those of normal height is so small as practically to defy analysis. Nor do such cases appear to follow any very clear law—for example, there does not seem to be any definite relation between the numbers of persons who reach 7 feet and those who reach 8 feet. And if such a law could be found, it is fairly certain that predictions based upon it would not be of much value. For example, I am confident that analysis of the authentic cases of gigantism recorded between 1800 and 1900 would have led to a reasonable conclu-

* *Daily Express*, March 23, 1927.

† *Evening Standard*, July 18, 1928.

‡ The case of Mark Thrash, an American negro who died early in December, 1943, is apparently authentic. Had he lived till Christmas, he would have been 123. See *The Times*, 18 & 24.xii.43.

sion that no human being could ever reach the height of 9 feet—or, a
least, that the chances against this ran into such astronomical figures that
it could be dismissed as a total impossibility. And yet, soon after 1900, two
separate instances of this height being exceeded came to light. Machnov,
the Russian giant, who was over here in 1905, certainly stood a full 9 feet
3 inches; and Jan van Albert, who visited London in 1924, was reputed
to be 9 feet 3½ inches.

Now, even if we discard the traditional years of the Psalmist, and say,
with the son of Sirach, "The number of a man's days at the most are an
hundred years",* a man of 152 is not proportionately so much beyond the
ordinary limit as one of 9 feet 3 inches.† And similarly no amount of
statistical evidence could, I suggest, prove definitely that such a span of
life was a physical impossibility.

Why one or two individuals should survive—if they do survive—so
much longer than their fellows is a question to which there is no clear
answer. It may be due to some small organic abnormality—just as gigantism is due to an abnormal condition of the pituitary gland. It does not
seem to depend much upon diet, or height, or build, or sex—or even upon
locality. It certainly is not due to any nostrum such as the notorious "Old
Parr's Life Pills",‡ which Bon Gaultier celebrated in verse,§ and which
have still, I believe, a certain sale among the poorer classes. Those better
able to indulge a yearning for longer life and renewed vitality no doubt
prefer the "monkey-gland" treatment of Dr. Voronoff—a process whose
somewhat repulsive details are, perhaps, best not further discussed in
print here.

There is, however, more to be said for the views enunciated by Mechnikov.‖ It is undoubtedly true that, broadly speaking, normal longevity
diminishes as we go up the scale of life. Organisms such as the amœbæ,
which multiply by fission, are (in a sense) immortal; reptiles, on the whole,
live longer than birds, and birds longer than mammals.¶ Mechnikov connected this, somewhat curiously, with a fact of his own observation—that
Russian peasants, who are accustomed to drink large quantities of sour
milk, are notably long-lived. He pointed out that the part of the digestive

* *Ecclesiasticus* xviii. 9.

† 6 feet: 9 feet 3 inches as 100 years: 154 years approximately.

‡ These are supposed to be compounded upon a secret recipe obtained from one of
Parr's descendants (but actually evolved by one T. Roberts, a Manchester druggist).
See the *Medical Circular*, 23. ii. 1853 and 2. iii. 1853.

§ In his *Ballad of Parr's Life Pills*—one of his seven examples of the "puff poetical".

‖ See, in particular, his *Nature of Man*, 1903.

¶ There is, I believe, a tradition to the effect that some mediæval forerunner of
Darwin was burned for maintaining that an Archbishop is a mammal.

apparatus which temporarily retains waste matter is relatively much larger in reptiles than in fishes, and in birds than in reptiles; and that it reaches its greatest proportionate development in mammals. He assumed that this part, which is of little importance in digestion, is the seat of extensive putrefactive changes whose products, reabsorbed by the blood, cause auto-intoxication, and in time favour the advance of senile decay. On this ground he considered that we should, if we wish to live long, prevent intestinal putrefaction—which can be effected by employing the bacilli which occur in sour milk. Accordingly, he recommended a diet which should include preparations of milk soured by cultures from selected lactic acid—a diet which, I believe, is still favoured by a good many people, although Ilya Mechnikov himself died in 1916 at the comparatively early age of 71.

It may be so.* In this or some similar way we may succeed in prolonging our lives, or at least in thinking that we have done so. But, unless we could at the same time ward off the physical changes accompanying old age, what use would it be? Turn to those few, immortal pages in which Swift tells of the ghastly life-in-death of the Struldbruggs, those wretched creatures who could not die. It is easy to say, as Browning did:

> Grow old along with me,
> The best is yet to be,
> The last of life, for which the first was made . . .

but is it really true? We have all met wonderful old men and women— the particular example in my mind is Admiral of the Fleet Sir Provo Wallis,† the only admiral to celebrate his hundredth birthday while still on the Active List—in whom old age really is the crown of life; but they are a small minority. Too often the closing years are spent in increasing infirmity and pain, for which there is no remedy but death. Often, too, the real personality dies years before the animal residue. Who can think, unmoved, of such a fate as that of Swift himself, or of Nietzsche, or of a very great lady who died not long ago? Man's body may, perhaps, survive to a century and a half; but in doing so the man himself becomes slowly but surely an object first of curiosity and then of pity; so that he comes to answer Petulengro's question as Borrow himself did—*I would wish to die.*

* Present-day medical opinion, I understand, does not endorse Mechnikov's views.

† He died in 1892, aged 100 years 10 months. By an Order in Council (22.2.1870), he was retained on the Active List, in consideration of his past services, for life. He had been first-lieutenant of the *Shannon* when she took the *Chesapeake* in 1813. Incidentally, James Coull, who lost an arm at the *Shannon's* wheel during the engagement, lived to be 94.

THE LANDFALL OF COLUMBUS

["Landfall"* is a "term of endearment used by seamen" to denote the first land which they sight when coming in from the high seas.]

About two o'clock in the morning of Friday, October 12, 1492,† Christopher Columbus, who had left Gomera, in the Canaries, steering westward into the unknown Atlantic, on September 6th, and had seen no land since, sighted in the moonlight, from the poop of his flagship the *Santa Maria*, the shores of a low island some miles ahead, and knew that, whatever trials Fate might have in store for him, he had made history, and that the dream of his life was a dream no longer.

The island, which he named San Salvador, and of which, a few hours later, he took possession in the names of Their Most Catholic Majesties, was undoubtedly one of the Bahamas; but its identification with any known member of that group offers a problem which has perplexed geographers ever since, and which cannot even now be said to have been absolutely resolved. In fact, one result of a prolonged controversy has been, I suggest, a gradually strengthening conviction in the minds of geographers that, to speak in mathematical language, a rigorous solution of the problem is impossible; that, as in the case of Euclid's fifth postulate, the available data, when scrutinized, implicitly forbid the attainment of such a solution.

If seven cities, so we are told, contended for the honour of being Homer's birthplace (as eleven, certainly, have disputed that of Columbus himself), at least six widely separated islands of the Bahama group have at different times been put forward, and their claims to be regarded as the only true landfall of Columbus strenuously advocated, by various authorities. None of these solutions is free from objection—in one or two cases grave objection—while on the other hand there is something to be said for each. That is, of course, nothing unusual. There is something to be said for any of the score or so of men who have been accused of having written the *Letters of Junius*; just as there was for each of the thirty-odd unfortunate gentlemen who, between 1800 and 1850, claimed to be

* After I had read this paper at the R.G.S., a friend present informed me that his wife was under the impression that he was attending a lecture on "The Landslip at Colombo".

† Old Style. By the Gregorian calendar it becomes October 21.

Louis XVII. The present problem, however, is less complicated than either of these vexed questions—less complicated, indeed, than even the comparatively simple one of identifying Hannibal's Pass over the Alps. I have said that a rigorous solution is impossible, owing to the conflicting nature of the data; but I hope to show that if one accepts the principle of assessing the value of the various solutions by the percentage of evidence which one is compelled to disregard in each particular case, it is not difficult to decide that a satisfactory solution can only be afforded by one of *two* islands—the final choice being largely a matter of personal preference.

The historical facts in connection with the various identifications of the landfall are briefly as follows:

Beginning from the earliest date at which it can be said that the cartography of the Bahamas was anything more than rudimentary, the island first claimed as the landfall of Columbus appears to be Cat I. This identification was suggested by Catesby in 1731* and by Knox in 1767,† and held the field unchallenged until 1793, when the learned Spanish historian Munoz put forward the claim of Watling I.‡

When Navarrete published, in 1825, his classic work upon which all subsequent investigation of the subject has necessarily been based,§ he propounded, for the first time, the theory that Columbus' landfall was Grand Turk I., and this was supported by his American translator, Kettell, in the Boston edition of 1827, by the Hon. George Gibbs in an article (containing arguments of much greater length than depth) in the *Proceedings* of the New York Historical Society, 1846, and by R. H. Major in the first edition of his *Select Letters of Columbus* (London, 1847).

On the other hand, the Cat I. theory was revived and strongly advocated in Washington Irving's great *Life* of Columbus (avowedly based in large measure upon Navarrete), which appeared in 1828. Irving, with his customary good sense, entrusted the discussion of the landfall to another hand; only referred to, in the first edition, as "an officer of the Navy of the United States" who preferred to remain anonymous—although in the revised edition of 1848 he was revealed as Commander Alexander S. Mackenzie, U.S.N. The claim of Cat I., in opposition to Navarrete's Grand Turk I., was also supported, at about the same period, by De La Roquette in the French translation of Navarrete (1828), and by Baron de

* *Natural History of Carolina*, 1731.
† *New Collection of Voyages and Travels*, 1767.
‡ *Historia del Nuevo Mundo*, Madrid, 1793.
§ *Coleccion de los Viages* . . . Madrid, 1825.

Montlezun,* while Humboldt† also lent the weight of his European reputation in support of the arguments adduced by Mackenzie.

The claim of Watling I., which (as already remarked) had originally been put forward by Munoz in 1793, and had since lain dormant, was revived and strenuously advocated by Captain A. B. Becher, R.N., Assistant Hydrographer of the Navy,‡ in an extensive work published in 1856.§ To him is due the presence, on Admiralty charts Nos. 761 and 2579, of a note against Watling I.—"Landfall of Columbus, Oct. 1492" —and also an unfortunate error, to which I will refer presently, in the ascription of two names on adjacent islands.

One of the principal advocates for Grand Turk I., R. H. Major, was converted by Becher's arguments (a rare event), and in the second edition of his *Select Letters of Columbus* (London, 1870) and in the *Geographical Journal* for May, 1871, he retracted his former views, and accepted Watling I. as the landfall. Becher was also supported by Oscar Peschel in a work published in 1858.

By this date, then, there were at least three Richmonds in the field— Cat, Grand Turk, and Watling Is.—all with a respectable array of advocates; and there was also a fourth, Mayaguana I., put forward by Varnhagen in 1864.‖ This theory, so far as I can discover, has never been endorsed by any other authority of standing; and the same remark applies to another, developed with great diligence and wealth of detail by Captain G. V. Fox, U.S.N., in a monograph published in 1882.¶ He selected Samana I. as the landfall. It should be added that his essay forms probably the most complete and scholarly (although also, I think, the most obviously biased) investigation of the subject extant, and on points of detail it is a perfect encyclopædia of information.

Captain Fox's conclusions were very ably and convincingly criticized by Lieutenant J. B. Murdock, U.S.N., in a paper published in 1884 (after the former's death). This is by very far the most competent and impartial examination of the question which I have been able to discover. Murdock concluded that Watling I. was in all probability the true land-

* *Nouvelles Annales des Voyages.* . . . Paris, 1828.

† *Examen critique de l'histoire* . . . *du nouveau continent*, 1837.

‡ This post had not then been officially established, but Becher performed equivalent duties.

§ *The Landfall of Columbus*, London, 1856. Some correspondence between Becher and Gibbs (already referred to as an advocate for Grand Turk I.) appears in the *Nautical Magazine* (founded and, at the time, edited by Becher) for March 1858.

‖ *La Verdadera Guanahani de Colon*, Chile, 1864; Vienna, 1869.

¶ Report of the Superintendent of the U.S. Coast and Geodetic Survey for the year ending June 1880, Washington, 1882. (Appendix 18, pp. 347-411).

fall, but he pointed out grave defects in the reasoning by which Becher had previously arrived at the same conclusion.

The subject was also discussed at length by Sir Clements Markham in his *Life of Columbus* (London, 1892). He adopted Murdock's views, giving at the same time a *résumé* of the other theories. His treatment of the question, however, was not altogether satisfactory. As Macaulay might have done, he wrote, apparently, with the sole object of implanting in his readers' minds the same settled conviction as he had formed himself, and his presentation, both of the facts and the arguments, is in consequence extremely one-sided, as well as being inaccurate in many points of detail. In the edition of Columbus' journal which he edited for the Hakluyt Society in the following year he abandoned argument and treated the identity of the landfall with Watling I. as a *res adjudicata*.

In addition to Markham's *Life*, referred to above, the fourth centenary of the landfall saw the appearance of three books of first-class importance in the bibliography of the Admiral—Asensio's monumental biography, Harrisse's *Discovery of North America*, and Fiske's *Discovery of America*. Of these the first-named author is in favour of Cat I., although he prints an appendix in which the case for Watling I. is ably advocated by Juan Ignacio de Armas. Harrisse and Fiske content themselves, as do Winsor (1890) and Thacher (1903),* with a summary of the various theories.

In a paper† which appeared in 1935 the late Mr. L. R. Crawshay brought forward some fresh evidence, of an entirely novel kind. This, he considered, went to show that the landfall was Cat I.—though he admitted that this solution had "its own difficulties".

Lastly, I am now putting forward, for the first time, the claim of Conception I.—which, on balance, I regard as being, in all probability, the true landfall of Columbus.

It should be added that the navigation of Columbus' first voyage was very ably discussed by the late Earl of Dunraven in an appendix to the second volume of Filson Young's *Columbus* (London, 1906). He did not, however, attempt to identify the landfall, but assumed that it was Watling I. The same course was adopted by Professor S. E. Morison‡ in his

* Thacher refers to an expedition financed by the Chicago *Herald* for the purpose of identifying the landfall. Presumably, so far as that powerful organ's public is concerned, the question is settled.

† "Possible Bearing of a Luminous Syllid on the Question of the Landfall of Columbus." *Nature*, 5.x.35.

‡ And by Lt. J. W. McElroy, U.S.N.R., who accompanied him, in an article "The Ocean Navigation of Columbus on his First Voyage". *The American Neptune*, vol. 1, no. 3, 1941.

Admiral of the Ocean Sea,* a valuable work based upon first-hand investigation of the localities visited by Columbus. It may, in fact, be fairly said that since the appearance of Becher's work in 1856 the Watling I. theory has gradually made more headway, in the opinion of geographers in general, than any other, and that it is now accepted by the majority, as well as in most standard works of reference. It is, however, of course open for any one to propound a new theory, or to champion an old one, and it will be useful here to take stock of the materials on which such theories must be based, and of the general lines on which the problem can best be attacked.

The original journal of Columbus, and the map which he is believed to have drawn to accompany it, are lost—probably irretrievably. The sole first-hand authority for the voyage which has survived is a lengthy *précis* of the journal, with verbatim extracts, in the handwriting of Bishop Las Casas, the historian of the Indies.† It was examined by Munoz, and published by Navarrete in his *Coleccion de los Viages . . .* previously referred to. Many English translations of the portions relevant to the present inquiry have been made at different times—by Kettell, Becher, Thomas (for Fox), Montaldo (for Murdock—a revision of Thomas's), Markham, and others. In the present essay I have followed Montaldo's version, which, after collating it with several of those instanced, I believe to be the most accurate.

No other contemporary account of the voyage has survived,‡ and the *précis* published by Navarrete must in consequence be regarded as the sole real authority for its events. It is therefore very unfortunate (although, in

---

* *Admiral of the Ocean Sea, a life of Christopher Columbus.* S. E. Morison. (Boston: Little, Brown. 1942.)

† The date of this MS. cannot be exactly fixed. Las Casas completed his *Historia de las Indias* in 1561, and died in 1566. There is some ground for believing that he worked from a copy of Columbus' journal, and not from the original.

‡ Some years before the War there were produced in Germany (by Rangette, of Düsseldorf) a number of what purported to be facsimile reproductions of that lost copy of Columbus' journal which he is known to have jettisoned (during a storm off the Azores) when returning to Spain from his first voyage. It is difficult to believe that they could ever have seriously been intended to impose upon any but the half-witted. The text, based on Las Casas, is written in a pseudo-Gothic semi-cursive hand, and in *English* (in my copy), the reason alleged for this being that Columbus had intentionally kept this "secret journal" in a foreign tongue. I believe that this hoax was published simultaneously in several countries, the language employed for the text being varied accordingly.

The book also contained what purported to be a facsimile of Columbus' commission as Admiral, and was appropriately bound in brown paper, decorated with sea-shells, pebbles, algæ, etc.

the circumstances of its production, not altogether surprising) that some of its statements, to which I will refer later, are obscure, if not actually unintelligible.

Contemporary first-hand maps, also, are almost entirely wanting. The nearest approach to one is the famous world-map of Juan de la Cosa, a companion of Columbus in his voyage (he was pilot and owner of the *Santa Maria*). It was drawn eight years after the landfall, in 1500. Measuring about 5 feet by 3, it necessarily shows the Bahamas on a small scale, and not very correctly; still, it gives a surprisingly good general idea of the group and has, I think, been somewhat unfairly criticizéd. Becher, for example, speaks of it as ". . . an old document that is not worthy to be called a chart. . . ."*

Many other post-Columbian world-maps, of course, are extant, but they are nearly all on such a scale as to be of little value for the identification of "Guanahani", the native name of Columbus' landfall. One map, however, although produced a century later than de la Cosa's, is of great importance. That is the map of the Bahamas given in Herrera's *Historia General de las Indias Occidentales* (1601). Herrera was the official Spanish historian of the Indies, and had access to all available official documents.

Apart from the above, there is little of fundamental importance in the way of material available, although, of course, much is to be learned from a study of the working out of the various theories and the arguments used for and against them. As regards local information and tradition, little is to be gleaned from this source. The gentle and unsuspicious natives who inhabited the Bahamas at the time of Columbus' arrival were, unfortunately but perhaps excusably, unversed in civilized warfare, and were in consequence rapidly and almost completely exterminated, leaving the islands swept and garnished for their subsequent exploitation by pirates, bootleggers, hijackers, and other predatory animals. One or two of the native names ascertained by Columbus are still in use, and assist in the identification of some of the islands which he fell in with, but there appears to be no reliable tradition, either in the Bahamas or in Spain, which throws any light on the subject of the landfall. In fact, such tradition as exists has a directly confusing effect—for example, the name "San Salvador" has, since the beginning of the seventeenth century, been applied at various times both to Cat and Watling Is., and the resulting

* The best reproduction of the Bahaman portion of this chart which I have seen is that given in Harrisse's *Discovery of North America* (Paris and London, 1892, opp. p. 91). It should, however, be remarked that the accompanying note "enlarged twice the original size" is incorrect. The actual enlargement is trifling—about 10 per cent.

confusion formed the subject of a well-meant Act passed by the Bahaman legislature in 1926.

No relics, inscriptions, or records which can be definitely associated with Columbus' landfall have been found on any of the Bahamas, nor does he appear to have taken any astronomical observations of its position—in fact, Las Casas's *précis*, as a whole, contains remarkably few of such observations. A small number of observed latitudes (some of which are obviously wrong) are given, but the earliest of these is dated October 30th. Even if available, Columbus' longitude of Guanahani would be practically valueless as a means of identification, both by reason of his primitive methods and of his well-known underestimate of the length of a degree; but an observed latitude* of the landfall would have been of considerable assistance.

The methods which, at first sight, would appear to be available for investigating the question of the landfall are as follows:

1. By working up the courses and distances sailed by Columbus between Guanahani and his last-known point of departure—Gomera.
2. By using the direct evidence afforded by the charts of de la Cosa and Herrera.
3. By comparing the description of Guanahani which Columbus gives with that of the various likely islands as they exist to-day.
4. By constructing, from the data given·in the journal, a plotting of the relative bearings and distances of the various islands discovered by Columbus, and fitting this in on a modern chart.

Before applying any of these methods, the following notes upon one or two general points may be useful.

The courses, bearings, distances, and dimensions given in Columbus' journal are, of course, only approximate. One could hardly expect them to be otherwise. He had no hand-log, and his dead-reckoning must therefore, even when unfalsified, have been quite sketchy, while the distances and dimensions of the islands which he sighted are probably no better than rough eye-estimates. The allowance, if any, which he made for leeway (which in the ships of his time was very considerable) is nowhere mentioned. His courses and bearings appear to have been usually given to the

---

* The nearest approach to this is Las Casas' remark (Oct. 13) that the landfall was "in the same latitude with the island of Hierro [Ferro] in the Canaries". This is clearly no more than a casual comparison—Ferro was then taken to be in about $24\frac{3}{4}°$N. It is actually in $28\frac{1}{4}°$ N—while the N. point of Cat I., the northernmost of the "Big Six", is only in $24°\ 42'$ N.

nearest two points; at least, while he occasionally logs intermediate points such as N.N.W., he very seldom employs by-points. His distances are generally given in round figures, and mostly in leagues. Captain Fox, in the monograph previously referred to, made a careful investigation of the probable values of Columbus' "league" and "mile", and reached the conclusion, which appears well founded, that no great error would be occasioned by calling the "league" 3 nautical miles, and the "mile" three-quarters of the present nautical mile. He also published in the same work a very careful investigation by C. A. Schott (U.S. Coast and Geodetic Survey) of the probable amount of variation obtaining in the Bahamas in 1492. This showed that, in all likelihood, such did not exceed a quarter of a point westerly.* In view of the approximate nature of Columbus' bearings and distances, therefore, it appears best to treat them as being "true", and to convert all quoted distances to nautical miles. While on the subject of distances, it is interesting to note that Columbus frequently speaks of short distances as "two lombard shots", or "two cross-bow shots". The lombard was a species of culverin—a smooth-bore cannon of small calibre and short range. I have not succeeded in obtaining conclusive evidence of its carrying power, but there would probably be no great error in regarding a "lombard shot" as two cables† and a "cross-bow shot" as half a cable.

The first method, that of working up Columbus' run from Gomera to the landfall, is impracticable. The great circle run from Gomera to the nearest point of the Bahamas is about 3,100 miles, and at this distance the whole chain of the Bahamas, from Bahama in the north-west to Grand Turk in the south-east, would subtend an angle of only about 11°; in other words, even if one could depend upon having worked out Columbus' "course made good" to within half a point, which is a much closer degree of approximation than one could reasonably expect from such data, one would still have all the Bahamas to choose from, while to identify any particular island with certainty one would have to be able to depend upon the "course made good" being correct to about a quarter of a degree—a total impossibility.

The second method—that of using the direct evidence afforded by the charts of de la Cosa and Herrera—is more promising, although not altogether conclusive in the result which it affords. As already stated, while de la Cosa's chart is, for its date, surprisingly accurate in the general idea

* Becher found it necessary, in support of his views, to assume that the variation was a point and a half westerly, but there seems to be absolutely no justification for this assumption. A "point" is $11\frac{1}{4}°$.

† 400 yards.

which it affords of the Bahama group, it is woefully inaccurate in detail. Broadly speaking, it indicates that Guanahani is a comparatively small island, standing out a little to the north-east from the general north-west: south-east line of the Bahamas and towards the centre of that line, approximately due northward of the strait dividing Cuba from San Domingo, and due eastward of the north-west point of Cuba.

On Herrera's chart, which supports this inference, the Bahamas are indicated with more precision, while in addition all the islands at present known to exist are shown (de la Cosa's chart is defective as regards the north-west islands). The topography of Herrera's chart is markedly inaccurate, but the *relative* shapes and sizes of his islands are not far from the truth, although their general trend, considered as a whole, has an anti-clockwise error of about 15°.

If we accept the evidence given by the charts of de la Cosa and Herrera, which is in essential concordance, there are *prima facie* grounds for immediately non-suiting two claimants out of our "Big Six"—Cat, Watling, Conception, Samana, Mayaguana, and Grand Turk Is. For on both charts we see Samana, Mayaguana, *and* Guanahani shown as three entirely separate and distinct islands. It has, indeed, been argued at length by Fox that the name "Samana" was, at the date of Columbus' discovery and for some time after, applied to one of the Crooked Is., while the present Samana was Guanahani. His arguments are ingenious, but little more. On the other hand, the position given for Samana by Herrera is admittedly very incorrect—much more so, relatively speaking, than that of any other island on his map.

Both charts, moreover, combine against the claim of Grand Turk. If this were accepted, we should have to assume that all the islands shown by both de la Cosa and Herrera to the south-eastward of Guanahani were figments of their imaginations—an assumption which a glance at the modern chart will show to be untenable. A reasonable deduction, it is suggested, from the evidence of the charts is that they show only three admissible hypotheses—namely, that Guanahani must have been either Cat I., Watling I., or Conception I.

I turn now to the third method—that of attempting to identify Guanahani from the description of its topography, etc., recorded by Columbus. That description, briefly, is as follows. It was an island of uncertain size,* low, well wooded, with abundance of water and fruit, having no high hills, with a large lagoon in its middle, and encircled by a reef. One side trended to the north-north-east, and Columbus especially noted a penin-

---

* Las Casas describes it, on Oct. 12, as "a small island"; but next day—now quoting Columbus—as "very large". He has no other reference to the subject.

sula—in appearance, an island—which, as he remarked, could be easily fortified.

The Bahamas, which have a total area of about 4,400 square miles, and contain some 700 islands and cays,* may be thought to offer a tolerably wide field to any one who, on the evidence of this somewhat vague description alone, should set out to identify the island to which it refers. But, as I hope to make plain later, any one who puts forward a considered theory as to the location of Columbus' landfall is morally bound, or so it appears to me, not only to select an island corresponding with this description, but also one from which Columbus' track—so far as this can be made out from the fragments of his journal preserved by Las Casas—and the islands and cays discovered along that track, can be brought into reasonable agreement with the topography of the Bahamas as at present known. This condition practically reduces the field of inquiry to the "Big Six" of which I have already spoken.

I take this opportunity of referring to a suggestion which has several times been mooted; namely, that our troubles in identifying the landfall of Columbus possibly arise from volcanic or other extensive changes which have taken place in the Bahamas at some date between 1492 and the beginning of the nineteenth century, by which time their topography (chiefly as the result of work done by H.M. Surveying vessels) had emerged from the comparative twilight of "sketch surveys" and other dangers to navigation, and was known in all essentials as it is known to-day. Such a theory is, of course, impossible to disprove satisfactorily, or even to dismiss as highly improbable: the calamity of Martinique in 1902 goes to show that volcanic disturbances on an almost unparalleled scale have before now given the West Indies a dreadful eminence in the history of seismology; but at the same time we should, I suggest, follow Newton in saying *hypotheses non fingo*. If a matter can be cleared up without the aid of suppositions which, however possible, are highly improbable, we have no right, on an ordinary estimate of probabilities, to invoke them. The volcanic changes which would destroy the general outlines of the topography of the Bahamas, or which would, in other words, allow us to "remould it nearer to our heart's desire" in respect of some particular theory, would connote an alteration in general level of many yards—and in support of such a sweeping and Wegener-like assumption there is, so far as I am aware, no evidence whatever.

* These figures are taken from the recent *Maps of the Bahamas published by authority*, 1926. This work states that "the island officially known as San Salvador is generally called Watlings (*read* Watling), and is now accepted as the island called San Salvador by Columbus".

Let us, therefore, turn to the question of comparing the description of Guanahani given by Columbus with that of the "Big Six" as contained in the Admiralty Sailing Directions and other standard sources of information.

Cat I. is roughly 40 miles long north-west and south-east by about 10 miles wide at its south-east end. Its maximum height is about 400 feet.* At the south-east end (the end likely to have been examined by Columbus) are several lagoons. It has no fringing reef (it should, however, be noted that such a reef would in all probability have suffered very extensive changes between 1492 and, say, 1830) and no pronounced portion of coast-line trending north-north-east.

Watling I. is 13 miles long by about 6 broad. It has a large lagoon at its centre, and is extensively wooded. The greater portion of its eastern shore runs north-north-east and south-south-west, and it is low, nowhere exceeding 140 feet. It has no fringing reef. On its eastern side is a narrow, inconspicuous peninsula—not resembling an island.

Conception I. is small, about 3 miles long by 2 broad. It has a central lagoon (and another in the northern portion). It is low (90 feet) and grows stunted brushwood. It has a partial fringing reef. The eastern side forms a shallow bight whose extremities lie roughly N.N.E. and S.S.W. of each other, while very close to the former is a conspicuous islet (Booby Cay— 130 feet) which, from most points of view, appears as a peninsula.

Samana I. (also called Samana Cay and/or Atwood's Cay) is about 8½ miles long by 1½ miles broad. It runs practically east and west, and has no eastern side at all. It has no lagoon or fringing reef, and no peninsula.

Mayaguana I. is 23 miles long, east to west, and from 2 to 6 miles broad. It has no real lagoon, but a few coastal ponds, the largest about 5 miles in length and, as they all are, very narrow. It is low-lying, nowhere exceeding 100 feet. Its south-east extremity has a short coast-line, some 5 miles in length, running about north-east and south-west. It has no fringing reef; on the other hand, there is a well-defined peninsula half-way along its northern coast.

Grand Turk I. is low and has large lagoons and an encircling reef. On the other hand, it is exceedingly small (only about 2 miles long by 1 mile in breadth), no portion of its coast-line runs for any distance north-north-east, and it has no woods, and no peninsula.

---

* Markham, in his *Columbus*, p. 95, remarks: "Guanahani was low; Cat Island is the loftiest in the Bahamas". It is undoubtedly true that Cat I. is slightly higher than its neighbours, but quite imperceptibly so. All alike are very low-lying, and "lofty" seems a somewhat misleading term to apply to an island 40 miles long and nowhere rising more than 400 feet above sea-level.

Let it be noted that the presence or absence of the "stigmata" is not necessarily a conclusive proof or disproof of a particular claim.* Much may have happened in four centuries: a lagoon may have formed or filled up; erosion may have converted a peninsula into an island, or accretion rendered it an indistinguishable part of the neighbouring coast-line; a belt of timber may have widened or withered. At the same time, since by the rules of probability it is unlikely that all these causes should have operated in the same direction in any one case, it is to be inferred that the fairest estimate of the relative merits of the six claims is to be arrived at by comparing the present facts with Columbus' description without making any allowance for subsequent changes, whose amount and extent it is quite impossible to ascertain or even to estimate.

If we do this, the account will run as follows: Conception I. complies with practically all, and Watling I. with most of, the requirements; after them, in order of minimum rejection, come Mayaguana, Cat Island, Grand Turk, and Samana.

Finally, we have to consider the information, with regard to the location of the landfall, afforded by the descriptions which have survived (in Las Casas' *précis*) of the relative sizes, shapes, distances, and bearings of the various islands seen by Columbus.

After leaving the landfall the Admiral—who had, he records, made up his mind to pass no island without taking possession of it—visited in turn three other islands and then, after sighting a group of small islets, fell in with a fifth island, much greater in size than any of the remainder. This island was undoubtedly Cuba.

There is sufficient information available in Las Casas' abstract of the journal to construct a rough charting of these islands, but certain assumptions are necessary, and there are one or two defects of importance. The fifth island, as I remarked above, was undoubtedly Cuba, and the fourth and third can be identified with a fair amount of certainty. The second is more doubtful; and, unfortunately, although we are given the distance of the second from the first—the landfall—we are not given its bearing.

It has been generally assumed, even by the usually very careful Murdock, that the second island bore south-west from the landfall, this assumption being based on the fact that Columbus stated (in his journal for Saturday, October 13th) that he intended to sail, on the following evening, south-west in search of other islands. But as evidence to his actual

* So far as one important feature, the lagoon, is concerned, there is another island, Great Inagua (21° N., 73S° W.), which can compete with any of the "Big Six". I do not, however, envy the lot of any one who endeavours to work out a consistent track for Columbus from Great Inagua to Cuba.

course this is entirely negatived by a statement, in the journal for the following day, that having set sail he saw so many islands that he did not know which to make for first, but that he finally selected the largest.

Actually this statement is very obscure, for it does not seem possible that from a position in the neighbourhood of any probable landfall he could have seen more than a very few islands. Crediting him with a mast-head height of 60 feet, which is probably excessive, the greatest number would appear to be:—

From the neighbourhood of Conception I.	3	(Cat I., Rum I., Long I.).
,,	,,	,,	,, Cat I.	1	(Conception I.).
,,	,,	,,	,, Watling I.	1	(Rum I.).
,,	,,	,,	,, Samana I.	1	(Crooked I.).

Possibly, but not probably, he was misled by clouds hanging over islands, not actually in sight, below his horizon. But in any event, whatever its value, I submit that it entirely inhibits us from assuming that he necessarily steered south-west to the second island.

Let me illustrate. Suppose that a friend told you that he was going next day to the Motor Show, and that he intended to buy a car of a certain make. If you simply heard later that he now owned a car, you would naturally conclude, on that evidence, that it was of the make he had mentioned. But supposing that he wrote to you and said that when he got to Olympia he saw so many cars that he couldn't make up his mind at first, but finally selected a car which suited him more than any other, you would then be left in complete uncertainty as to what particular make of car it was. I apologize for labouring the point, but it is of some importance, and does not seem to have been fully appreciated in the past.

Summarizing all the evidence contained in the journal as to the size, bearings, distances, etc., of the five islands, it amounts roughly to the following:

The second island ("Santa Maria de la Concepcion") lay about 20 miles from the first island ("San Salvador" or "Guanahani")—bearing not stated. The side towards Guanahani ran north and south 15 miles, the other east and west 30 miles. It was probably in sight from a point somewhere near Guanahani, but not from that island itself.

The third island ("Fernandina") was in sight from the second, and about 24 miles west of it. It extended about 75 miles or more in a direction roughly N. 25° W. to S. 35° E. On the east side was an inviting-looking harbour which was found to be shallow. This had a narrow entrance, with a rocky islet on the east side of its centre.

The fourth island ("Isabela") was not in sight from the third. Off its northern shore was a rocky islet, bearing east from the third island; distance not stated, but about four hours' run with a fair wind. From this islet the coast ran south-south-west* to a prominent cape. The native name of the island was "Saometo" or "Samaot". It was even more beautifully wooded than the other islands, and somewhat higher, but by no means mountainous. It was suspected to consist of two closely contiguous islands, and had large lagoons.

The group of islets ("Islas de Arena") formed a chain extending in a north and south direction. On their south side was shallow water for some 15 miles. They were situated roughly 70 miles west of the west side of the fourth island.

The fifth island ("Juana") was sighted after running about 70 miles south-south-west from an anchorage to the southward of the group of islets.

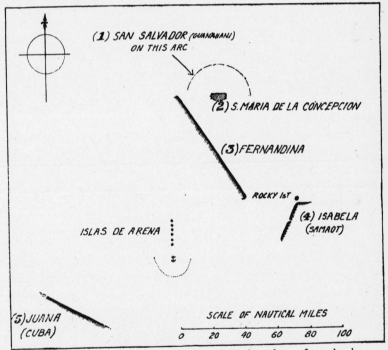

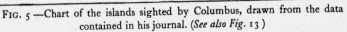

FIG. 5 —Chart of the islands sighted by Columbus, drawn from the data contained in his journal. (*See also* Fig. 13)

It is possible, with these materials, to put together a very rough sketch-chart† which should give some idea of what Columbus' own map, if he

* This bearing is partly inferred. At another place in the journal it is given as west 35 miles, which would make the cape in sight from the third island.

† See Fig. 5.

ever drew one, would have resembled. In so doing, strictly speaking, where the bearing of one island from another is given with no indication of the particular portion of the island to which the bearing refers, one should put the centre of the island on the bearing. But as, in the present case, both the second and fourth islands are stated to lie about the same distance eastward of the third (a long island running about north-north-west and south-south-east) and not to have been in sight from each other, it seems a fair assumption that the second lay somewhere off the north-north-west end of the third and the fourth somewhere off the south-south-east end.

It should be noted that this sketch-chart has been put together, almost entirely, by means of the relative bearings and distances of the various islands one from another, as given in the journal; and that no use has been made, except where absolutely necessary, of the courses and distances logged by Columbus' ships, which are vitiated by all sorts of errors—such as over- or under-estimation of speed, errors of steering, leeway, current, etc.—uncertain both in amount and in direction.

It is not, of course, claimed that so rough a chart can give more than an indication of the relative configuration of the islands visited by Columbus, but it will, I think, be found amply sufficient to assist in testing the comparative merits of the seven complete tracks (from the landfall to Cuba) which have been put forward by different authorities; and such a test is, I suggest, the most searching and the most efficient to which any theory of the landfall can be subjected.

Taking these tracks in chronological order, the first is that of Navarrete, who selected Grand Turk I. as the landfall, and who also assumed, on no authority that I have been able to discover, that Columbus always sailed towards the westward in his courses from the landfall to Cuba.

Navarrete makes the Caicos group the second island, Little Inagua the third, Great Inagua the fourth, and Cuba the fifth (all the tracks agree upon this last point). The courses and distances which Columbus must have traversed to follow such a route are entirely at variance with anything to be found in the journal, as also are the dimensions of the various islands; for example, the selected third island, Little Inagua, is only $7\frac{1}{2}$ miles long, instead of Columbus' 75 or so. The "Islas de Arena" are not identified but simply omitted.* As Murdock severely but justly remarks, ". . . It is hardly possible to imagine that this track is derived from the log at all".

Mackenzie starts from Cat I., which he assumed to be the landfall;

---

* Murdock states that Navarrete omitted the fourth island, as well as the "Islas de Arena", but this is incorrect. See above.

FIG. 6 —*Navarrete*, 1824

FIG. 7 —*Mackenzie*, 1828

and it should here be noted that there is one argument in favour of Cat I.
—and equally of Conception I.—which is not applicable to the rest of
the "Big Six". That is, that the selection of either island as the landfall
would explain what, following Dr. Watson (the celebrated and Bœotian
companion of Sherlock Holmes) might well be called "the singular incident of the light in the night-time"—an incident which has always been
one of the standing puzzles in connection with this subject. About 10
p.m. on the night of October 11—i.e. about four hours before making the
landfall and an hour and a half before moonrise*—Columbus and others
with him on the poop of the *Santa Maria* saw, or thought they saw, a
light some distance away in the darkness. It is described as looking like the
flame of a small candle, alternately raised and lowered. It seems to have
gone out of sight again not long after.

Judging by the speed of the ships, as given in the journal for this night,
the light must have been some 35 miles or so eastward of the landfall, and
well to windward of it. Markham considers that it must have been in a
native canoe—an "arawak"—which is certainly possible:† but the supposition entails consequences to which, I think, he shut his eyes. He
assumes that Watling I. was the landfall; his canoe, then, must have been
some 35 miles to the eastward of that island—dead to windward, and in
some 2500 fathoms of water! Why should it have made so laborious and
purposeless an excursion?

Murdock, another and far sounder advocate for Watling I., appreciates
this difficulty, and cuts the Gordian knot by suggesting that the light was
non-existent—a figment of excited imaginations. This theory of collective
hallucination is certainly possible, but it seems rather a drastic way of
treating inconvenient evidence—which, by the way, Las Casas gives in
some detail and clearly regards as important. Mackenzie, on the other
hand, supposes that the light was on Watling I.; and that Columbus,
owing to the darkness, missed that island, although seeing the light, and
passed northward of it, making his landfall at Cat I. This theory, taken by
itself, seems reasonable, as the run between light and landfall would then
fit in quite well. It is equally reasonable (a point which Mackenzie
missed) to suppose that Columbus passed southward of Watling I., and
made his landfall at Conception I. But in any event, so long as we accept

* According to information very kindly furnished by the Astronomer-Royal.

† Writing to me from Nassau, Bahamas, in 1941, Commdr. P. Langton-Jones, R.N.,
remarks: " . . . even the smallest fishing and sponging sloops and schooners of small
size still use the open hearth under the mainsail as did the arawaks several centuries ago.
The wind when causing the charcoal embers to glow illuminates the sail with a soft
light, making a picturesque and charming sight".

the light as a reality, then—whether it were on land, in an arawak, or (as will be seen later) in shallow water off-shore—it must have been in the vicinity of Watling I. Consequently, on that assumption Watling I. *cannot* have been the landfall—which *must* have been either Cat I. or Conception I. Incidentally, on any supposition it is very surprising that if Columbus (as he seems to have done) looked on the light as a sure indication of the long-expected land, he should have calmly proceeded under all plain sail and let it go out of sight astern, instead of clewing up and waiting for daylight, or even for moonrise.

From Cat I. Mackenzie sends Columbus to Conception I., which he selects as the second island, making Great Exuma the third, and Long I. the fourth; after which he dispatches him south-westward to Cuba, straight across the Great Bahama Bank. This portion of the route (and also that between Exuma and Long I.) is, and probably always has been, practically unnavigable.

In addition to this fatal defect in Mackenzie's track, his second island is far too small, and his third island is not in sight from it. Moreover, he makes Columbus go from Conception I. to Exuma without apparently noticing Long I., although we are told in the journal that the Admiral resolved to pass no island without taking possession of it.

Becher, having fixed on Watling I. as the landfall, makes Rum I. the second island. As explained, the latter's bearing from the landfall is uncertain, while as regards distance Rum I. fills the bill more or less satisfac-

FIG. 8 —*Becher*, 1856

torily. Columbus, however, describes the second island as about 5 *leagues* north and south by 10 east and west, while Rum I. extends only about those numbers of *miles* in such directions. Becher neglected this point; but it does not seem to be a fatal objection. It was later shown by Murdock, and I think conclusively, that Rum I. is a more generally satisfactory "second island" than any other yet proposed. It is possible that Las Casas, or the copyist, simply wrote "leagues" for "miles",* which would explain the whole difficulty; but one hesitates to make such assumptions, since it is fatally easy, in this manner, to twist facts to suit theories.

But Becher, having gone so far, proceeds to go definitely and demonstrably wrong in his further discussion of the track. Mistranslating an expression in the journal, ". . . cargué las velas . . ." ("clewed up the sails") as ". . . I made sail . . ." he sends Columbus, in flat defiance of the journal, past the second island, Rum Cay, without stopping, and thence to the third island, which, like Mackenzie, he identifies as Great Exuma. He next, to the confusion of common sense and, one would think, in utter forgetfulness of his own very considerable nautical experience, assumes that during the night of October 16–17 Columbus, in a gale and off an unknown coast, ran 100 miles in ten hours along the east coast of Long I. without noticing that it was not part of Exuma, and so arrived on the following day at Crooked I., which Becher selects as the fourth island. Putting aside the fact that no sane man would navigate in so utterly reckless a manner, it need merely be pointed out that the gale in question only existed in Becher's imagination, the journal for that night recording ". . . the wind was light and did not allow me to reach the land to anchor. . . ." As Fox rather caustically suggests, Becher appears to have confused Columbus with Vanderdecken.

From Crooked I. Becher makes Columbus anchor south of the Ragged I., which he identifies with the "Islas de Arena", and then lets him go on his way, without further perilous adventures, to Cuba.

A curious error, arising directly out of Becher's resolve not to let Columbus stop at the second island, still appears on the Admiralty charts. The name of that island, "Santa Maria de la Concepcion", is divided, one-half appearing as C. Santa Maria (Long Island), and the other half as Conception I.!

Varnhagen, assuming Mayaguana as the landfall, makes the second island Acklin I. Regarding Acklin and Crooked Is. as one (they are closely contiguous), this would agree fairly well with the dimensions given in the journal, although not at all with the distance between the first and

---

* Markham, having mooted this assumption in his *Columbus*, states it as a simple fact in his translation of the journal.

second islands. He fixes on Long I. for the third island, and makes Columbus circumnavigate it—after which he brings him back to Crooked I., which he must have passed on his way to Long I., and makes him regard it as an entirely new discovery—the fourth island! Like Becher, he identifies the "Islas de Arena" with the Ragged Is. chain.

FIG. 9 —*Varnhagen,* 1864

Fox, although selecting Samana as his Guanahani in place of Mayaguana, is otherwise in substantial agreement with Varnhagen. Like him, he goes to the Crooked Is. group for the second island, although he selects Crooked I. itself, and not Acklin. He, too, makes Long I. the third island, and brings Columbus back afterwards to the Crooked Is. group for the fourth island, this time selecting Fortune I. (close south-west of Crooked I.). He agrees with Varnhagen (and with Becher) as to the identity of the Ragged Is. group with the "Islas de Arena".

From the text of the journal itself, and on such grounds alone, the plan, followed by Varnhagen and Fox, of making Columbus sail half-way round the Crooked Is. group, proceed to Long I., and return again to the Crooked Is. group under the impression that it was an entirely new and different "fourth island", out of sight of the "second island"—i.e. practically, of itself—seems entirely untenable, and remarkable only as an excellent example of the extent to which very able and honest men can, under the influence of theories, shut their eyes to facts. It seems scarcely necessary to "flog the dead horse" any further, but it may be pointed out that Long I., for instance, is not visible from any part of the Crooked Is.

group, whereas Columbus most distinctly stated that the third island was in sight from the second.

The track worked out by Murdock in 1883 differs greatly from its predecessors—not only in its configuration but in its superior plausibility, and also in the method by which it was obtained. Instead of starting with some island assumed as the landfall and then constructing a track from this to Cuba, Murdock reversed this plan, and worked backwards from Cuba until he reached the landfall.*

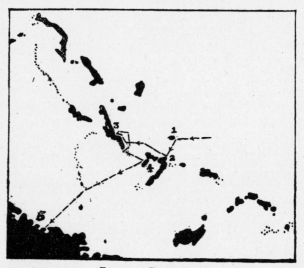

FIG. 10 —*Fox*, 1882

At the outset of applying this method, however, there appears to be an almost insuperable difficulty. Although the fifth island of Columbus can only—in view of its size, the trend of its shores, the corroborative evidence of Columbus' successors and his own later voyages, and the persistence of its native name from then till now—be identified with Cuba, it is not so easy to locate the part of it which Columbus first sighted and the harbour in which he first anchored. There are at least five candidates for the latter—Port Nipe, Port Gibura, Port Padre, the Boca de Caravela, and Bahia Bariai. The only real clue is a statement in the journal that the harbour had a wide entrance with 11 fathoms of water. Morison, *the*

* This is undoubtedly the more scientific method. It is, however, curious to note that Caleb Cushing, in an article in the *North American Review*, remarks that after applying it "we . . . shall be convinced that Guanahani is no other than Turk's Island"!

authority on such matters, unhesitatingly identifies Bahia Bariai—the
only one of the five possessing this feature—as Columbus' anchorage.

It might be thought, then, that whether you work out the track for-
wards or backwards you have to assume a starting-point. But, as Murdock

FIG. 11 —*Murdock*, 1884

showed, this can be avoided in working from Cuba to the landfall. The
first point to identify from Cuba is the anchorage at the "Islas de Arena",
which, from the journal, is found to have been about 75 miles north-east
from the harbour in Cuba. If, therefore, one takes the outline of the north-
east coast of Cuba, and transfers it bodily 75 miles north-east this line should
pass through or near the anchorage south of the "Islas de Arena", and a
short examination shows that these can only have been the Ragged Is.

Having determined this point, it is similarly possible to work backwards
to the position, off the fourth island, from which Columbus took his
departure for the "Islas de Arena". This is given in the journal as being
south-east 21 miles from the south point of the third island, and about
west-south-west from the rocky islet at the north end of the fourth island,
while it was about 65 miles east $\frac{1}{2}$ north from the "Islas de Arena"
(which have just been identified as the Ragged Is.). These data point with
practical certainty to Long I. as the third island and Crooked I. as the
fourth,* the rocky islet being Bird Rock off Crooked I., which agrees

* It may be noted that the native name of Crooked I. is "Samoete": compare the
name "Samaot" recorded in the journal as being given by the natives to the fourth
island.

exactly, both in position and appearance, with the account given in the journal. The harbour on the east side of the third island was probably Clarence Harbour, Long I.

So far then, working backwards from Cuba, the "Islas de Arena" and the fourth and third islands have been identified with very fair certainty. It remains to identify the second island, and thence, if possible, the landfall. And it is here that the real difficulties begin.

As previously suggested, since the fourth and the second islands are both stated to be situated about the same distance—25 miles or so—eastward of the third, and out of sight of each other, it is a reasonable assumption that the fourth lay off its south-east extremity, and the second off its north-west. If this is accepted, the second island almost selects itself—it must be Rum I.; there is no other available. On the other hand, there are two objections to this identification. One is, that the distance to Long I. is smaller than Columbus states, being only 15 miles instead of 21 or so; and the other is the discrepancy in size, although not in shape, already mentioned. The distance, however, was probably overestimated by Columbus; in fact, it must have been, for if it had really been 21 miles the third island could not have been seen from the second unless it were far higher than any land now known to exist in the Bahamas. Murdock considers that the fact that Rum I. is the only possible "second island" in sight from Long I. must be set off against the discrepancy in distance; but I suggest that he might with more reason have argued that this discrepancy was in fact unimportant, and that the only difficulty was the discrepancy in size. On the whole I think that, reviewing and balancing all the data, there cannot be much doubt that Rum I. has a pre-eminent claim to be regarded as the second island, although it must be admitted that the identification is not so convincing as in the cases of the islands sighted subsequently.

So far I have, in essentials, simply followed and endorsed Murdock's argument. But, for the reasons I have already given, I cannot assent to his final step. Having reached Rum I., he says in effect this: "The second island lay about 21 miles south-west from the landfall. Rum I. is the second island, and it lies about 19 miles south-west $\frac{1}{4}$ south from Watling I. Therefore Watling I. must be the landfall."

The correct conclusion, I suggest, should be this: "Rum I. is, in all probability, the second island. That island, so far as can be gathered, lay some 15* miles from the landfall, bearing not stated. The landfall must be

* Las Casas, quoting Columbus, says (Oct. 14) that the second island was "probably distant five leagues from this of *San Salvador*"; but amends this (Oct. 15) to "over five leagues distant, rather seven". We have seen that he was prone to over-estimate, since he put the distance from the second island to the third, which is actually 15 miles, at

an island agreeing with Columbus' description and lying on or near a circle of 15 miles' radius drawn from Rum I."

FIG. 12 —*Gould*, 1945

If, as a starting-point, we draw such a circle from the centre of Rum I. we find two—and only two—islands lying close to it. It passes close to Conception I. in the N.W., and within six miles of Watling I. in the N.E. Or if, to mean the errors, we increase the radius of the circle to 20 miles— which is nearer to Columbus' own estimate—it will then pass within 2 miles of the nearest point of both islands, Conception lying inside the circle, and Watling outside it. *Both* agree, *in most respects*, with Columbus' description of the landfall, and there is no other possible claimant—at least, no other now rising above the surface of the Atlantic.

21—seven leagues. Presumably, then, since he also estimated the distance from the second island to the first at the same amount—seven leagues—it is safest to take this, at first, at some 15 miles.

Another clue—unfortunately ambiguous—to the landfall may be noted here. On Oct. 15 the journal, as quoted by Las Casas, also remarks of the second island "that side which is towards the island of *San Salvador* runs north and south, and is five leagues in length". Rum I., which (although much smaller than Columbus states) is probably the second island, has no stretch of coastline extending so much as 15 miles in any direction: but it has two which run approximately north and south. Of these, its eastern extremity, some 4½ miles in extent, faces obliquely "towards" Watling I. in the N.E.: while its western, extending some 2¾ miles, similarly looks towards Conception I., in the N.W.!

Murdock, scouting the mysterious light, and tacitly disregarding the claim of Conception I. as conflicting with his view that Columbus *must* have sailed S.W. to his second island, naturally plumped for Watling I. as the landfall. This conclusion, which he expounded most ably, was generally accepted—and still is. But in 1935 Mr. Crawshay, a marine biologist who had worked in the Bahamas, re-opened the whole question by his paper, already referred to, dealing with the subject of the mysterious light.

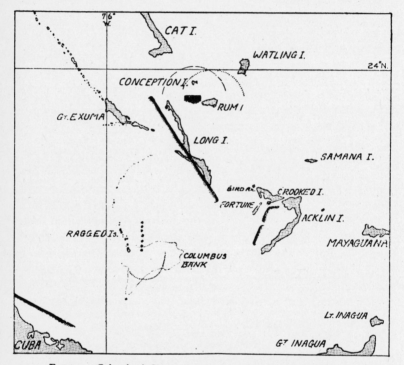

FIG. 13 —Columbus' Chart, superposed upon a modern chart

He suggested that Las Casas' account of it went "strongly to support the view that it was due to a surface display at the time of luminous marine annelids of the genus *Odontosyllis*". He pointed out that such a display would produce a light of exactly the intermittent, short-lived character described by Columbus; that the syllids producing such make their home in shallow water; and that the displays, which are associated with the reproductive process, generally occur once a month, some time after sunset, on or very near the day when the moon enters her last quarter, and within 2½ hours of low water. *All these conditions were fulfilled on the night of Oct. 11, 1492.**

Here, then, is a natural and highly probable explanation of the mysterious light. It fits the facts better than the supposition that the light came from the fire on board an arawak, since in the latter case this, while it might well be intermittent, would probably be visible, off and on, for a good many minutes. On the other hand, the syllid displays are generally very short—as Mr. Crawshay pointed out, "the strange and unaccountable light would disappear almost as soon as there was time to report it".

There is, then, excellent reason for supposing that the light seen from the *Santa Maria* was not a hallucination, but a reality; and that it was probably emitted by a congregation of luminous syllids in the shallows off Watling I. Conceivably, but less probably, it came from a native canoe in the vicinity of that island, or from some point on its shore.

In any event, if we accept the light as a reality it follows, as already remarked, that the landfall *cannot* be Watling I., and *must* be either Cat I.† or Conception I. If, again, we accept as the best method of investigating the *Santa Maria*'s track Murdock's admirable plan of working backwards from Cuba to the landfall, we find that the landfall *must* have been either Watling I. or Conception I., and *cannot* have been Cat I. The conclusion seems inevitable—*the landfall of Columbus was Conception I.*

Yet this is not really inevitable—only highly probable. Any result which one reaches is conditioned by the particular interpretation which one chooses to put upon the language of Las Casas' defective and obscure narrative: or, in places where his statements are self-contradictory, which of them one decides to accept and which to reject. Personally, I now accept Conception I. as the landfall, since I regard the evidence in its favour as outweighing that which originally led me, following Murdock, to accept his Watling I. theory‡—but I should be the last to claim that I had finally settled this long-mooted point.

In this connection, it may be salutary to indicate a question, in connec-

---

* The light was seen about two hours after sunset, and the same period after low water (at Watling I.). The age of the moon was 21 days.

† In an unpublished paper of which he very kindly gave me a copy, Mr. Crawshay inclined to the view that Cat I. was the landfall! But by no efforts could he get over the gap of 34 miles between it and Rum Cay (which he accepted as the second island)—or explain how, in that case, Columbus had sailed very close to Conception I. at mid-day without seeing it!

‡ In re-reading the original form of this paper, I have been both amused and mortified to notice how often I skirted the question of identifying Conception I. as the landfall without coming to grips with it. I *did* say, though, that I should class Conception I. as *proxime accessit* to Watling I.

tion with the identification of Guanahani, to which it does not seem likely that any satisfactory answer will ever be given. It arises from an entry in Columbus' journal about a month later (November 20, 1492). He there states that, being in a position east-south-east of Babeque, he was at the same time 12 leagues from Isabela (the fourth island), adding the exasperating note that Isabela is 8 leagues from Guanahani, or San Salvador. It seems quite impossible to reconcile the courses, distances, and bearings given in the journal between October 12th and 20th with the statement that the landfall and the fourth island, or any part of them, are only some 24 miles apart. The minimum distance between our pair and Crooked I. is about 67 miles. We must, I think, take refuge in the last resort of the baffled investigator, and declare that the passage in question is corrupt.

It may be noted that while Columbus himself never revisited the Bahamas, and while they were not much explored by his immediate successors, there is a passage in the account of Ponce de Leon's first voyage to Florida in 1512 which seems, at first sight, likely to throw a good deal of light on the identity of Guanahani. Unfortunately, it flatters only to deceive. According to Herrera, de Leon on his sixth day out from Porto Rico arrived at Caicos, in the Bahamas, and on the eighth at an island named Yaguna, in lat. 24° N. From this he went to another, named Manuega, in lat. 24° 30', and on the eleventh day arrived at Guanahani, in lat. 25° 40' N., which, it is added, was the same island as that first discovered by Columbus, and by him named San Salvador.

Whatever the actual error of these latitudes might be (and it is probably considerable) we could, assuming that it was fairly constant for all, use them to identify Guanahani if we were certain of Yaguna and Manuega; or, conversely, we could, if we were certain of Guanahani, identify the other two. But we are not certain of any of them, and it is fatally easy, in hunting round for Yaguna and Manuega, to fit these names on to some promiscuous pair of islands which agrees with that theory of the identity of Guanahani which one happens to hold. Both Humboldt and Fox certainly appear to have done so. I am afraid that this itinerary of de Leon's is not of much assistance.

But I suggest that while we may never, in the absence of Columbus' full journal and/or map, have absolutely irrefutable evidence as to the identity of Guanahani, we have at least enough to support a strong and reasonable conviction. Like many other celebrated historical mysteries, research has narrowed the issue down to a comparatively small compass. Just as it is fairly certain that the Man in the Iron Mask was either Mattioli or Eustache Dauger; just as it is long odds on Sir Philip Francis for the Junius Stakes against any other nominee; so, I suggest, is it reasonable to take the view that nearly two centuries of discussion and research have by no means been barren of result—that they have ventilated the question pretty thoroughly and shown that, although the data that we possess embody so many and to some extent so conflicting requirements that it is highly improbable and probably impossible that any one island will ever be found to satisfy them entirely, there are unquestionably two,—Conception I. and Watling I.—which stand head and shoulders above the

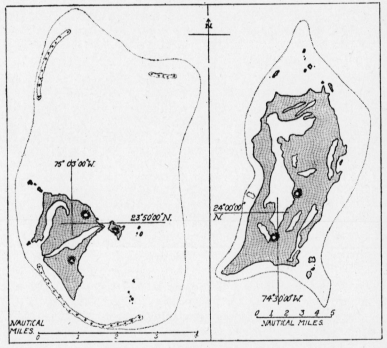

FIG. 14.—Conception I. and Watling I.

others in the number which they satisfy and the fewness of those which their selection compels us to reject. Whether we go by the evidence of the charts of de la Cosa and Herrera, by that of the description of the landfall given by Columbus himself or by that of the track which he followed from the landfall to Cuba—and on whatever system we "weight" the results of these examinations—we are, I submit, independently led in each case to the same conclusion, while the cumulative effect of this triple agreement is almost irresistible. In rejecting, if we decide to reject, the claims of Cat I., Mayaguana, Samana, and Grand Turk, we imply no censure upon their advocates—rather, I suggest, do we actually honour such men's labours, all of which have, indirectly, contributed to at least a provisional solution of this famous problem.

But while few geographers, I fancy, will disagree with this reduction of the field from six runners to two, many will doubtless question the wisdom of backing a rank outsider against an established favourite. My reason for preferring Conception I. to Watling I. is, that in my judgment it succeeds —and its rival fails—in complying with three additional criteria. Columbus could have seen several islands from it—but, at best, only one from Watling I.; it has the conspicuous island-peninsula which Watling I. lacks; and its selection as the landfall fully explains the mysterious light which, if accepted as real, utterly demolishes Watling I.'s pretensions. Still, I would emphasise that these are merely the views of an arm-chair geographer—I have never visited the Bahamas, and it does not seem in the least likely, now, that I ever shall. *Lusisti satis.* . . .

BEALINGS BELLS

On March 1, 1834, there appeared in the *Ipswich Journal* a long and remarkable letter. It was from Major Edward Moor,* F.R.S., and described the extraordinary disturbances which had occurred, and were still occurring, in his house at Great Bealings, Suffolk.

An occasional "runaway ring" is not very uncommon, especially when small boys are about; but at Great Bealings peals of four or five house-bells would often be rung simultaneously (and with extraordinary violence) while a watch was actually being kept on them, and when it seemed absolutely out of the question that this could have been done by any human agency. These peals, and occasional single rings, continued to occur at frequent and irregular intervals during a period of some seven weeks—and, in spite of repeated efforts, no definite cause for them could be discovered.

The *Ipswich Journal*, not unnaturally, opened its (fortnightly) columns to further correspondence on the subject; and to this Moor (whose good faith was unquestionable) contributed, from time to time, further bulletins as to the progress of the disturbances. And when these had finally stopped, and the matter had become a mere nine days' wonder, he devoted his leisure (of which he seems to have had a good deal) to further investigations. He had already confessed himself baffled as to the cause of the bell-ringing in his own house, and to this he gave no further attention; but he made it his business to track down, as far as possible, the particulars of any other similar cases.

He seems, when he began his researches, to have been under the impression that the bell-ringing at Great Bealings was an entirely novel phenomenon. To him it probably was. Nowadays, those who are well-read in such matters would probably classify the Bealings bells as a somewhat unusual, but not unique, variety of the manifestations generally associated with the "poltergeist"—that irritating entity whom sceptics regard as being, invariably, a mischievous child or servant; while those more

---

* A well-known writer on Hindoo mythology. He was born in 1771, and served in the East India Company's forces from 1782 to 1806, when he retired, with a special pension for his distinguished service. In character, he seems to have been a more prudent Colonel Newcome. Edward ("Omar") Fitzgerald and he were old friends. He died on February 26, 1848, aged 77.

credulous consider him an "elemental", possessed of a somewhat crude sense of humour.

During 1834–41 Moor accumulated details of some thirty cases which he regarded as similar to his own, and in the latter year he published his results in a small book entitled *Bealings Bells*.* The motive for its publicâtion was, avowedly, the very common one of trying to make a little money—but for a "worthy object". A new church was to be built at Woodbridge, about five miles east of Great Bealings; and it was hoped, with the usual optimism, that the present "scanty funds" would be augmented as the result of a bazaar. *Bealings Bells* was written for sale at that dismal function. I have no information as to the result, although this can perhaps be inferred from the fact that the book is extremely rare.

Such being the case, it seems worth while to compile from Moor's monograph—which, after all, is the *locus classicus* of a singular and rare phenomenon—an account of what happened at Great Bealings, and an outline of some of the other cases collected by him. A good deal of selection and compression is necessary. The book is not very well arranged, and details are alternately piled and withheld in a most exasperating manner. What conceivable purpose, for example, is served by beginning a chapter† like this?

"No. 29 THE —— HOUSE GHOST

"The facts I am about to tell, belong to —— House — or ——, as it was formerly called; a respectable old manor house in the north-eastern part of ——shire. It was, in very early times, the seat of the ——; a family of some distinction in the County."

Some of the cases cited as analogous, too, are quite otherwise. Moor solemnly sets down particulars of two cases in which public clocks have struck more often than they should, and ascribes this to the same mysterious agency which pealed his own house-bells. We are also told of a quite ordinary "haunted house" at Windsor (strongly suspected to be a fraud); of a poltergeist at Sydersterne, Norfolk; of the apparition of a man on horseback, both "of colossal stature" and seeming "as if they had been flayed alive", which appeared to two Army officers out shooting; and of

---

* BEALINGS BELLS. // An Account / of the / Mysterious Ringing of Bells / at / Great Bealings, Suffolk, / in 1834; / and in other parts of England: / with Relations of farther / Unaccountable Occurrences, / in / Various Places: / by / Major Edward Moor, / F.R.S. &c. // Woodbridge: / Printed and sold by John Loder, / For the Benefit of the New Church. // 1841. (12mo. xiii + 142 pp.)

† *Loc. cit.*, p. 112.

mysterious thuds, like those of a pile-driver, which were at first thought to be produced by beetles. In the last-named case the reader's natural curiosity as to their species is gratified by a footnote: "Not the insect; it is believed—but the implement.—E.M."*

Even when dealing with the disturbances in his own house, Moor is sometimes a little difficult to follow. For example, he gives the most meticulously-detailed description of the arrangements of the bell-wires; yet it is, so far as I can judge, quite impossible to construct from this description a diagram showing that arrangement. It may be as well to point out that his bells, like those in every case which he describes, were of the old-fashioned kind, hung on spiral springs, and rung by pulling; this pull being transmitted from the "bell-pull" by means of thin wires led either through detachable casings secured to the walls of the house, or inside the walls themselves. The direction of the wires was changed where necessary by "bell-cranks"—L-shaped levers, pivoted at the angle of the L, and having the wires made fast to the two arms. Drawing out the bell-pull† about half an inch is usually enough to ring all such bells; on releasing the pull, a spring returns the wires to their original position.

But while it is easy to censure Moor's book as badly arranged, and its author as pedantic—and, in spite of the letters after his name, unscientific —there is another side to the picture. He wrote at a time when such subjects were not taken very seriously; he took a great deal of trouble to investigate various recondite matters which, but for his labours, would not have been permanently recorded; he may not always, or even frequently, get hold of the right end of the stick, but it is his own painstaking record of his labours that enables this to be seen; he is perfectly frank and obviously honest. And he has a very remarkable story to tell.

Returning from church on the afternoon of Sunday, February 2, 1834, he was told that the dining-room bell had been rung three times between two and five o'clock. There was no one then in the room, and no apparent cause for the ringing. On Monday, much the same thing occurred. Moor considered that birds must have shaken the bell-wires—these, at one end of the house, ran outside it, and close to a pear-tree much frequented by blackbirds. On Tuesday the 4th, returning home about 5 p.m., he learned

---

* An engineer friend of mine once contributed to *The Times* an account of the demolition of a lighthouse, concluding with the statement that the last few stones had been removed by crabs. This excited so much astonishment that he was compelled to explain, in a later issue, that they were steam-crabs.

† Bells rung from outside a house generally have horizontal bell-pulls: inside the house the wires are usually pulled by a crank-handle.

that five of the nine bells hung in the kitchen had been ringing peals, at
intervals of about a quarter of an hour, for the last two hours.

With his son, he visited the kitchen, and while he was looking at the
bells, they rang again, very violently—so much so that, although he knew
what to expect, he was greatly startled. Ten minutes later, the same thing
happened again, not quite so violently; and a third peal followed some
fifteen minutes later. This went on, the interval between the peals gradually increasing, until a quarter to eight, when the disturbance stopped,
except that about an hour after silence had fallen an attic bell, hanging by
itself in the kitchen, sounded gently.

For a period of fifty-four* days—February 2 to March 27, 1834—
these strange ringings continued. Their character was more or less
uniform—peals of five bells, or of a different three, varied by occasional
rings from the single bell mentioned previously, or from another single
bell hanging in an attic, and connected with a bedroom. A curious feature
of the peals was the extreme violence with which the bells were agitated—
this could not be duplicated by ringing them from the bell-pulls in the
ordinary way.

Moor does not state whether the bell-pulls and/or the wires (which
could be sighted along practically their entire extent from pull to bell)
were observed to move when the bells were pealed. But he is careful to
point out that, so far as he could judge, no human agency could have produced what he heard.

"The bells rang scores of times when no one was in the passage, or
back-house, or house, or grounds, unseen. I have waited in the kitchen,
for a repetition of the ringings, with all the servants present—when no
one—hardly 'so much as a mouse'—could be in concealment. But what
matters?—neither I, nor the servants—singly or together—nor any one
—be he whom he may, could or can, I aver, work the wonderment, that
I, and more than half a score others, saw. . . ."†

"I will here, note, once for all‡—that after much consideration, I cannot reach any procedure by which they (these effects)§ have been, or can
be, produced.

If I had a year to devote to such considerations, and the promise of a
thousand pounds in the event of discovery, I should despair of success. I
would not, indeed, attempt it."‖

* Moor, in a footnote to p. 68 of his book, calls this fifty-three days.
† Pp. 17, 18.
‡ The punctuation is that of the original: I am inclined to blame the printer, who
seems to have followed the old tradition of "three stops to every line".
§ This is interpolated.   ‖ P. 21.

At the time of the ringings, he had stated, in a letter to the *Ipswich Journal*:

"*February* 25, 1834

"P.S. I had on the above date (25.ii.34) an opportunity of reading the above proceedings . . . to six or eight very intelligent gentlemen at Woodbridge—and add, as my answer to some of their queries—that I keep no monkey—that my house is not infested by rats—that the wires of the five, and of the three, *pealers*, are visible in their whole course, from their pull to the bells, save where they go through walls, in which the holes seem no bigger than is necessary. The wires of the two single bells are also visible, except where they go through floors or walls. One or two of my friends, said it was '*all a trick*'. It is *possible*. I have for many years of my life passed over large arcs of the earth's surface, and have seen divers tricks of distant people. If this be one, it surpasses all that I have seen. . . ."

Needless to say, the theory mooted by his friends had several supporters —notably a correspondent* of the *Ipswich Journal* who appears, from his letter,† to have been a retired acrobat living in a house designed by the late J. N. Maskelyne.

"In my house, which compared with Mr. Moor's, is of a limited extent, a person may, in a second, set three bells ringing violently by touching the wires, which all pass along a passage and through a hole in the wall, and in less than two seconds may get out of the passage at any one of the five doors, and may almost instantaneously set other bells ringing, and within two seconds may enter the kitchen in a different direction from that of the passage where the three bells were set ringing."

He suggested to Moor, however, a very sensible plan of action— namely, to send for a few trustworthy neighbours, seat his entire establishment in one room with a friend, lock them in, station a friend on each staircase, and search the house, locking each room as he proceeded. "If this plan be pursued I will . . . make any moderate bet, either that the bells will not ring at all during the search, or that, if they do ring, the party searching the house will find some relative, or friend, of one of his establishment concealed in some part of the house."

It would certainly have been more satisfactory if this had been done. But the letter did not commend itself to Moor. He remarks, rather loftily: ". . . I did not in any way, follow the advice therein offered". It

* One still sees his name in the papers. He signs "Constant Reader".
† *Loc. cit.*, p. 11.

must be remembered, though, that he had previously satisfied himself that the bells could not be rung from any of the rooms in a way which reproduced the violence of the mysterious peals; and he also ascertained that they could not be so rung even by tampering with the wires at a point intermediate between the bell-pull and the bell.

To do this he tried the effect of pulling down with a hoe the wires of the five "pealer" bells at a point where they all ran parallel, and close together, along a passage between the kitchen and the back-house. By his description, it seems to have been about the most favourable spot at which to pull if one wished to disturb the bells—although no one could do so without being observed from the kitchen. The effect of his test was to show that if he pulled the wires violently the bells did not ring at all; while if he pulled them gently, the bells would tinkle, but no more. He admits, though, that it took less force to set the bells in motion than he would have expected.

He also admits that there is one point, that at which the five wires first converge, from which they could be made to ring.

". . . A rope led horizontally . . . and so pulled would ring them. But they could not be rung with the violent jerks witnessed and described. With no vigour of pull could that be effected. The cranks and wires might be broken: and I have no doubt but they would be, with very much less violence of pull. This is the only mode that occurs to me by which I could, even gently, ring the four or five bells. I confess, however, that the ringing in the passage, by the direct downward pull, moved the whole six bells into sound, easier than I had foreseen, or expected, before trial.*

"But it does not shake my expressed conviction—that my bells were not so rung by any mortal hand."

He is very non-committal as to any possible explanation; he gets no nearer to one than this extraordinary rigmarole:†

"The question ever recurs—what can be the cause? An adequate cause must exist; for these effects, and for every effect; moral and physical, in nature. But, in this case, no one has yet pretended, so far as I know, to develope (sic) it.

"It may be no advance to say—that, possibly, some hitherto undiscovered law of electricity or galvanism—latent—brought into activity, only by certain combinations of metallic alloys, in certain co-extension of

* He afterwards ascertained that no downward pull, applied anywhere along the whole run of the wires, could do more than tinkle the bells.
† Loc. cit., pp. 57, 58.

parallelisms, straightness, or angles—certain concurring, or varied, degrees of tension—in connexion with certain conditions of atmospheric influences—acted upon by agencies, subtle and occult, &c. &c.

"These possibilities—whose combined eventualities may, or may not, ever be developed—may be only another link in the amazing chain of results, that recent researches into the mysterious operations of science and galvanics, have brought under the wondering eye and contemplation of chymical philosophy.

"Who can say, or imagine, where they are to end? . . ."

There is a good deal more of this sort of thing, which may be all very well for the wrapper of a patent medicine, but seems a little out of place in a book written by a Fellow of the Royal Society.

I turn to the cases collected by Moor. He omits—whether designedly or otherwise there is nothing to show—the bell-ringing at Sampford Rectory in 1810, of which an account was published by "Lacon" Colton, who then held the living.* Some of his instances, too, are so shorn of detail by excisions that they are of no value; in one or two cases, no details seem to have been vouchsafed. The following, for example, might as well not have been printed:

"No. 19. A gentleman, whom I do not know, called on me, and stated that his father took a house in the country, that had been a lady's school.— The dinner-bell frequently rang during the night; and the bells in the house, were frequently ringing.—He tried an experiment, by fixing a bell to the wall; and it rang. . . ."

Two of the cases, however—the ringings at Greenwich Hospital in 1834 and at Stapleton, near Bristol, in 1836—deserve mention.

The Ringings at Greenwich.

The best authority for the Greenwich ringings is a letter from Lieutenant William Rivers, R.N.,† in whose rooms they occurred, to Major Moor. His account is supported by a very similar one written by his wife, and by contemporary newspaper reports. I may say that I heard something of the story, as a still-lingering tradition, when I was at Greenwich Hospital (now Greenwich Naval College) in 1911.

* *A Plain and Authentic Narrative of the Sampford Ghost* (1810). There is a copy of the Appendix to this in the British Museum, but none of the pamphlet itself. Colton's bells rang all night, apparently untouched.

† Rivers (b. 1788) had served in the *Victory* at Trafalgar, where he lost a leg. He was Warden of Woolwich Dockyard from 1824 to 1826, when he became a Lieutenant of Greenwich Hospital. He died there in 1856.

(Rivers to Moor *)   GREENWICH HOSPITAL
                                        April 26, 1841

"The bells in my apartments in Greenwich Hospital, from some unknown cause, commenced ringing at half-past six o'clock, on the morning
of the 30th September, 1834; and continued, first one, and then another,
at intervals of four or five minutes, and sometimes all four at once. The
first day, I had a minute examination made by the clerk of the works, and
the bell-hanger; and in the evening, at eight o'clock, I had the wires cut
off from them. The bells then ceased to ring; but the wires were agitated
for some minutes afterwards. All remained quiet during the night. At
nine o'clock next morning, the bell-hanger came, and re-united the wires
to the bells; which had no sooner been done to the first, when it rang; the
second the same; and they continued at intervals, as before, all that day:
and many persons witnessed the performance.

"In the evening, about eight o'clock, I tied up the clappers; while so
doing, the bells were much agitated and shook violently. They ceased to
ring during that night. In the morning I loosed them again; when they
began to ring again. The clerk of the works, his assistant, and Mr.
Thame the bell-hanger came and had another examination, without discovery as to the cause. They requested the family and servants would
leave the apartments to themselves. We did so, and dined at four o'clock
at our neighbours opposite; and while at our dinner there we heard the
bells ring a peal. Mr. Thame, and the assistant to the clerk of the works,
remained until eleven at night, one watching the cranks, the other the
bells below, with perfect astonishment: but they† ceased at their
accustomed time, about nine o'clock or half-past. At eleven o'clock I
requested them‡ to retire, having made up my mind to sleep there by myself; but my brother-in-law, Capt. Watts, and my wife, determined like-
wise to do so. I searched the apartment before I went to bed, and retired
at half-past eleven o'clock. In the morning they began to ring again; but
more faintly than before. I was then fully resolved to let them have their
play out. . . . [They stopped about 3 p.m. on Friday, October 3rd.]

"I must here mention, that what appeared most extraordinary was the
movement of the cranks, which (the bell-hanger said) could not cause the
bells to ring without being pulled downwards; which they did, of themselves, in every room, working like pump-handles. . . ."

* The punctuation of this letter, and Mrs. Castle's, departs so widely from accepted
rules that I have had to alter it. The printer appears to have run short of commas, and
to have used semicolons instead (*loc. cit.*, pp. 81–83).

† The bells.

‡ Thame and the other man.

The Ringings at Stapleton

The account which Moor prints of the Stapleton case* is contained in a letter from a Mrs. Castle (who, with her husband, was living in the house where the ringing occurred) to a Mrs. Shawe, of Kesgrave Hall, Woodbridge, by whom it was forwarded to Moor.

STAPLETON GROVE
May 8, 1841

". . . One afternoon in July 1836, the bell of one of the sitting-rooms was observed to ring loudly several times; no person having touched it. In the course of half an hour the same thing occurred with nearly (if not) every bell in the house. Sometimes one would ring singly; then three or four together. The wires were distinctly seen to descend, as if pulled violently.

I sent for the bell-hanger; but before he arrived, the noise had ceased. He examined all the wires, without being able to discover any cause for this singular occurrence; and was about to take his leave, as it was growing dusk, when the bells' again began to ring more violently than before. One we particularly noticed at this time, belonging to a room immediately over the passage in which the bells hang. It is pulled by drawing up a little slide against the wall; and the wire merely passes through the floor to the bell below. The slide we watched for more than five minutes. It was constantly shaken; even making a rattling noise, and the bell ringing.

When it had continued about an hour, I desired the bell-hanger to take down every bell, as our only chance of passing a quiet night. The maidservants (who, as you may imagine, were a good deal alarmed) assured me that the wires continued to shake through the night; but I cannot vouch for the correctness of this statement, and think it was probably a little fancy on their parts. The weather was rather hot, but we were not aware of any thunder during that week.

I think it impossible that there could have been any trick, as I assembled all the servants in one place, and had the house thoroughly searched. The bells had all been newly hung† about twelve months before with stout copper wire. They were all replaced the next morning, and have never shown a disposition to be riotous from that time. . . . We have always supposed it to have been caused by electricity.‡

"MARY CASTLE "

* *Loc. cit.*, pp. 97–99.

† *I.e.* the operating wires renewed. The bells are actually hung on spiral springs, formed from flat steel strips about an inch wide.

‡ "All done by mirrors", so to speak.

In all such cases—and, indeed, in all disturbances of the poltergeist type—there must be a very strong presumption that the whole thing is the result of human agency. If a servant, or a child, has a grudge against the occupants of a house—or if any one desires to unsettle them, or to induce them to quit it—their bells offer a simple means (at least, for a time) of causing them a maximum of annoyance at a minimum risk to one's self. Nowadays, of course, the best method is to keep on ringing them up on the telephone—although if one takes the obvious precaution of using a series of call-boxes it is likely to prove a somewhat expensive amusement. But in the days before telephones, or even electric bells—and the Bealings, Greenwich, and Stapleton cases all occurred between 1834 and 1836— the facilities which house-bells offered to persons desirous of paying off a score of any kind were certainly second to none.

If the disturbances at Bealings, Greenwich, and Stapleton had been of short duration, there could be little doubt that each was either a practical joke or a piece of spite. It is their duration which makes them remarkable. The longer they went on, the more attention they would attract; and, consequently, the greater would be the risk of the operator being discovered. Besides, we all know what familiarity breeds; if he did not effect his purpose in a short time, he was not likely to do so by persisting with what had ceased to be a startling and unnerving thrill, and had become merely a nuisance, to be inquired into and, if possible, abated. It is easy to imagine many ways in which a fraud might have been perpetrated for a short time; but it is difficult to conceive why it should have been persisted in for so long—and still more so how the *modus operandi* failed to be discovered once curiosity was thoroughly aroused. Moor, as we have seen, was most thoroughly convinced that no human agency moved his bells; the minions of the Board of Works were equally baffled at Greenwich; Mrs. Castle took effective measures which certainly should have exposed a mere trick.

As the Senior Wrangler remarked of the *Ode to a Nightingale*, such occurrences, however well authenticated, "prove nothing" and lead no-where. They may have some natural explanation—most probably there is one, if we knew exactly where to look for it. On the other hand, it is an indisputable fact that the persons chiefly desirous of finding such an explanation, who may be presumed to have known more of the facts than we can hope to do now, were not successful. If Major Moor and the others were merely the victims of a prolonged and annoying hoax, its perpetrator may at least be congratulated upon having outshone Caglio-stro, the Davenport Brothers, and many "mediums" of our own day—in that he went to his grave undetected and unexposed.

POSTSCRIPT

In his *Recollections of a Geographer* (London, 1935) the late Mr. E. A. Reeves related a personal experience (*c.* 1890) which closely resembled the Stapleton case, and which proved equally insoluble.

Another example occurred during the first World War. The bells all over an old house in the heart of Greenock developed a habit of ringing, without apparent cause, in the middle of the night. Investigation revealed that Diesel engines for submarines were being tested, by night, at a neighbouring factory, and that the vibration thus produced, while imperceptible to human beings, was enough to set the bells in motion—their "period" of swing happening to coincide with it. But no explanation of this kind will cover the sudden, appalling peals heard at Great Bealings, or the independent movement of the bell-pulls at Greenwich and Stapleton— quite apart from the fact that at the epoch of those ringings there were, so far as I can discover, no factories in operation anywhere in the vicinity.

THE *VICTORIA* TRAGEDY

For the moment, it is the afternoon of June 22, 1893. In bright, calm weather the Mediterranean Fleet are steaming eastward towards the coast of Lebanon. On their starboard bow is the old roadstead of Tripoli, where they will shortly anchor. The day being Thursday, the sailor's half-holiday, all hands are officially "making and mending clothes"— but, in fact, mostly indulging in a nap before being summoned to their anchor-stations.

Along the narrow fore-and aft-bridge of the flagship *Victoria* a little procession makes its way forward—a Vice-Admiral, a flag-lieutenant, a midshipman, and a signalman. The leader, a tall, burly, bearded man, is the Commander-in-chief, Sir George Tryon, K.C.B. He is well fitted to make his way—he has been doing so, by sheer merit, all his life. He has seen war-service in the Crimea, has commanded battleships with marked ability, and has made a name for himself at the Admiralty: he is the last naval officer ever to hold what is now a jealously-guarded plum of the Civil Service—the post of Secretary to the Admiralty. Since reaching flag-rank, he has had charge of the Australian Station, and of the Reserves; and in these posts he has won for himself an enormous and well-deserved reputation as a master of all that appertains to the handling of squadrons and fleets.

The flag flying at the *Victoria's* masthead bears silent but eloquent witness that he has reached the most coveted position which the Navy of his day offers—that of Commander-in-Chief, Mediterranean Station. He stands at the summit of his career—and at the instant of its utter catastrophe. Within twenty minutes, he will be dead—and with him will go his flagship and more than half of her company.

The *Victoria* tragedy—the Naval counterpart of the Charge of the Light Brigade—came as a stunning blow to all who had the Navy's welfare at heart. We had lost ironclads before—the unstable *Captain*, blown over by a squall in the Bay, and the *Vanguard*, through collision in fog— but never in such utterly incredible circumstances. That the flagship and second flagship of the world's crack fleet should collide in broad daylight, while manoeuvring with ample sea-room and in perfect weather—that a modern battleship, with watertight doors, should capsize and sink within ten minutes of being rammed far forward at a speed of no more than six knots—and that this catastrophe should be the direct result of an order, given by a past-master of manœuvre, which was impossible of literal execution and fraught with the gravest danger to every ship of the Fleet— these events lay quite outside normal experience, and were for some little time scouted as both incredible and impossible. Yet they happened—and might conceivably happen again. The real tragedy of the *Victoria* was the exaggerated conception of discipline which was revealed as then existing among the officers of the Mediterranean Fleet—a state of matters which, paradoxically, was largely due to Tryon's great ability and masterful personality. Confronted with the fact—obvious to the most junior mid-shipman with an open mind—that the leader whom they admired and trusted had committed an egregious blunder in mental arithmetic *and did not realise this*, most of Tryon's captains took refuge in the assumption that the C. in C. had something up his sleeve—some novel manœuvre which would "clear up the mess"; while the few who anticipated trouble contented themselves with planning to keep their own ships clear of dis-aster. Admittedly, unquestioning obedience is the fundamental basis of discipline—but there is a point when such obedience passes into crass stupidity. A strong man realises that it may sometimes be his duty not only to remonstrate, but even to disobey—and he is not afraid, if need be, to act on that knowledge.

The story of the disaster, and of the events leading up to it, has often been told—sometimes, temperately and accurately. The chief source of information, of course, is the Command Paper* containing the minutes of the court-martial which sat at Malta (July 17–27, 1893): nominally, to try the survivors of the *Victoria* for losing their ship—actually, to ascer-tain the cause and details of the catastrophe. This is a mine of information —but, like most mines, the ore calls for a good deal of reduction; and there are one or two singular omissions of vitally important facts. I have done my best to fill these gaps from various sources—notably, from the late Admiral C. C. P. Fitzgerald's "Life" of Tryon.† The whole story, as re-told here, is naturally at second and remoter hands—I was less than three years old when the *Victoria* went down: but I can, I think, claim

---

* (C.—7178. 1893). In what follows, information from this source is distinguished by the reference-number of the question, as put at the trial, with the letters "C.M." prefixed. Information from Admiral Fitzgerald's *Life of Vice-Admiral Sir George Tryon, K.C.B.* is noted as *Fitzgerald*.

† *Life of Vice-Admiral Sir George Tryon, K.C.B.* By Rear-Admiral C. C. Penrose Fitzgerald. Wm. Blackwood & Sons, Edinburgh & London, 1897.

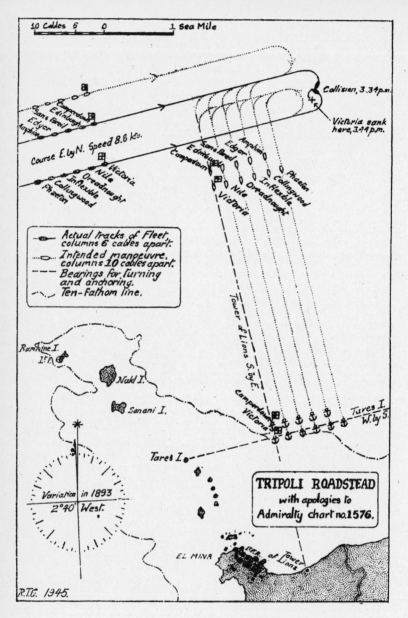

FIG. 15 —Tryon's intended manœuvre off Tripoli

that fig. 15 is a fresh contribution to the subject. It shows graphically—for the first time, so far as I know—the whole manœuvre which Tryon had planned, together with the mistake which he committed, and the consequences of that mistake.

On the morning of June 22, 1893, the Mediterranean Fleet was lying at anchor off Beyrout. It consisted of eight battleships—*Victoria, Camperdown, Nile, Dreadnought, Inflexible, Collingwood, Edinburgh* and *Sans Pareil*—three cruisers—*Amphion, Edgar* and *Phaeton*—and two 3rd class cruisers, *Fearless* and *Barham*. To modern eyes, a curious feature of the ironclads, apart from their comparatively small size,* would be their lack of homogeneity. The advantage of having squadrons composed of sister-ships had only begun to be realised. True, a beginning had been made with the six "Admirals",† and the next two decades were to see several classes of eight identical ships (*e.g.* the *Royal Sovereigns, Majestics,* and *King Edward VIIs,* otherwise known as the "Wobbly Eight"), but Tryon's eight ships were either pairs or units, and of widely divergent types.

Of these his flagship the *Victoria,*‡ completed in 1890, was the latest. Like her sister-ship, the *Sans Pareil,* she was an improved "Admiral", and embodied the large unarmoured ends which constituted the main defect of that class. But, unlike their predecessors, whose fore- and after-barbettes each mounted a pair of 13.5" guns,§ the *Victoria* and *Sans Pareil* carried their main armament—two 16.25" 110-ton guns—in a single large fore-turret, their lack of stern-fire being inadequately met by mounting a single 9.2" gun aft, in a shield. This curious disposition of their guns‖ gave them, at a distance, a shoe-like outline, their freeboard being notably low forward and high aft.

Had the second-flagship, the *Trafalgar,* been in company with the Fleet, she and her sister-ship the *Nile*¶ would have formed a second pair. But she was in dock at Malta, and Tryon's second-in-command, Rear Admiral A. H. Markham, had temporarily hoisted his flag in the *Camper-*

---

* None exceeded 12,000 tons.

† *Anson, Benbow, Camperdown, Collingwood, Howe*—generally known, for sufficient reason, as the *Anyhow*—and *Rodney.*

‡ The superstitious will like to note that her name, originally *Renown,* was changed while she was on the stocks.

§ Except the *Benbow,* who carried a single 16·25" gun in each barbette. The *Collingwood's* guns were 12".

‖ It had previously been employed in some small "coast defence" ships: the *Hero, Conqueror, Clatton, Hotspur,* and *Rupert.*

¶ Known, for obvious reasons (see Plate III) as the *Lincoln & Bennett.* The *Trafalgar* had no top-hats.

down. She was of the "Admiral" class, as was the very similar but slightly smaller *Collingwood.* Then came the *Inflexible,*[*] carrying four 81-ton *muzzle-loading* guns in two midships-turrets, arranged *en echelon*; and the *Edinburgh,* a reduced version of the *Inflexible,* who shared with the cruiser *Edgar* the unenviable distinction of being the unhandiest ship in the fleet. The list closes with the old *Dreadnought*—another exponent of M.L. guns—a precursor of the *Nile,* entirely destitute of secondary armament.

In the light of after events, an important point must be noted. The turning-powers of this motley collection of ships differed widely—very widely. For example, when using full helm (34°) the diameter of the *Dreadnought's* turning-circle was some 430 yards—that of the *Edinburgh,* about four cables (800 yards). Those of the other ships varied between these two extremes. To ensure uniformity of manoeuvring, therefore, it became necessary for all ships to use such helm as would bring their turning-circle to the size of the *Edinburgh's.*[†] To do this, the *Victoria* and *Camperdown* required 28° helm; the *Nile* and *Inflexible* considerably less; and the *Dreadnought* no more than 12°–15°.

The Fleet weighed and left for Beyrout at 10 a.m.; performing, as soon as the anchors were out of the ground, an unusual and brilliant manoeuvre of the kind with which Tryon delighted to surprise his captains. The Fleet had anchored in two lines parallel with the shore, the first division being the inshore column; and, as soon as aweigh, all ships turned together as if to steam out in divisions, line abreast, second column leading. But Tryon next took the first division, in line abreast, through the intervals of the second; and, having done so, directed the second division to steam, in line abreast, on a slightly diverging course at 7½ knots, while his own division continued on its original course at 6. The result of these joint movements was to bring the second division, diagonally, exactly into line and station with the first—after which the ships of the second division altered course, together, to conform with that of the flagship, and the whole Fleet proceeded together, in single line abreast, northward along the Lebanon coast.[‡]

The ships were due to arrive off Tripoli about 4 p.m.; and shortly after noon the *Victoria* hoisted the customary "anchoring signal", indicating

[*] She had been Lord Alcester's flagship at the bombardment of Alexandria in 1882. Even more wildly unprotected than the "Admirals", only about a quarter of her water-line was armoured—with wrought-iron, *two feet* thick.

[†] Or, if anything, a little more. In a signal made by Tryon to Capt. Vander Meulen, *Inflexible,* on June 30, 1892 (C.M. 1701) he stated "The tactical diameter of the circle of manoeuvring is 850 yards, which suits all ships". But it seems, in practice, to have been generally taken as four cables.

[‡] *Fitzgerald,* p. 389.

the formation in which the Fleet would anchor. As will appear, this signal was, actually, of much more than routine importance; yet the Court-martial seems to have attached none at all to it, and there is no published record of its actual text. According to Capt. Brackenbury of the *Edinburgh*,* its purport was as follows:—

"(Fleet will) anchor in columns of divisions—guides of columns N. by W. from the guide of the fleet (*i.e.* the *Victoria*), ships in column E. by N. from their guides. Columns two cables apart, ships in column two cables apart."†

At 2.20 p.m. the signal was made for the Fleet to form columns of divisions in line ahead, columns disposed abeam to port, columns to be *six* cables apart. This brought the Fleet into the following order:—

	Camperdown	*Victoria*	
Port	*Edinburgh*	*Nile*	Starboard
column	*Sans Pareil*	*Dreadnought*	column
	Edgar	*Inflexible*	
	Amphion	*Collingwood*	
		Phaëton	

the columns being six cables apart, and the ships in column two cables. This formation-signal puzzled Capt. Noel of the *Nile* (afterwards Admiral of the Fleet Sir Gerard Noel) considerably. As he told the Court-martial (C.M. 1580):—

"As a rule, after the anchoring signal has been made, I have always found that I could foretell how the fleet was to be got into the necessary formation for anchoring. On the fatal 22nd of June 1893, the anchoring signal was made soon after noon. About half past two the columns were closed to six cables. It then occurred to me that there was some error, and at 2.55 I made a signal "Please repeat third hoist of anchoring signal", as I thought we had taken it in wrong, which was done, repeating the former signal. I still thought there was something wrong, but of course it was impossible for me to say where the mistake might have lain."

Noel's difficulty is not hard to discover. To pass from the new cruising formation to that already signalled for anchoring, the two columns would have to be inverted—the leading ships of each column turning simultaneously through 16 points (a half-circle) and the remaining ships of the

* *Fitzgerald*, p. 367.
† See Fig. 15. The various billets are indicated by the rings of the anchors.

column following in the wake. At the same time, or soon after, the distance separating the columns must be closed from six cables to two.

In that case, why on earth had Tryon disposed them, so recently, at six cables apart? If *ten* cables had divided them, it would have at once been clear that he intended to turn the two columns inwards, "leaders together, remainder in succession" through sixteen points. Using the 4-cable "circle of manœuvre", this would simultaneously invert the columns and reduce the inter-column distance to 2 cables, thus bringing the fleet into its anchoring formation in one act. But such a manœuvre was quite impossible with the columns only 6 cables apart; even at 8 cables, each ship would come uncommonly near rubbing the paint off her opposite number as she completed her turn. Tryon must, then, intend to turn both leaders *the same* way (both to starboard, or both to port) and then close the columns by turning all ships slightly inwards simultaneously— although this would be a slovenly way of doing things, and a long way below his form of that morning. No wonder that Noel "still thought there was something wrong".

The Hon. Maurice Bourke, the *Victoria's* captain, was also disquieted —and with more reason, since he knew exactly what Tryon intended to do. Here is his account, from his official report to Markham on the day following the catastrophe:—

"Shortly after 2 p.m. the Commander-in-Chief told me he wished to see me and Staff-Commander Hawkins-Smith* with the charts. At about 2.10 p.m. we went down to his cabin. . . .

"The Commander-in-Chief then said that he should form the Fleet in two divisions disposed to port, columns 6 cables apart, and when sufficiently past the line of bearing, namely the Tower of the Lions, S. by E., which was the line we were going to turn up and anchor on, he would invert the lines by turning the columns inwards 16 points, so that on reaching the line of bearing for turning up for anchoring, the Fleet should alter course together 8 points to port, bringing the Fleet in columns of divisions line abreast to port, columns disposed astern, steering S. by E., and anchoring on these bearings when Tares Island bore W. by S.†

"The Staff-Commander then suggested that 8 cables would be a better distance to form up in two divisions than 6 cables, and the Admiral said 'Yes, it should be 8 cables'.

"The Staff-Commander then went on deck, and at about 2.15 or 2.20 the signal was made for the Fleet to form columns of divisions in line

* The *Victoria's* navigating-officer.
† This is the "Intended Manœuvre" shown, in dotted line, on Fig. 15.

PLATE III

THE LAST SEEN OF H.M.S. "VICTORIA"

Facing page 112

ahead, columns disposed abeam to port, columns to be 6 cables apart. The Staff-Commander then sent down by the Flag-Lieutenant to the Admiral to say that 6 cables was flying, and he had said 8 cables.* I was then in the Admiral's cabin, who said it was to remain at 6 cables. I then went on deck."

Reading between the lines, it is clear that Bourke, in his account of what passed between Tryon and himself in the former's cabin, had said as little as he could. At the Court-martial, even under pressure from the President (Admiral Sir Michael Culme-Seymour) he avoided amplifying his statement to any material extent:—

"(C.M. 12). . . . After the Flag-Lieutenant left the cabin the Commander-in-Chief went and sat in the stern walk and I stayed in the stern walk. It was then the Flag-Lieutenant came down to the Admiral to say that the Staff-Commander had told him that eight cables was to be the signal and he had ordered six. I am now going to say something that I did not put in the statement.

"The COURT: Yes, you can do anything you wish.

"Captain BOURKE: I then said to the Admiral words to the effect that he had certainly said that it was to be more than six cables. The Admiral then said to the Flag-Lieutenant 'Leave it at six cables', and the Flag-Lieutenant went on deck. I was left in the stern walk with the Admiral, and I must beg the Court to excuse me as I have no proof of any sort of what did pass between myself and the Admiral. I must beg the Court to excuse me saying anything about what I said to the Admiral, we being alone in the stern walk. I have no proof, and under the circumstances I am afraid I must decline to make any statement.

"13. By the COURT: Do you state that on the ground that you do not wish to incriminate yourself?—No, Sir. I do not wish to have anything said about it at all. The subject was discussed between the Admiral and myself. I can go as far as that. The question is a very serious one for me. The only person I said anything to was the Admiral. Whatever I said, he is gone, and cannot qualify my statement. I am on my oath, but under the circumstances I would rather not say anything at all about it.

"14. I am afraid there is no option with you. You are before the Court, and you must say everything to the best of your knowledge and belief. I am afraid we cannot take it from you that you would rather not say any-

* Before going back to the C. in C. with the Staff-Commander's query, Gillford showed Hawkins-Smith a slip of paper on which Tryon had written the figure "6". This had accompanied Tryon's verbal order to Gillford, that the columns were to be six cables apart. (C.M. 119, 120).

thing in the absence of proof.—The question was discussed between the Admiral and myself.

"15. I have no doubt of it; but I am afraid we cannot take that reply. You can only refuse to answer any question on the plea that it tends to incriminate yourself. I am afraid we cannot take anything else. You are bound to answer any question put to you except upon that plea. That is the law which we have got to carry out. We will put everything else aside. —The interview was very short, and I very shortly went on deck after that.

"16. That is not the point. The point is, you are asked a question as to what passed, and there is no doubt by the law you can only refuse to answer on the plea that it tends to incriminate yourself. There is no question about that.—I reminded the Admiral that our circle was 800 yards. He said the columns were to remain at six cables. I then went on deck.

"17. By the Prosecutor:* In your answer to the Court, is that all that passed between you and the Admiral in the stern walk?—Yes."

Next day, Sir Michael Culme-Seymour returned to the subject. He gave Bourke a direct order:—

"(C.M. 78). State to the Court, to the best of your recollection, all that took place between you and the Commander-in-Chief when he was in the stern walk after the Flag-Lieutenant left.—The Commander-in-Chief was sitting in a seat in the stern walk on the port side. I was standing in the stern walk between him and the door leading into the after cabin. After the Flag-Lieutenant left, I reminded the Commander-in-Chief that our circle was 800 yards. The interview I am referring to did not last more than a minute. I left the stern walk about a minute after the Flag-Lieutenant had left the stern walk. To the best of my belief the Commander-in-Chief said to me, rather shortly, something to the effect of 'That's all right. Leave it at six cables', and then I left the cabin. That was all that passed between us. It was a very short interview. I went on deck almost immediately afterwards."

And so the matter had to be left. Either Bourke had been making a mountain of what proved a molehill or else—which seems far more probable—he was doing his best to withhold some information which, in his judgment, was to Tryon's discredit. What was it?

I cannot believe that it was anything of very great importance; on the other hand, I have no doubt that Bourke's curious reluctance to discuss

* Capt. A. L. Winsloe.

the matter, coupled with the strange contrast between Tryon's brilliant handling of the fleet when leaving Beyrout and his lamentable blunder a few hours later off Tripoli, did much to give rise to a "whispering campaign", whose echoes may not have entirely died away even now,* to the effect that in the interval he had been drinking heavily.

Such rumours are not only baseless and uncharitable, but sheerly absurd. One of the most striking features of the *Victoria* tragedy is the prompt and unswerving obedience shown by Tryon's captains to an order which, clearly, they did not and could not fully understand. Their action, in such circumstances, indicated unequivocally that, *even then*, they trusted their leader implicitly. Is it conceivable that they should have acted in this way towards a man of whom they had even the slightest suspicion that he occasionally drank to excess?

The truth of the matter, I fancy, is this. Tryon was an impulsive and hot-tempered man; and, while he was in good general health, he was suffering—in hot weather, too—from a small ulcer on his leg which had obstinately refused to heal.† His newly-joined Staff-Commander had, for the second time in a few minutes, queried his dispositions for what he himself regarded as a perfectly straightforward manoeuvre—and now here was his own flag-captain backing the man up! It is quite natural to suppose that Tryon may have suddenly boiled over—flared up and said, with an oath or two, that he didn't wish to hear another word on the subject. It is equally natural that Bourke—who, quite clearly, was devoted to his chief, and his chief's memory—should have brooded with pain and regret over the incident, and have resolved that no power on earth should make him repeat in public, and as matter of permanent record, the last words which they ever exchanged in private. The pity of it is, that his entirely well-meant effort to safeguard Tryon's reputation should, in the event, have had precisely the opposite effect.

At 3.20 p.m. Tryon came forward, and went up to the top of the *Victoria's* chart-house. With him here were Bourke, Gillford, and Hawkins-Smith. The flagship had just crossed the line of bearing—Tower of Lions S. by E.—on which the C. in C. intended to close the anchorage, and she stood on for another ten minutes, so as to allow the *Phæton*, the rearmost ship of the longer column, time to complete her forthcoming 16-point turn, and steady up, before again altering course to port (see fig. 15).

At 3.27 Gillford, at Tryon's order, hoisted a pair of "divisional"

* I have heard them myself—though they have never, so far as I know, found their way into print before. Their explicit contradiction is long overdue.

† (C.M. 1146).

signals—one, at the mast-head,¶ addressing the second division (led by the
Camperdown); the other, at the yard-arm, addressing the first (led by the
Victoria). They ran:—

Second division alter course in succession 16 points to starboard, preserving the order of the division.†	First division alter course in succession 16 points to port, preserving the order of the division.†

For the reason already given—the insufficient distance between the
two columns—this pair of signals must have come as a complete surprise
to Tryon's second-in-command, Markham, and to the captains of the
fleet. With Markham's reactions I shall deal shortly; here are those of the
captains,‡ as attested in Court:—

FIRST DIVISION (starboard column)

Capt. Bourke, *Victoria*, while appreciating that, on the face of it, his
ship would go very close to the *Camperdown*, thought that "the Commander-in-Chief had some way out of it".

Capt. Noel, *Nile*, expected that the leaders, by reversing their inner
screws, would reduce their turning-circles to less than three cables. Anyhow, he would. "I made up my mind that I should turn inside the
Victoria whatever she did."

Capt. Moore, *Dreadnought*, thought "we were about to see something
unusual in the way of an evolution". He decided, as Noel had, to turn
inside his leader whatever happened. He knew his ship—the handiest in
the fleet—was in no danger; and he did not at once appreciate that less
handy ships might be.

*Capt. Vander Meulen,§ *Inflexible*, expected that, once the *Victoria* and
Camperdown had come end-on to each other, the former—realising that

¶ The *Victoria* had, practically, only one mast—the main, crossing two yards and
carrying a fighting-top. She also had a small pole-mast stepped forward of the fore-
bridge. See the *Nile* (Plate III) whose masting was similar, except that her pole-mast
was much longer than the *Victoria's*.

† Not, as is generally stated, "preserving the order of the *fleet*". The flag used—the
compass pendant—only had this significance when used as a "general signal" to the
whole fleet: not when used (as on this occasion) with a distinguishing signal, addressing
a particular division, hoisted superior to it. Actually, Tryon said nothing about preserving the order of the fleet (C.M. 124).

‡ Except two—Capt. Dickinson (*Fearless*), and Commdr. Aylen (*Barham*)—
neither of whom gave evidence.

§ The Court-martial minutes speak of him as "Rear Admiral Vander Meulen"—he
got his flag soon after the catastrophe and before the Court-martial.

the manœuvre, as signalled, was impossible, or at best highly dangerous—would ease her helm, and circle outside the latter.

Capt. Jenkings, *Collingwood*, considered that, the manœuvre as signalled being impossible, a wrong signal must have been made to the first division. He expected to see this turn to *starboard*.

Capt. Custance, *Phæton*, at first saw nothing wrong with the signal, and said to himself, "That gives us two cables to turn in". Immediately afterwards, he realised that he had mistaken the radius of the fleet's turning-circle for its diameter, and concluded that Tryon had done the same.

SECOND DIVISION (port column)

Capt. Johnstone, *Camperdown*, at first thought a mistake had been made in the signal, the manœuvre being impossible with the columns so close together. He then accepted Markham's suggestion that the C. in C. was going to circle round outside their column.

*Capt. Brackenbury, *Edinburgh*, also thought that Tryon's division would circle round outside Markham's.

Capt. Wilson, *Sans Pareil*, noticing that the *Victoria* and *Camperdown* were exchanging semaphore signals, concluded that the leaders were arranging which should pass outside the other.

*Capt. Acland, *Amphion*, expected that Tryon would lead the first division round outside the second.

It will be observed that the only point upon which Tryon's captains were agreed was, that the manœuvre, as signalled, was impossible without taking extraordinary measures—and that while, in general, the first division—the handier ships—expected to reduce their turning-circle by the help of their screws, the second division, on the other hand, anticipated that their opposite numbers would *increase* this, by easing thei· helm, and pass on the outside of the port column. In view of this complete cleavage of ideas, it is depressing to note that every ship of the fleet, with one exception, at once acknowledged Tryon's two signals by hoisting her answering pendant "close up"—indicating that these were both seen *and understood*.

The exception was the *Camperdown*. Markham, on the signal being reported to him, at once remarked, "It's impossible—it's an impracticable manœuvre". He directed his flag-lieutenant to keep the repeat-hoist "at

---

* The Captains marked with an asterisk were called, at Markham's request, to testify to their interpretation of the signal (already intimated by them to Markham, spontaneously); namely, that Tryon intended to circle the first division outside the second.

the dip"*—indicating that the signal was seen, but not understood—and to semaphore to the C. in C.: "Do you wish the evolution to be performed as indicated by the signal?" But, before this could be done, Tryon had already semaphored to the luckless *Camperdown*: "What are you waiting for?"

Markham was no weakling—as second-in-command of the *Alert* in the Arctic (1875–6) he had led the sledge-party which, painfully toiling over very heavy pack-ice while handicapped (and ultimately routed) by scurvy, had reached the then "farthest North", 83° 20′ N. But he was a sensitive, abnormally-courteous man who fully realised his Chief's superiority in manœuvre, and had grown accustomed to obeying him blindly.† He realised that he, and he alone, was delaying an important manœuvre and, possibly, endangering the fleet—which was heading for the shore:‡ and he must, for a brief period, have been immensely relieved when a reasonable explanation of Tryon's astonishing signal flashed into his mind. The signals were completely separate; he must turn as soon as that to the second column came down;§ Tryon, no doubt, would keep that to his own column flying a few seconds longer, to give a safe margin of clearance and then, on hauling it down, circle round the second division under reduced helm, and come up on the other side of it, afterwards closing the columns. He communicated this idea to Johnstone, who welcomed it, and showed his repeat-hoist close up. Down came the flagship's two hoists§—*simultaneously*—and the two leaders put their helms over: the *Camperdown*, at 28°, which would turn her in the standard four cables—the *Victoria, hard over* (34°).

The wide separation of the flagship's helm-signals must speedily have warned Markham that his conception of the intended manœuvre was quite wrong, and that a collision was imminent. The fact had already become obvious to the little knot of men gathered around the Commander-in-Chief; that was why Hawkins-Smith, on his own initiative, had given the order "extreme starboard helm" as soon as the turning-signal came down. The impending disaster might still, or even a little

* Hoisted half-way, or little more—not close up. The fleet being in two columns, the *Camperdown* would repeat all signals made by the *Victoria*—which, owing to smoke, etc., might otherwise be missed by ships astern of the flagship.

† (C.M. 412). "We used to carry out many evolutions in the Mediterranean Squadron of which at the time, I must acknowledge, I hardly knew what was the object, and they were only afterwards fully explained to me by the Commander-in-Chief, in his cabin."

‡ Actually, there was no reason for hurry on this score—the fleet could have maintained its present course and speed for another hour before crossing the 10-fathom line.

§ A manœuvring-signal "becomes effective" immediately it is hauled down.

later, have been averted if one ship or the other (not, of course, both) had reversed her helm;* but Markham was most firmly of opinion that "I should have been utterly wrong in doing it"†—and Tryon, apparently, was temporarily stunned at realising that he had committed an appalling blunder. He stood silent, with his eyes fixed on the *Camperdown*: and although Bourke more than once said to him, with urgency in his tone, "We shall be very close to that ship, Sir. May I go astern with the port screw?", it was not until the two flagships were end-on, and rapidly converging, that he gave the required permission. Soon after, Bourke went "Full astern both engines" on his own responsibility; and the *Camperdown* followed suit.‡ At the same time—far too late to be of any real use—both ships piped "Close watertight doors".

The peaceful, sunny, afternoon scene had suddenly become charged with stark tragedy. Tryon's intended reversal and reformation of the fleet had transformed itself into a terribly convincing demonstration of the power of that obsolescent weapon, the Ram§—and, also, of its basic weakness. This was, that in most cases it was impossible to be certain whether an attacking ship would ram or be rammed. It was generally a toss-up—but on this occasion the issue was decided by the fact that the *Victoria*, using more helm than her opponent, had turned in a slightly smaller circle. About four minutes after the signals were hauled down, the *Camperdown* rammed the *Victoria*, practically at right angles, on the starboard bow and cut her wide open with a resounding crash.

The *Camperdown's* speed, at the moment of impact, can hardly have exceeded six knots, but even then the momentum of her 10,600 tons was enough to send the *Victoria* bodily sideways for some 70–80 feet. Suddenly brought up, the two battleships remained locked together for a minute or so—then, as the *Camperdown* gathered sternway and backed out, observers aboard her could see a huge, gaping rent in the flagship's side.

* Such, at least, was the opinion of the *Camperdown's* navigator, Lt. Barr. (C.M. 661, 662). He considered that, even when they were end-on, the ships would have cleared if one of them had reversed her helm—and so do I.

† (C.M. 401). He held that any evasive action must be taken by Tryon—he himself must strictly perform the evolution signalled to his division, since he had acknowledged it as "understood".

‡ Actually, it would have been better if both ships had gone full astern with their inner screws, and full *ahead* with their outer. This could not have averted collision—but it *would* have ensured that they collided broadside-on, and that neither rammed the other. By error, the *Camperdown's* starboard telegraph was only put at ¾ speed astern.

§ It was fitted to the first ironclad ever in action, the Confederate *Virginia* (ex-*Merrimac*) and was first discarded in the French battleship *Brennus*, completed in 1891.

The *Victoria* had been struck a little abaft the bed of the starboard anchor, over the bulkhead * dividing the fore mess-deck from that of the stokers. Men on this deck actually saw the *Camperdown's* stem come crushing its way in, attended by a cloud of coal-dust—below, the spur of the ram had ploughed through a reserve bunker, and entered a cable-locker. An unfortunate stoker petty-officer,† sitting close to the point of impact, was carried to the sick-bay with a broken leg, and black as a sweep. Meanwhile, the ram withdrew—leaving a V-shaped hole, some twelve feet wide at the upper deck and descending to about eighteen feet below the waterline, naked to the sea.‡

At this juncture, by one of those grim ironies in which Fate delights, a semaphore message from Markham was handed to Tryon—who was, at the moment, within hailing distance of him. It was the (delayed) reply to his peremptory enquiry, "What are you waiting for?" and it ran:—"*Because I did not quite understand the signal!*"

The fleet, of course, was in confusion: but the ships were well handled, and there were no other collisions. Noel in the *Nile*, next astern of the *Victoria*, had carried out his intention of keeping clear of her whatever happened; he passed close to her port quarter, drew a little ahead, and stopped. *His* next astern, the *Dreadnought*, turned even shorter, and brought up almost level with the flagship, a little further off than the *Nile*. On the other hand Brackenbury, in the unwieldy *Edinburgh*, who had started to turn a little beforehand in order to off-set his ship's sluggishness, and who was swinging rapidly towards the motionless *Camperdown*, reversed his helm very promptly, and passed outside her.§

It was clear to all that the *Victoria* was doomed. She was considerably down by the head—so, to a less extent, was the *Camperdown*—and steadily sinking deeper, at the same time heeling gradually over to starboard. The *Dreadnought* was already lowering her boats, and the rest of the fleet were following suit when Tryon signalled "Negative sending boats, but hold them in readiness". At the same time, he assumed charge of the engines, and sent Bourke below to find out the full extent of the damage. Learning from Hawkins-Smith that they were in deep water (about 75 fathoms) he turned his stricken flagship (by the screws) southward towards the shore, and gave orders to go ahead at seven knots; but before the *Victoria* could gather steerage-way the quartermaster on the

* No. 22.

† Stoker P. O. Wheeler—drowned.

‡ Such a hole would admit, initially, some 3000 tons of water per minute.

§ This goes far to support the view that the *Victoria* and *Camperdown* *might* have avoided collision, even when end-on to each other.

fore-bridge reported, "I can't right the helm, Sir—the pressure's off". The hydraulic steering-engine had failed—so had the hydraulic boat-hoist of the main derrick, with which Jellicóe,* the *Victoria's* commander (officially on the sick-list with Malta fever) was struggling to hoist out the boom-boats.

What Tryon thought, during those last, agonising minutes when the sea, after submerging the foc'sle, was slowly rising around the base of the great turret, no one will ever know: but what he said is on record, for Hawkins-Smith, who stood by him to the end, was saved. He made but one reference to the disaster—addressed to no one in particular, but over-heard both by the navigator and by Gillford.† His words were, "It's all my doing—all my fault". A little later, he remarked to Hawkins-Smith, "I think she's going"—and was answered, "Yes, Sir, I think she is". And, just at the last, turning to the midshipman‡ in attendance, he said, "Don't stop there, youngster—go to a boat".

Meanwhile Bourke, unescorted, was making his last "Captain's Rounds" in the *Victoria*. As he left the deck, he saw a party headed by Lieutenant Heath§ (the executive officer pro tem.||) vainly struggling to get the collision-mat over the hole: then he went down to the "flats" on the starboard side, below the mess-deck, and satisfied himself that their doors and scuttles had been properly closed. He was then standing some-what abaft the actual damaged-area, and many feet below sea-level, for the whole of the forecastle was already submerged—while the forward compartments must have been full right up to the upper deck. At this moment he heard the order given, far above him, "All hands on deck". In spite of what that order implied, he regained the mess-deck, and went aft, down into the starboard engine-room. This was dry, and he could hear the gongs of the telegraphs—the main engines were still being worked, and all the engine-room staff at their posts. Coming up, Bourke met the Fleet-Engineer,¶ who told him that, so far as he knew, there was no flooding abaft the foremost boiler-room bulkhead—about 40% of the ship's length from her stem. Bourke then came on deck, where he found the bulk of the ship's company clustering on the higher (*i.e.* port) side of the quarter-deck and in the port battery. Telling Heath to fall them in,

---

* Afterwards Admiral of the Fleet Earl Jellicoe of Jutland.

† (C.M. 157, 158, 202). Gillford testified on this point with obvious reluctance, and only under pressure from the Court.

‡ Midshipman Herbert M. Lanyon—drowned.

§ Now Admiral Sir Herbert L. Heath.

|| Commdr. Jellicoe being on the sick list, and Lieut. Inglefield in hospital at Malta.

¶ Fleet Engineer Felix Foreman—drowned.

four deep, on the quarter-deck, he went up to the after-bridge and started forward, along the steeply-tilted fore-and-aft bridge, to rejoin Tryon.

But, before he had got more than half-way, the end came. It was a matter of seconds. Ever since the collision, ten minutes earlier, the *Victoria* had been slowly putting her bows down, and also heeling to starboard: until now most of the upper half of the port screw was clearly visible as it flailed at the water, while the ports of the turret, and of the forward starboard battery-guns—*none of which had been closed**—were down to sea-level. There followed a fresh inrush of water—a few seconds of agonising suspense—and then Heath, who had turned the ship's company about, to face seaward, felt the ship lurch heavily to starboard, and gave the order "Jump". The *Victoria* turned right over—at first slowly, then with increasing speed. In a few seconds there was nothing to be seen of her but the aftermost portion of her bottom-plating (down which a few men were crawling), her screws—still revolving—and her rudder. Then, as the watchers held their breath, these vestiges slid steeply forward and downward, and disappeared. The flagship was gone.

A few seconds later there rose from the depths an enormous swirl of mingled air and water,† accompanied by masses of miscellaneous lumber—everything that would float and could come loose. The first boat on the scene had the narrowest possible escape from being stove in by the *Victoria's* wooden main-derrick; which, fifty feet long and weighing several tons, reared itself vertically out of water within a few feet of her. It was this huge vortex which, perhaps even more than the sinking itself, occasioned the heavy death-roll. It was enough to overwhelm all but the strongest swimmers; and, unhappily, many of the flagship's crew, strange though it may seem nowadays, could not swim at all—while those who could, all too frequently found themselves so hemmed-in by their drowning shipmates that they literally had no room to do so. At first, the water outside the ever-widening belt of white foam caused by the swirl was dark with human heads—after this had passed, comparatively few were to be seen. Many men, too, must have been killed or stunned by the screws —which were still turning as they disappeared.

---

* No order seems to have been given about the battery-ports until too late—while the foc'sle was under water before the turret-port plugs could be placed.

† This was not due, as generally stated at the time, to the boilers having exploded. Actually, there is *no* authentic case on record of such a thing having occurred. The sudden external cooling of a boiler full of steam would cause it to collapse *inwards*, not to explode. It seems very probable that the *Victoria* must have righted herself on hitting the bottom (in about 75 fathoms), thus releasing the great volume of air trapped in her hull, and also her deck-lumber, etc.

The Fleet remained near the site of the disaster until 5.30 when, as the *Camperdown* was making a good deal of water, Markham anchored the main body off Tripoli. Three ships (*Amphion*, *Barham*, and *Fearless*) stayed behind till night fell. Bubbles of air and oil kept rising for several hours, but they picked up nothing of importance. Nor were the searches made in succeeding days much more successful, apart from the fact that a few bodies were recovered and buried in the Christian Cemetery, Tripoli. Admiral Tryon's was not among them. He was never seen after the final lurch. In all probability he found himself trapped, as Hawkins-Smith did, among the network of stays, awning-guys, etc., on top of the chart-house and was unable to get clear in time. Hawkins-Smith's own view* was:—

"He went down, and was seen by no one again; and I never expected to see him, as I am sure he, being a short-breathed man, could not have kept the water out of his lungs as long as I was able to do, and I could not have done so a second or two longer.

"He was perfectly calm and collected to the last, and died as he had lived, a brave man."

As the *Camperdown* lay at anchor off Tripoli, with her stern cocked up and her hawse-pipes awash,† she offered a striking proof of the fact that the ram is a weapon almost as dangerous to the ship using it as to her adversary. A hole ten feet by six had been torn in her stem—through which hole, by the way, a diver was sent down to close two water-tight doors which would otherwise have remained inaccessible, the adjacent compartments being flooded. Her fighting-power had, temporarily, been reduced almost to nothing—she could not have repeated her blow, or steamed at more than a crawl—and in heavy weather she would have been in grave danger. A few days' hard work, however, saw her patched-up sufficiently to make the return voyage to Malta under easy steam.

The inevitable Court-martial to try Capt. Bourke, and the surviving officers and men‡ of the *Victoria* for the loss of their ship was held at Malta, in H.M.S. *Hibernia*, on July 17-27, 1893. The President was

---

* *Fitzgerald*, p. 364.

† Shortly before the collision, she had been drawing 27′ 9″ forward, and 29′ 4″ aft. After it, her draught was 32′ forward and 27′ 6″ aft.

‡ This was, of course, a *pro forma* citation. Actually, all the "prisoners" except Bourke were allowed to withdraw from the court as soon as they had appeared—and Bourke's sword was taken as representing those of all the officers.

the new Commander-in-Chief, Admiral Sir Michael Culme-Seymour, Bart., and the final composition of the Court* was as follows:—

Vice-Admiral R. E. Tracey (Supt. of Malta Dockyard).
Capt. A. P. M. Lake, A.D.C. (S. NCO., Gibraltar).
Capt. Pelham Aldrich (*Hawke*).
Capt. W. C. Karslake (*Colossus*).
Capt. R. F. Hammick (*Triumph*).
Capt. E. F. Jeffreys (*Hood*).
Capt. C. G. Robinson (*Trafalgar*).

The Prosecutor† was Capt. (afterwards Admiral Sir) A. L. Winsloe, who had been sent out from England for this duty, and the Deputy Judge Advocate‡ Mr. H. H. Rickard (the C. in C.'s Secretary).

It was generally conceded on all hands that no member of the *Victoria's* crew—not even her captain—stood in danger of being found "guilty" of occasioning her loss: and attention was chiefly concentrated on the anomalous position of two other officers who were actually, though not technically, on trial. These, of course, were Markham and his flag-captain Johnstone, of the *Camperdown*. They were, naturally, anxious to take this—the first, and quite possibly the only§—opportunity of justify-ing their actions in connection with the catastrophe; yet, although far more truly on trial than Bourke and his shipmates, they were technically debarred from putting questions, from addressing the Court, or even from being present in it‖—except when actually giving evidence. Culme-Seymour and his colleagues had no power to relax the Queen's Regula-tions governing such matters; but, with an obvious desire to off-set what was recognised as a hardship, they made, in the exercise of their discretion, a material concession in Markham's favour. It was known that more than one of the captains present at the collision agreed with Markham's inter-pretation of Tryon's signal—that the first column would circle round the

* Bourke naturally and successfully objected to three officers (Captains Johnstone, Acland and Custance) on the ground that they were to give evidence. A fourth, Capt. Langley (*Arethusa*) was accidentally allowed by the President to absent himself while the Court was sitting—taking, as soon as this was discovered, no further part in its proceedings.

† The officer detailed to take charge of the prosecution, select and examine wit-nesses, etc.

‡ An officer, usually of the Paymaster branch, who is the Court's adviser on points of Naval Law.

§ So it proved. In view of the Court's finding, they could not themselves have been court-martialled, even at their own request.

‖ On the ground that they were material witnesses.

second—and the Court in consequence intimated to him that it intended to call *all* the captains of ships present at the disaster. During their examination (but then only) there would be no objection to his being present in court as a spectator. He could not question them himself, but he might submit questions, in writing, to the Court—which questions the Court would, if it saw fit, then put to the witness.*

During the ten days which the court-martial occupied, its members heard a great deal of—in general—highly technical evidence. There was one dramatic moment when Noel, of the *Nile*, in answer to the question:

"1580. When the signal was made for the divisions to turn inward, did it occur to you that it was a dangerous manœuvre?"

replied (in part, and in Markham's presence):—

". . . My hope was, and it is with great reluctance that I give evidence against the Rear-Admiral, my hope was up to the last moment that he would not turn. On the other hand, I felt that if the two leaders used all their efforts to turn, they could do so without collision. Undoubtedly it was an impossible signal as an evolution, that is, for the ships turning on the usual arc".†

There were also one or two humorous moments, as when the Prosecutor naïvely enquired of Fleet Engineer Newton (*Camperdown*) whether his ship's main drains (whose pipes were many feet below sea-level) were used for letting water *out of* the ship; and, again, when Newton explained that an extra 170 tons of water had found their way, some time after the collision, into the hull because the drains of the carpenter's storeroom had suddenly been opened. The cause of this singular action—which might have sunk the *Camperdown*—was promptly elucidated thus:—

"789. By whose order were they opened?—They were opened by my order.

"790. Were you aware at the time that the water was still coming into the ship?—I thought it was partly stopped by the collision mat.

"791. And did you ask nobody?—I did not ask anybody."

---

* In most cases he suggested, and the Court put, eight or nine leading questions, tending to support his own interpretation of the signal. The answers were not always quite what he wanted.

† Markham, next day, requested that this statement of Noel's hopes might be struck out of the minutes, as being "perfectly irrelevant" and "not evidence". The Court decided that it must stand.

But the bulk of the evidence—1886 questions, all told—was, as already remarked, highly technical and largely devoted to matters of mere detail. For instance, the Court showed admirable persistence in putting on record every scrap of evidence it could obtain, from a procession of witnesses, as to which of the *Victoria's* water-tight doors had actually been closed, and which had perforce had to be left open: yet it left the crucial question—what was in Tryon's mind when he made that fatal signal?—entirely unsolved.

On the final day (July 27) the Court gave a sympathetic hearing to a straightforward, sincere, and eloquent defence by Bourke, and clewed up one or two loose ends of evidence: then, after the usual recess, it delivered its finding. The first paragraph ran as follows:—

"The Court finds that the loss of Her Majesty's Ship "Victoria" off Tripoli, on the Coast of Syria, on the Twenty-Second day of June, 1893, was caused by a collision with Her Majesty's Ship "Camperdown"; and it is with the deepest sorrow and regret that the Court further finds that this collision was due to an order given by the then Commander-in-Chief, the late Vice-Admiral Sir George Tryon, to the two Divisions in which the Fleet was formed to turn sixteen points inwards, leaders first, the others in succession, the columns at that time being only six cables apart."

The Court found that everything possible had been done to save life; and considered that Tryon's signal "Negative sending boats" was, in the circumstances, a wise one.* It found no blame attributable to Bourke or to any of his officers and men, and acquitted them accordingly.
The Finding continued:—

"Fourthly.—The Court strongly feels that although it is much to be regretted that Rear-Admiral Albert Hastings Markham did not carry out his first intention of semaphoring to the Commander-in-Chief his doubt as to the signal, it would be fatal to the best interests of the Service to say he was to blame for carrying out the directions of his Commander-in-Chief present in person."

And it wound up by saying that while the Court had collected all available evidence about the closing of the *Victoria's* doors, it did not feel either called upon or competent to express an opinion as to the cause of her capsizing.

* Had the boats been clustering round the *Victoria* when she sank, the ensuing swirl would probably have capsized or overwhelmed a good many.

This Finding came, in due course, before the Admiralty; and Their Lordships took the unusual course of promulgating a Minute* reviewing it. In general, They concurred with its terms; but They did not entirely approve of Markham's proceedings, and quite definitely disapproved of Johnstone's. They deemed it "necessary to point out that the Rear-Admiral's belief that the Commander-in-Chief would circle round him was not justified by the proper interpretation of the signal", while They regretted that Johnstone "did not manifest the promptitude and decision which the occasion demanded for the security of the ship under his command, and to diminish the risk of collision".

The "proper interpretation" of Tryon's order—a disputable point which Their Lordships did nothing to elucidate—may be deferred for a moment: but They were clearly wrong in referring to it as "the signal". It was *two* signals—for the sufficient reason that the manœuvre which Tryon intended had never been contemplated by the framers of the Signal-book, so that there was no single signal which covered it. To Their strictures on Johnstone there is, unfortunately, less exception to be taken. He had done well in the past; in particular, at Tamatave, Madagascar, when Commander of the *Dryad* in the summer of 1883. France was then engaged in deposing the native King *vi et armis* and annexing the island, showing in the process scant respect to the interests of other Powers, or their subjects; and Johnstone, in the face of overwhelmingly superior force, showed great courage and firmness in his dealings with the French S.N.O., Admiral Pierre—who was unquestionably *non compos mentis*. For this, he had been deservedly promoted to Captain. But, in my judgment, it is impossible to read through the evidence given at the *Victoria* Court-martial without deriving the impression that the *Camperdown* was neither a smart ship nor very competently handled.†

Their Lordships also intimated that a special Minute would be issued dealing with the stability of the *Victoria*; and this duly appeared (Oct. 30, 1893) accompanied by a long and detailed report from the Director of Naval Construction.‡ The latter's main conclusions were:—

---

* Oct.28, 1893. It may be noted that the Admiralty have no power to increase—though they can diminish—the sentence of a court-martial upon the person or persons tried before it: but they can censure, or take disciplinary action against, anyone else subject to Naval discipline whose conduct appears to them, from the evidence, to deserve this.

† *E.g.* Her second-in-command was not on deck at the time of the collision; and although the Fleet was manœuvring, there was then no one stationed at her starboard telegraph—so that this had to be worked by a midshipman who did not understand it, and put it to "¾ astern" instead of "full astern".

‡ Mr. (afterwards Sir) W. H. White.

(a) That the *Victoria* would have remained afloat, if all her watertight doors, hatches, etc, had been closed before the collision.

(b) That, although there was insufficient time to close some of these, she would not even then have capsized (though she might have eventually foundered) if her turret-ports and upper-deck battery ports had been closed.

(c) That, even if the *Victoria* had had an all-round belt of armour, this would not have saved her.

Conclusion (a) may be admitted; and the Admiralty gave immediate effect to it by issuing orders that, whenever ships were manœuvring, *all* watertight doors, etc., should as far as possible be kept closed, and men stationed at any left open. At the time, this salutary precaution—obvious though it may now seem to us—came as a complete novelty to the Fleet: *not one* of the ships under Tryon's command had closed her doors until Bourke took the initiative just before the collision. And in the circumstances he could not have done so sooner without appearing to have passed a public censure upon his Commander-in-Chief—a very serious breach of discipline indeed.

But conclusions (b) and (c), taken together, are purely ludicrous. In the first place, the blow struck by the *Camperdown's* ram was about equal in striking-force to that of a $12''$ shell. If an armour-belt were no protection against the former, it would be of little avail against the latter—from which it followed that the injury which the *Victoria* received was one she was very liable to sustain *in action*. And she could not conceivably have gone into action with her turret- and battery-ports closed, since then she could not possibly have been fought, and therefore might as well not have been built. In other words, on the Chief Constructor's own showing the *Victoria*, like other ships with large unarmoured ends (a type, happily, now long obsolete), deserved to be regarded, for serious purposes, less as an effective fighting-ship than as a floating death-trap.

And now for the crux of the whole matter—which both the Court-martial and the Admiralty evaded discussing. Was Tryon's manœuvre, *as signalled*, impossible of execution? Was Markham's interpretation of it correct—or Noel's—or any other? Or had the Commander-in-Chief, in disposing the columns only six cables apart, simply made an elementary blunder?

Well, in the first place, Markham was over-hasty in stigmatising the manœuvre, when the purport of Tryon's signals was first reported to him, as "impossible". A simple and feasible explanation—though not, unfortunately, the right one—escaped him. There was nothing, beforehand, to show that the two signals would be hauled down simultaneously (as, in fact, they were) and not successively: Tryon might easily have hauled down the signal addressed to his own division as soon as he saw Markham's repeat-hoist "close up", leaving that to the second division still flying. In that case the first division, led by the *Victoria*, would have turned, in succession, well clear of the second: while the signal addressed to the latter would, presumably, have been hauled down at the right moment to let the *Camperdown*, leading her division, turn inward and take station astern of the *Phæton*, thus bringing the whole fleet into line ahead, first division leading. This, *in itself*, is a quite satisfactory interpretation of the two signals.

But the resulting formation would be far removed from that in which Tryon had already signalled—to Noel's disquietude—that the fleet would anchor: and there is convincing evidence that Tryon had never contemplated re-forming the fleet in single line ahead. Gillford has recorded* that as soon as the "fatal" signals were hoisted Tryon ordered him to get two others (never hoisted, as it happened) bent on. They were:

$$\left\{\begin{array}{c}\text{Columns to be two cables}\\ \text{apart}\end{array}\right. \quad \text{and} \quad \left\{\begin{array}{l}\text{All ships will turn together}\\ \text{with their guides as the guide}\\ \text{of the fleet turns}\end{array}\right.$$

These, of course, are conclusive. After the evolution, whatever it may be, the ships will be in two columns, and are all to turn simultaneously as the *Victoria* turns. Furthermore—an important point—when taken in conjunction with the anchoring-signal they make it practically a foregone conclusion that, when the evolution is completed, the ships will be in formation for anchoring, with the first division the *inshore* column. In other words, they are entirely compatible with the manœuvre which Tryon outlined, in his after-cabin, to Bourke and Hawkins-Smith (which is shown in fig. 15)—*and with no other.*

For the same reason—the formation enjoined by the anchoring-signal —we may rule out Markham's idea, that Tryon's column was going to circle round outside his own: and, equally, the view—very ably maintained by the late Sir William Laird Clowes in his book,† *The Royal Navy*—that Tryon was expecting to see Markham lead the second division round outside his own.

Apart from their being inconsistent with the anchoring-signal—a

* In a written statement made to Markham on the day of the tragedy, and forwarded to the Admiralty. It is printed with the Court-martial minutes.

† *The Royal Navy*, vol. vii., pp. 415-426. London, Sampson Low, Marston & Co. 1903.

point which neither Markham nor Laird Clowes seems to have noticed—there was something, but not very much, to be said for both these interpretations. Markham, as we have seen, took the view that while Tryon was free to use reduced helm, he was not: and, also, that by the Rule of the Road at Sea the *Victoria* was bound, when she had come end-on to the *Camperdown*, to pass her "port side to port side"—and, hence, to take the wider circle. This sweeping conception of the Rule of the Road's authority did not commend itself to the Court; and seems, in fact, not a little absurd. One might contend, with almost equal force, that the Rule must be observed by ships when in action.

Laird Clowes, writing at leisure some time after the event, was able to develop his views more at length, and with—at first sight—considerable appearance of weight. Summarised, they were these.   (a) The manœuvre actually performed was not the one Tryon intended. His apparent indifference to the precise distance of the columns—first fixed at 6 cables, then at 8 (on Hawkins-Smith's suggestion), and finally at 6 again—indicated a manœuvre in which the distance of the columns was, within limits, immaterial. Consequently, he *must* have meant one column to circle round the other—an evolution which, with perhaps a little help from the screws, could have been safely performed with the columns four cables apart, let alone six.   (b) He must have expected Markham to go outside him, since a junior officer does not, without express permission, cross his senior officer's bows!   (c) He gave the *Victoria* extreme helm to allow Markham as much room as possible when passing outside; and he would not let Bourke go astern with the port screw until the ships were end-on, because until then he could not be certain that Markham had failed to grasp what was expected of him.   (d) His expression, "It's all my fault" should be taken as meaning "It's all my fault, for trusting too much to my second-in-command's initiative".   (e) Lastly, the signals said ". . . preserving the order of the fleet", and this *would* have been preserved if Markham had led his column round outside Tryon's—while otherwise, even if the leaders had contrived to reduce their turning-circles sufficiently, the order of the fleet would have been changed, the starboard column now becoming the port column, and *vice versa*.

It is all very plausible—and, at first sight, almost convincing. But it will not stand examination. (a) and (e) are inconsistent with the anchoring-signal. (b) is absurd—Markham would, technically, have crossed Tryon's bows whether he went inside or outside: or, for that matter, if he had contrived to turn short of the *Victoria* altogether! (c) is unwarranted —it was not Tryon who ordered "extreme helm", but Hawkins-Smith: and he did so because he did *not* expect Markham to pass outside them.

(d) is far-fetched—an example of twisting facts to suit theories. And (e), in addition, is based upon a mis-translation of the signals—as already remarked, being addressed to separate divisions they did *not* signify "preserving the order of the fleet".

On the point of initiative, a word must here be said about Tryon's "TA" system, of which a good deal was heard at the Court-martial. He had long maintained that, when in action, the fewer the signals that were made the better: with fast-moving ships, an opportunity might be lost while signalling how it should be used—and signal-masts, -yards, and -halyards were liable to be shot away just when most needed. So under his command the Mediterranean Fleet often engaged in exercises which began by his hoisting "TA", which signified "Observe attentively the Admiral's motions" and hence notified his second-in-command, and the captains of ships, that he might at any time alter course, or do something which they were to follow, without further orders. Thereafter, the fleet manœuvred without signals—or, at most, a one-flag hoist to denote a simultaneous turn.

It is hardly necessary to say that this system shared the fate of its author—*spurlos versunkt*—though rather unjustly; for the signals which brought about the sinking of the *Victoria* had nothing to do with the "TA" system, while (in pre-W/T days) the latter would probably have been found very useful in action. But one must admit that "TA" may easily have tended to make his subordinates consider that it was no uncommon thing for their C. in C. to take some unexpected action without previously signalling what it would be—and consequently to make them prone, in emergencies, to rely on his initiative rather than their own.

Revenons. . . . On the joint evidence of the anchoring-signal, the views which Tryon outlined to Bourke and Hawkins-Smith in his aftercabin, the two "fatal signals", and the pair which were intended to follow them, it is quite certain that the manœuvre which Tryon intended is that shown in fig. 15. It is equally certain that, using the ordinary manœuvring-circle, this manœuvre was impossible with the columns only six cables apart—at which distance Tryon had disposed them only an hour earlier. Was Noel, then, right in his belief that the C. in C. expected all ships, without further explanation on his part, to turn short by "jockeying" with their screws?

Unquestionably, no. In the first place, the practice was one which Tryon discountenanced, as his captains well knew.* Secondly, with such

* Notice how Brackenbury, in the unhandy *Edinburgh,* began his turn a little beforehand, as a substitute for the more effective plan of giving a "kick" with his inner screw.

a miscellaneous assemblage of ships, grave risk of collision—and, nor-
mally, Tryon never took such risks—could only have been avoided by his
making an explanatory signal, "All ships will reduce their turning-circle
to two cables by reversing the inner screw". And, lastly, even if Tryon
had decided to take the risk and make no such signal, he must at least have
known that the *Victoria*, like the rest of the fleet, would *have* to reverse
her inner screw as soon as the turning-signals came down: and, if he had
then found Bourke not taking the initiative—failing, so to speak, to pass
his test of immediate and independent thinking—Tryon must have
immediately corrected the omission. But actually, as we know, he was by
no means eager to let Bourke reverse the inner screw.

No, the inevitable conclusion is, that the manœuvre which Tryon signalled only ended in disaster because he had made a simple and natural
slip in working-out the distance required between the columns. He seems
to have reasoned thus: "*Diameter* of each leader's turning-circle, 2
cables. Hence, sum of the two, 4 cables. Distance columns must be apart
when semi-circles are completed, 2 cables. Total of all, 4 + 2, which is
6 cables".* And, having once firmly made his mind up on this simple
point, he could not be brought to see any necessity for changing it. As
Bourke said, in the course of his defence, "Sir George Tryon had a
master mind. He loved argument, but he was a strict disciplinarian".
Earlier, he had told the Court ". . . no one was ever consulted on the subject of manœuvres".

At the Court-martial evidence was given that Tryon, for all his great
ability, was capable of occasionally confusing the radius of a ship's turning-
circle with its diameter: in fact, that he was rather prone to do so—that
his brain had a "blind spot"† in this connection. Here is part of the
testimony given by Capt. Custance‡ (*Phæton*):—

"1661. By the Court: You say that you thought at the time the signal
was made that the late Commander-in-Chief had mistaken the radius of
the turning-circle of the fleet for the diameter. Do I understand that that

---

* He should, of course, have reasoned thus. "Diameter of each leader's turning-
circle, 4 cables. Hence, sum of the two, 8 cables. Distance columns must be apart when
semi-circles are completed, 2 cables. Total of all, 8 + 2, which is 10 cables." We have
all made similar slips, in our time—and even defended them when they were first
pointed out to us.

† A metaphor based, of course, on the *punctum cæcum* where the optic nerve enters
the retina. I owe this apt expression to my friend Mr. J. G. Lockhart, who used it
when discussing the loss of the *Victoria* in his *Mysteries of the Sea* (London, Philip
Allan, 1924).

‡ See also p. 117 for his opinion of the "fatal signals".

struck you at the time?—At the time, but not immediately the signal was reported; very shortly afterwards. The Court will observe that I made that same mistake myself.

"1662. Is that the reason you think that the Commander-in-Chief made the same mistake?—Not altogether. On a previous occasion, when the Captains had met the Admiral after manœuvres, I remarked that the Commander-in-Chief made a mistake about the number of cables and diameter, about which he had to be corrected. Not about yards, but about cables.

"1663. Do you remember the occasion?—No, I cannot fix the occasion.

"1664. Only once?—I think it was only once."

Much stronger evidence to the same effect was, I am quite certain, brought to the Court's notice *in private*, although no mention of this appears in its minutes. Three years earlier Vice-Admiral R. E. Tracey, one of its members,* had undergone an experience of Tryon's methods very similar to Markham's own—though with a happier ending.† When a Rear-Admiral, flying his flag in the *Anson*, he had been second-in-command of the fleet commanded by Tryon in the Naval Manœuvres of 1890. One afternoon, when exercising the fleet off the Eddystone, Tryon signalled *precisely the same "fatal" manœuvre*, the columns being insufficiently far apart. Bouverie-Clark, Tracey's flag-captain, maintained so stoutly that the evolution was impossible that Tracey flew his repeat-hoist at the dip, *and kept it there*: with the result that, as the fleet was getting uncomfortably near the Eddystone, Tryon "negatived" the manœuvre, and then made a general signal to the effect that it had been rendered abortive by the *Anson's* slackness in acknowledging signals! When dining with Tryon afterwards, Bouverie-Clark succeeded in obtaining from him a half-admission that this censure had been unjust.

Writing some forty years after the event (which he had not witnessed) the late Admiral Mark Kerr made a series of most curious misstatements in attempting to give, *more suo*, proof that Tryon had not only confused the radius and diameter of the manœuvring-circle, but *had explicitly said so after the collision*. In a letter‡ to the *Evening Standard* (25-VI-36) he remarked:—

* Debarred, in consequence, from giving evidence before it.

† Communicated to me privately, some years ago, by a retired flag-officer very well placed for knowing the facts.

‡ The gist of his letter was taken from his book of reminiscences, *The Navy in My Time*, published in 1933.

"Shortly, the proof is as follows.

"A little over a year after the loss of the *Victoria* I met a Lieutenant who had been in the ship with me and who was Officer of the Watch on the Bridge by the Admiral when the collision occurred.

"I gave my opinion that the cause of the accident was mistaking the amount to be allowed for a half-circle turn. It was very easily done, as a quarter-circle is constantly used in manœuvres and a half-circle very seldom.

"My friend replied: 'That was exactly the reason. The Admiral himself told me that that was the mistake he had made. I could not make up my mind what to do if I was called as a witness, for we had all been told by Captain Maurice Bourke that we were to do everything to preserve Sir George's reputation.

"Fortunately I was not called to give evidence'."

Now for the facts, which differ *toto cœlo* from this farrago.

The *Victoria's* officer of the watch at the time of the collision was Lieut. Charles James Collins, R.N. Being among those saved, he naturally *was* called upon to testify at the Court-martial—it would have been in the highest degree astonishing if he were not. He gave his evidence on the second day. It comprises fifteen questions and answers,* and covers nearly a page of the minutes. From his own statements, it is perfectly clear that he did not have, and (after the collision) could not have had, any conversation with Tryon at all. Here is his account of his movements:—

"323. After the collision, where did you go?—I went aft, along the fore and aft bridge, and put the marines I found on the bridges on to the large collision mat. . . I then jumped down over the screen . . . I then went aft, and tried to get the ridge rope set up. . . . I then went up through the battery on to the bridge again. . . . When I got on the bridge, I had not been there, I suppose, 10 or 20 seconds when the Admiral called me, and said, 'Go and tell them to make a general signal "send boats in tow ahead".' I left him, and went from the chart-house to the fore-bridge, and, I think, had just given the order to a yeoman of signals, when the ship gave a heavy lurch which threw me on the deck. I had time to scramble up and get hold of the shield of a 3-pounder quick-firing gun on the port side, when the ship capsized. I remember no more."

It is clear that, between the collision and the capsizing, Collins had no opportunity whatever of any "heart to heart talk" with Tryon. Admiral Mark Kerr's romance was simply a good example of the rapid accretion of myth around a striking event. Of such myths several—one or two,

* (C.M.) 309–323.

perhaps, better founded—have clustered around the *Victoria* catastrophe. For example, Tryon is said to have been seen, the same afternoon, at Lady Tryon's "At Home" in London; two hours after the collision a large crowd had already gathered at Malta Dockyard gate, convinced that some disaster had befallen the fleet; and Col. Drury records* that, hours beforehand, hundreds of the natives had gathered on the hills overlooking Tripoli roadstead, agog to witness the calamity with which, they had been assured (by a fakir) *a week earlier*, Allah had determined to visit the ships of the infidels. It is, at least, a fact that Tryon once unconsciously prophesied his own fate. Discussing with Mr. J. R. Thursfield† the loss of H.M.S. *Serpent*,‡ he remarked:—

"An error of judgment, I fear; but we are all liable to it, and those poor fellows have paid for it with their lives".

And so did he, and with him more than three hundred others§—victims of a totally unnecessary disaster which illustrated the apparently-unsuspected fact that even Admirals can make mulish mistakes: and that their subordinates ought to bear this in mind and, if necessary, act accordingly.

But it illustrated something else as well. One thing, and one alone, throws a sunset-glow over the whole futile, needless tragedy of the *Victoria*. The behaviour of the ship's company was beyond praise—even the *Birkenhead* saw nothing finer. Here is Bourke's tribute:—‖

"There was absolutely no panic, no shouting, no rushing aimlessly about. . . . The men on the forecastle worked with a will until the water was up to their waists, and it was only when ordered aft that they left their work. . . .

"In the case of the men working below, I was a witness to their coolness. When the order was passed down for everyone to go on deck, there was no haste or hurry . . . all were in their stations, the engineer officer was there, the artificer, and the stokers. . . . In all the details of this terrible accident one spot especially stands out, and that is the heroic conduct of those who, to the end, remained below stolidly, yet boldly, at their place of duty. . . .

---

* In his *In Many Parts* (London, Fisher Unwin, 1926). He was the *Edinburgh's* Major of Marines at the time of the collision; and he afterwards made it the theme of two excellent short stories, "The Passing of the Flagship" and "In the Bag Flat".

†Who related the incident in an excellent article published in Brassey's *Naval Annual* for 1894.

‡ Wrecked on the N. coast of Spain, 10-XI-90.

§ In all, 365 lives were lost out of a total of 659.

‖ In (C.M. 1879)—his formal "defence".

"The men fallen in on the upper deck also showed the same spirit. . . . When the men were turned about to face the ship's side, it must have passed through the minds of many that to 'look out for oneself' would be the best thing to do. The men must have seen the others coming from forward wet. . . . This order to turn about was given apparently about a minute before the end, and I can hear of not one single instance of any man rushing to the side . . . not one was found who had not that control over himself which characterizes true discipline and order . . . no one jumped from the ship until just as she gave the lurch, which ended in her capsizing."

" IN MORTE TALIUM
STAT MATRIS GLORIA "

THE LAST OF THE ALCHEMISTS

The title of this essay is misleading. There have been alchemists in all ages, and there always will be: and by "alchemists" I do not mean fools or impostors, but men who have soberly and patiently attempted (and, in my judgment, occasionally accomplished) the transmutation of certain of the "base" metals, such as lead, silver, and mercury, into gold.

The subject is one which it is difficult to approach with an open mind —although that difficulty has been considerably lessened by the chemical and physical discoveries of this century. But in most people's minds the term "alchemist" is, I think, as surely and naturally associated with "impostor" as "succulent" with "bivalve", or "temporary" with "embarrassment". We know, or we knew until recently, that the chemical elements are immutable—such, we say, is a "Law of Nature", and since it does not conflict with our private inclinations we are under no temptation to infringe it, or to let others do so. In Science, as in religion, orthodoxy pays best, and the heretic questions accepted views at his peril. He must be prepared for a long and bitter fight—and, if in the long run he should succeed in extorting a grudging acquiescence from his opponents, he generally finds that his victory has been dearly bought. The dust of conflict besmirches the victor's crown. As has been truly said, public opinion on the subject of a novel and heterodox point of view generally goes through three well-marked stages.

(a) It is anti-scriptural.
(b) (say ten years later.) At all events, it can never be of any practical value.
(c) (after a similar interval). It has been well-known and accepted for a long time. Where is the originality in it?

And yet it is not in the least paradoxical to say that every advance in human knowledge has been made by men who were not content to take anything whatever on trust, but proceeded in strict accordance with the precept "Prove all things; hold fast to those that are good". It is perfectly true that, in science as in architecture, one cannot build durably without foundations; but it is equally true that these are the better for periodical inspection.

Macaulay, the apostle of mid-Victorian complacency, once wrote* (no doubt with general approval):

"There are branches of knowledge with respect to which the law of the human mind is progress. In mathematics, when once a proposition has been demonstrated, it is never afterwards contested. Every fresh story is as solid a basis for a new superstructure as the original foundation was. Here, therefore, there is a constant addition to the stock of truth. In the inductive sciences, again, the law is progress. Every day furnishes new facts, and thus brings theory nearer and nearer to perfection. There is no chance that either in the purely demonstrative, or in the purely experimental sciences, the world will ever go back or even remain stationary. Nobody ever heard of a reaction against Taylor's theorem† or of a reaction against Harvey's doctrine of the circulation of the blood."

If this passage illustrates anything except its author's proverbial "cocksureness",‡ it is the extreme difficulty of recording dogmatic truth without providing amusement for succeeding generations. In passing, it may be stated that Macaulay's mathematical knowledge was so scanty that he was "gulfed" in the Cambridge Tripos of 1822; i.e. he obtained Honours in Classics, but failed in mathematics.

If Macaulay had wished to expand his argument by a geometrical illustration, he would probably have selected, as an example of a universally-accepted truth, Euclid's theorem§ that the three interior angles of any plane triangle are together equal to two right angles; or Playfair's Axiom.‖ These lie at the very roots of Euclid's system of geometry; a system which stood unquestioned for nearly two thousand years, and which Kant and his school regarded as an irrefragable proof of the existence of intuitive truth—truth, that is, apprehended independently of the senses, or of experience. Yet neither can be proved, and we know now that neither is necessarily true. Some years before Macaulay wrote the passage just quoted, the foundations of geometry had been, for the first

* Review of Von Ranke's *History of the Popes, Edinburgh Review*, October 1840.

† $f(x+z) = f(x) + zf'(x) + \dfrac{z^2}{2!}f''(x) + \ldots$

‡ "I wish", said Sydney Smith, "that I could be as cocksure of any one thing as Macaulay is of everything". Incidentally Macaulay—who, according to his biographer Trevelyan, regarded "every successive mathematical proposition as an open question" —was ill-advised in selecting Taylor's theorem as an illustration of his argument. There *was* a reaction against it. Cauchy showed, in 1815, that as enunciated by Taylor it was too general—and, in certain cases, untrue. Taylor's "proof" of it has long been regarded as unsound.

§ *Euclid*, i. 32.

‖ "Two intersecting straight lines cannot both be parallel to a third straight line."

time,* independently examined and reconstructed by N. Lobachevski,† of Kasan, and János Bolyai,‡ of Maros-Vásárhely, in Hungary. Through their work, and that of their successors, such as G. B. F. Riemann, we know that there are other systems of geometry, free from the inconsistencies of Euclid's, in which the angles of a plane triangle may amount, in the aggregate, to more or less than two right angles; and that in such systems two§ intersecting straight lines may both be parallel to a third. In consequence Geometry, long regarded as the crown of "pure mathematics", has now taken its rightful place as one of the experimental sciences.

It does not follow, then, because a point of view appears to be well-founded, and because it has been unquestioned for centuries, that it is necessarily correct. There is probably no popularly-received belief which is absolutely true; and certainly none whose foundations would not be the better for stringent re-examination at intervals. But in such matters the voice of authority is still far too prone to echo the unfortunate remark of a mathematical writer well-known in his day, Isaac Todhunter:

" . . . If he (the student) does not believe the statements of his tutor— probably a clergyman of mature knowledge, recognised ability, and blameless character—his suspicion is irrational, and manifests a want of the power of appreciating evidence."

It is human, I suppose, to prefer one's old *mumpsimus* to the new *sumpsimus*; but the result generally is that inconvenient truth seldom has a fair hearing. In the geometrical case just instanced, I doubt whether one boy in a hundred, when learning geometry, ever hears of the existence, or even the possibility, of the non-Euclidean systems. And, to take another example, how many clergymen are accustomed to tell their flocks the accepted results of modern Biblical criticism? How many of them even know those results?

It has come, rightly or wrongly, to be an accepted popular belief that alchemy—the transmutation of baser metals into gold—is, always has been, and always will be a physical impossibility. And yet it is strictly true that there is a considerable body of historical evidence pointing to the

---

* In saying this, I am not forgetting the work of Saccheri, Lambert, Gauss, and Schweikart. But the latter two never published their investigations, and neither Saccheri nor Lambert could bring himself to accept the logical conclusion to be drawn from his own results. Lobachevski and Bolyai are unquestionably the first two geometers to have the courage of their convictions upon this subject.

† *Geometrical Researches on the Theory of Parallels*, Berlin, 1840 (and various earlier papers).

‡ *The Absolute Science of Space*—appendix to W. Bolyai's *Tentamen*, Maros Vásárhely, 1832–33.

§ Or, none. In Riemann's system of non-Euclidean geometry no parallel lines exist.

conclusion that such transmutation has, in the past, been occasionally effected—evidence of such weight that, did it relate to any more probable event, we should be compelled either to accept it or to cease putting any faith in recorded testimony.

It is unquestionably true that the modern prejudice against any serious discussion of alchemy arises, in great measure, from the general trickiness and chicanery of its professors. In what are loosely called the Middle Ages—in, that is to say, the infancy of scientific knowledge—an investigator whose conscience debarred him from entering the Church found it even harder to gain a living by purely scientific researches than is the case to-day. If he were inclined to astronomy, then in the intervals of his observations he cast horoscopes and "ruled the planets", blessing his stars that, as Kepler remarked, "Nature, which has given to every animal the means of subsistence, has designed Astrology to be the support and hand-maid of Astronomy". And if his tastes were chemical, his energies were directed, either by natural inclination or by the compulsion of necessity, towards alchemy. Here was something which even princes could understand. Just as Gladstone was attracted to one of Faraday's discoveries by the latter's assurance that it would soon be taxable, so the mediæval monarch, Prince, Markgraf or what-not readily afforded shelter and stipend to a professed alchemist for a period depending principally upon the length of his purse and the "cunning man's" adroitness in parrying inconvenient inquiries as to the progress of his labours. In those days the tide of opinion ran as strongly in favour of the possibility of transmutation as it has now set the other way; and one can scarcely blame the early chemists if, as the price of carrying on their researches, they encouraged—or, at least, did nothing to discourage—this idea. And even if they knew in their hearts that they possessed no method of accomplishing transmutation, that is not to say that they disbelieved in its theoretical possibility. The evidence is all the other way. It is undeniable that a chemist of, say, A.D. 1600 would have been far less astounded had he succeeded in transforming a bar of lead into one of gold than if he had combined hydrogen and oxygen to form water (then regarded as a typical element): or than if he had been shown that a poisonous metal and an equally poisonous gas were the sole constituents of one of the most necessary things in the world—common salt.

But in all ages rogues, as the Tichborne Claimant acutely remarked,*

* "Some folk has money and no brains, some has brains and no money. Surely them as has money, no brains, was made for them as has brains, no money." (Arthur Orton, *alias* Thomas Castro, *alias* Sir Roger Charles Tichborne, Bart., *alias* C.33, Dartmoor—in a pocket-book found at Wagga-Wagga.)

have been on the look-out for their natural prey, of whom, according to the American estimate, one is born every second. And they found the credulous and embarrassed potentates of mediæval Europe a flock well worth shearing; while as the most convenient means of separating any given fool from his money they employed, in lieu of the three-card juggle, or the confidence trick beloved of "Patsy" and other practitioners in demand at Scotland Yard, the profession of alchemy. And if alchemy be defined simply as the "making" of gold, some of them were, for a limited time, quite successful.

Their methods were various. To quote Thomson's *History of Chemistry*:

"Sometimes they made use of crucibles with a false bottom; at the real bottom they put a quantity of oxide of gold or silver, this was covered with a portion of powdered crucible, glued together by a little gummed water or a little wax; the materials being put into this crucible and heat applied, the false bottom disappears, the oxide of gold or silver is reduced, and at the end of the process is found at the bottom of the crucible, and is considered as the product of the operation.

"Sometimes they make a hole in a piece of charcoal and fill it with oxide of gold or silver, and stop up the mouth with a little wax; or they soak charcoal in solutions of these metals; or they stir the mixtures in the crucible with hollow rods containing oxide of gold or silver within, and the bottom shut with wax:* by these means the gold or silver wanted is introduced during the process, and considered as a product of the operation.

"Sometimes they have a solution of silver in nitric acid, or of gold in aqua regia,† or an amalgam of gold or silver, which being adroitly introduced, furnishes the requisite quantity of metal. A common exhibition was to dip nails into a liquid, and take them out half converted into gold. The nails consisted of one-half gold, neatly soldered to the iron, and covered with something to conceal the colour, which the liquid removed. Sometimes they had metals one-half gold the other half silver, soldered together, and the gold side whitened with mercury; the gold half was dipped into the transmuting liquid and then the metal heated; the mercury was dissipated, and the gold half of the metal appeared."

In view of the foregoing it may, perhaps, not be entirely a coincidence that the decline of belief in alchemy corresponds roughly, in point of date,

* There is a vivid account of a transmutation of this kind, supposed to have been effected by one Galeotto in the presence (but not to the satisfaction) of Leonardo da Vinci, in Merejkowski's novel, *The Forerunner*.

† A mixture of nitric and hydrochloric acids.

with the appearance of the professional conjurer. Had J. N. Maskelyne or
Buatier de Kolta lived in those piping times, and escaped (which seems
unlikely) the penalties meted out to sorcerers, what a harvest they must
have reaped!

But, just as in former days the Church of England numbered Titus
Oates among her ministers along with the saintly Bishop Ken; and as in
our own day the profession of letters has embraced both myself and the
late Mrs. Amanda McKittrick Ros; so among the mediæval alchemists
and their successors are to be found not only many charlatans of the
Cagliostro type, but also men of high ideals and scrupulous honesty—
such men as Van Helmont, Helvetius, and Robert Boyle, all three of
whom, as will shortly appear, have testified to having personally effected
transmutation in their own laboratories, albeit under somewhat peculiar
circumstances. I have selected these three cases because of the eminence
of the principal actors, but I could easily give many more; while a list of
the eminent men who have affirmed their belief in the possibility of transmutation would also include the names of Sir Isaac Newton, Leibniz, Sir
Humphry Davy, and (in our own day) Sir William Crookes and others.
Newton spent a considerable time in alchemical experiments, and left
several (unpublished) MSS. on the subject—Leibniz acted for some time
as secretary of a German alchemical society—Davy declared that he could
not stigmatize the doctrines of the alchemists as "unphilosophical"—and
Crookes, as will be seen, constructed a "force-engine" for the purpose of
transforming silver into gold. I may mention, in passing, that the student
of the subject will find a very full and accurate account of the historical
evidence for transmutation in Schmieder's *Geschichte der Alchemie,** if he
can obtain it.

Van Helmont

Jean Baptiste van Helmont (1577–1644), a Belgian, is generally regarded as the greatest chemist of the seventeenth century. It will interest
politicians to know that he invented the term "gas". That he was no
friend of the professed alchemists of his day is shown by his referring to
them as "a diabolical crew of gold and silver sucking flies and leeches".
Yet here is his account† of a transmutation which he himself performed:

" . . . For truly, I have divers times seen it (the philosopher's stone)
and handled it with my hands: but it was of colour, such as is in Saffron in

---

* *Geschichte der Alchemie,* Karl Christoph Schmieder (Doktor der Philosophie und
Professor zu Kassel). Halle, 1832. It was reprinted, with a good introduction, in 1931.
† In his *Oriatrike* (translated by one J. C.), London, 1662.

its powder, yet weighty, and shining like powdered glass: There was once given unto me one-fourth part of one grain: But I call a grain the six hundredth part of one Ounce: This quarter of one Grain therefore, being rouled up in Paper, I projected* upon eight Ounces of Quicksilver made hot in a Crucible; and straightway all the Quick-silver, with a certain degree of Noise, stood still from flowing, and being congealed, settled like unto a yellow Lump: but after pouring it out, the Bellows blowing, there were found eight Ounces, and a little less than eleven Grains of the purest Gold. Therefore one only Grain of that Powder, had transchanged 19,186† Parts of Quick-silver, equal to itself, into the best Gold. . . ."

Elsewhere, Van Helmont says that he was given the "stone" by a stranger, "a friend of one evening's acquaintance". Figuier, in his *L'Alchimie*, says that Van Helmont came by it in 1618, in his laboratory at Vilvorde, near Brussels. He gives a faithful version of Van Helmont's narrative, but finds himself compelled to explain it away; and, *faute de mieux*, has perforce to suggest that some emissary of the mysterious "stranger" had craftily substituted a trick crucible of the pattern already described—or, failing this, that the mercury employed was, actually, an amalgam of mercury and gold. How a practised chemist like Van Helmont (whose personal honesty has never been impugned) could have failed to detect the substitution, or to perceive the residual mercury (on the second hypothesis) he does not attempt to explain. He continues:

"Van Helmont . . . became an avowed partisan of alchemy. In honour of the incident he named his newly-born son Mercurius.‡ This Mercurius Van Helmont bore out his alchemical baptism; he converted Leibniz to the view; during his whole life he sought for the philosopher's stone, and though he never found it, he died a fervent believer in its existence."

Helvetius

Johann Frederic Helvetius, physician to the Prince of Orange, a man of eminence in his profession who also stood very high as a chemist,

---

* *I.e.*, placed.

† There is some arithmetical blunder here. If, as seems most likely, he means by "Eight Ounces and a little less than eleven Grains" 8 oz. less 11 gr., the proportion would be as 19,156 to 1: if he actually obtained 10¾ grs. more matter from the crucible than he put into it, the proportion would be as 19,244 to 1.

‡ Francis Mercurius Van Helmont, 1618-91.

published in 1667 a work* giving an account of a transmutation much resembling that described by Van Helmont. Here are some extracts from the rather copious original:

"On the 27 December, 1666, in the forenoon, there came to my house a certain man, who was a complete stranger to me, but of an honest, grave countenance, and an authoritative mien, clothed in a simple garb. . . .

"After we had exchanged salutations, he asked me whether he might have some conversation with me. . . . After some further conversation, the Artist Elias (for it was he) thus addressed me.

" 'Since you have read so much in the works of the Alchemists about this Stone, its substance, its colour, and its wonderful effects, may I be allowed the question, whether you have not yourself prepared it?' On my answering his question in the negative, he took out of his bag a cunningly-worked ivory box, in which there were three large pieces of a substance resembling glass, or pale sulphur, and informed me that here was enough of the Tincture for the production of twenty tons of gold. When I had held the precious treasure in my hand for a quarter of an hour (during which time I listened to a recital of its wonderful curative properties) I was compelled to restore it to its owner, which I could not help doing with a certain degree of reluctance. After thanking him for his kindness in showing it to me, I then asked him how it was that his Stone did not display that ruby colour, which I had been taught to regard as characteristic of the Philosopher's Stone. He replied that the colour made no difference, and that the substance was sufficiently mature for all practical purposes.

"My request that he would give me a piece of his Stone (though it were no larger than a coriander seed) he somewhat brusquely refused, adding, in a milder tone, that he could not give it to me for all the wealth I possessed, and that not on account of its great preciousness, but for some other reason that it was not lawful for him to divulge. . . .

"When my strange visitor had concluded his narrative, I besought him to give me a proof of his assertion, by performing the transmutatory operation on some metals in my presence. He answered evasively, that he could not do so then, but that he would return in three weeks, and that, if he were then at liberty to do so, he would show me something that would make me open my eyes.

"He appeared punctually to the promised day, and invited me to take a walk with him. . . . At last I asked him point-blank to show me the

---

* Brief of the Golden Calf; Discovering the Rarest Miracle in Nature; how by the smallest piece of the Philosopher's Stone, a great piece of common lead was totally transmuted into the purest transplendent gold, at the Hague in 1666 (Translation). The actual date of the transmutation appears to have been January 19, 1667.

transmutation of metals. I besought him to come and dine with me, and to spend the night at my house; I entreated; I expostulated; but in vain. He remained firm. I reminded him of his promise. He retorted that his promise had been conditional upon his being permitted to reveal the secret to me. At last, however, I prevailed upon him to give me a piece of his precious Stone—a piece no larger than a grain of rape seed. He delivered it to me as if it were the most princely donation in the world.

"Upon my uttering a doubt whether it would be sufficient to tinge more than four grains of lead, he eagerly demanded it back. I complied, in the hope that he would exchange it for a larger piece; instead of which he divided it in two with his thumb, threw away one half, and gave me back the other, saying: 'Even now it is sufficient for you'. Then I was still more heavily disappointed, as I could not believe that anything could be done with so small a particle of the Medecine.

"He, however, bade me take two drachms, or half an ounce, of lead, or even a little more, and to melt it in the crucible; for the Medecine would certainly not tinge more of the base metal than it was sufficient for. I answered that I could not believe that so small a quantity of Tincture could transform so large a mass of lead. But I had to be satisfied with what he had given me, and my chief difficulty was about the application of the Tincture.

"I confessed that when I held his ivory box in my hand, I had managed to extract a few crumbs of his Stone, but that they had changed my lead, not into gold, but only into glass. He laughed, and said that I was more expert at theft than at the application of the Tincture. 'You should have protected your spoil with yellow wax, then it would have been able to penetrate the lead and transform it into gold. . . .'

"With a promise to return at nine o'clock the next morning, he left me. But at the stated hour on the following day he did not make his appearance; in his stead, however, there came, a few hours later, a stranger, who told me that his friend the Artist was unavoidably detained, but that he would call at three o'clock in the afternoon. The afternoon came; I waited for him till half past seven o'clock. He did not appear.

"Thereupon my wife came and tempted me* to try the transmutation myself. I determined, however, to wait till the morrow, and in the meantime, ordered my son to light the fire, as I was now almost sure that he was an impostor.† On the morrow, however, I thought that I might at least make an experiment with the piece of Tincture which I had

* Whether her name was Eve, is not stated.

† This is obscure. I do not imagine, however, that Helvetius contemplated offering Elias, should he return, any personal violence, or making him the subject of an *auto da fé*—he is probably speaking of the fire in his laboratory furnace.

received; if it turned out a failure, in spite of my following his directions closely, I might then be quite certain that my visitor had been a mere pretender to a knowledge of this Art.

"So I asked my wife to put the Tincture in wax, and I myself, in the meantime, prepared six drachms of lead; I then cast the Tincture, enveloped as it was in wax, on the lead; as soon as it was melted, there was a hissing sound and a slight effervescence, and after a quarter of an hour I found that the whole mass of lead had been turned into the finest gold. Before this transmutation took place, the compound became intensely green, but as soon as I had poured it into the melting pot it assumed a hue like blood. When it cooled, it glittered and shone like gold. We immediately took it to the goldsmith, who at once declared it to be the finest gold he had ever seen, and he offered to pay fifty florins an ounce for it.

"The rumour, of course, spread at once like wild-fire through the whole city; and in the afternoon I had visits from many illustrious students of this Art; I also received a call from the Master of the Mint and some other gentlemen, who requested me to place at their disposal a small piece of the gold, in order that they might subject it to the usual tests. I consented, and we betook ourselves to the house of a certain silversmith, named Brechtil, who submitted a small piece of my gold to the test called the 'fourth': three or four parts of silver are melted in the crucible with one part of gold, and then beaten out into thin plates, upon which some strong *aqua fortis** is poured. The usual result of this experiment is that the silver is dissolved, while the gold sinks to the bottom in the shape of a black powder, and after the *aqua fortis* has been poured off, melted again in the crucible, resumes its former shape. . . .

"When we now performed this experiment, we thought at first that one-half of the gold had evaporated; but afterwards we found that this was not the case, but that, on the contrary, two scruples of the silver had undergone a change into gold.

"Then we tried another test, *viz.* that which is performed by means of a septuple of Antimony; at first it seemed as if eight grains of the gold had been lost, but afterwards, not only had two scruples of the silver been converted into gold, but the silver itself was greatly improved both in quality and malleability. Thrice I performed this infallible test, discovering that every drachm of gold produced an increase of a scruple of gold. . . .

"The gold I still retain in my possession, but I cannot tell you what has become of the Artist Elias. Before he left me, on the last day of our friendly intercourse, he told me that he was on the point of undertaking a journey to the Holy Land. . . ."

* Nitric acid.

This strange story does not rest on Helvetius' unsupported testimony alone. Here is an excellent piece of corroborative evidence, in a letter written by one of the most upright men who ever lived—Baruch Spinoza the philosopher.

(Spinoza to Jarrig Jellis)
" . . . The Helvetius matter having been mentioned by me to Voss, he laughed at me, and was surprised to find me occupying myself about such nonsense. In order, therefore, to clear up the business I went to the assayer Brechtel, who had tested the gold. He assured me that when the metal was fused he had added some silver, with the result that the quantity of gold had become augmented. This shows that there must have been something uncommon about the gold, seeing that it had the power of transmuting some of the silver into additional gold.

"And not only Brechtel, but other persons who had been present at the test informed me that such were the facts of the case. I afterwards went to Helvetius himself, who showed me the gold and the crucible with a little gold still sticking to it. He told me he had projected upon the fused lead barely a quarter of a grain of the philosopher's stone. He added that he would tell everybody of the circumstance. It seems that the same alchemist has done something similar in Amsterdam, where he may perhaps be found. This is all I have learned respecting the affair. . . ."

Helvetius, it will be noticed, speaks of "the Artist Elias" as if his name were well known. It may have been, at the time; but I have not succeeded in tracing him—at least, under that name. The speculative may, perhaps, amuse themselves in identifying him with John Buttadeus, alias Ahasuerus (otherwise styled "the Wandering Jew"), or with the "deathless" Count St. Germain who cured Louis XV's flawed diamond, or with the stranger who gave similar portions of his "Stone" to Van Helmont and, possibly, to Boyle. Like almost every alchemist in history, there is an irritating flavour of mystery and superior knowledge in what we hear of him; but it must be conceded that Helvetius' behaviour was not exactly such as to encourage Elias to put much confidence in a man who was not above confessing that he had stolen and wasted a valuable piece of property. On the other hand we must allow that, to an ardent student of alchemy, the temptation offered by Elias's "Stone" was extreme; and in similar circumstances greater men than Helvetius have fallen. Pope Innocent X, in his early days, was kicked out of a French artist's studio, its enraged owner having caught him in the act of purloining a book which he especially coveted.

Boyle

The Hon. Robert Boyle (1627–91) is generally regarded as the founder of modern chemistry, a distinction which he deservedly won by a long life of single-minded devotion to science. The amount of chemical and physical spade-work which he accomplished, and of which an account is given in the five folio volumes of his collected works, is almost incredible. By his rejection of all fanciful theories, and his patient accumulation of facts and observations, he showed himself possessed of a scientific mind in the true and only sense of the term. It is not a little remarkable, therefore, that he continued all through his long life to believe in the possibility of transmutation; an opinion which led him, in 1689, to procure the repeal of the Statute V Henry IV, c. iv, which decreed heavy penalties against any person convicted of "multiplying gold".* He had already published (in 1678) a most singular pamphlet entitled, *Of a Degradation of Gold . . .*† in which he gave a narrative of an experiment, performed by himself, which bears a curious resemblance to the experiences of Van Helmont and Helvetius. It may be added that a paper of his, entitled "Statement Concerning the Incalescence of Quicksilver with Gold",‡ influenced several of Newton's alchemical experiments.§

Although there is little doubt that the pamphlet is intended to describe Boyle's actual experience, this is shrouded in a good deal of mystery. Not only is the work anonymous, but there is a preliminary advertisement, headed "The Publisher to the Reader", in which the former invites the latter to believe that he was allowed to peruse the MS. at his lodging, and proceeded to give it to the world without the trifling formality of asking its author's permission. Such may have been the case, for in those days an author was classed as *feræ naturæ*, with every man's hand against him, and no real copyright or other protection. But I think that in this case the "Advertisement" is simply a gentle mystification, written by Boyle himself, and not seriously intended to deceive.

The narrative is tedious and verbose. It is supposed to be told by one "Pyrophilus" (Boyle) to a company of fellow-chemists, afflicted with such names as "Simplicius", "Aristander", "Crattipus", and "Heliodorus". Subject to occasional interruptions Pyrophilus tells, in substance, the following tale.

* Repealed by I William and Mary. St. I, c. 30.

† *Of a Degradation of Gold, made by an Anti-Elixir: a Strange Chemical Narrative* (Anonymous). London: Printed by T. N. for Henry Herringman. (n.d. = 1678.)
    This pamphlet was reprinted, practically unaltered, after an interval of no less than sixty-one years—in 1739. In this edition, Boyle's name appears on the title-page as the author.

‡ *Philosophical Transactions,* 21. 2. 1676.

§ See his letter to Oldenburg, in Boyle's *Works,* v. 396.

Being in London, he called one day on "an ingenious Foreigner" who had visited him occasionally, in order to return a call. While there, a stranger, whom he had only once seen, came to visit his host, and Boyle and he got talking. The stranger had been to the East, and was about to go back there. Boyle asked him whether he had met any Oriental chemists, and was told he had encountered some as skilful as any in Europe, but fewer in number, and secretive as to their accomplishments. Civilities were exchanged,

" . . . and before he left the Town to go aboard the Ship he was to overtake, he in a very obliging way put into my hands at parting a little piece of paper, folded up; which he said contained all that he had left of a rarity he had received from an Eastern *Virtuoso*, and which he intimated would give me occasion both to Remember him, and to exercise my thoughts in uncommon Speculations."

Having obtained some hints as to the experiment he was to attempt, Boyle procured the services of a "Doctor of Physick"* to assist him. The paper was found to contain a tiny quantity of powder—so small in amount that they could scarcely determine its colour, which they judged to be dark red. Its weight was estimated at one-eighth to one-tenth of a grain.

Weighing out two drachms of refined gold, they fused this without a flux and added the powder, maintaining the fusion for about a quarter of an hour longer. On allowing the crucible to cool, they found that while the gold had not lost any weight it was much altered in appearance, looking dirty, and being coated with a substance like "half-vitrified litharge".† Adhering to the side of the crucible was a globule, apparently of silver; while its bottom was covered with a glassy substance, partly clear yellow and partly deep brown, in which were five or six similar globules.

They tried the "debased gold" in various ways. Tested on a touchstone, it showed more like silver than gold. It was brittle—almost as brittle as bell-metal.‡ It could be cupelled, but with difficulty. They did not test it with nitric acid, having none handy.§ They determined its

---

* The company are represented as being loud in their commendation of this prudent precaution.

† Lead oxide—PbO.

‡ Approximately three parts of copper to one of tin. As anyone knows who has listened to "Big Ben" (which was intended by Lord Grimthorpe, its designer, to be 22 copper, 7 tin, but was badly cast), bell-metal is easily fractured.

§ Nitric acid dissolves silver, and most other metals, but does not affect gold.

specific gravity, à la Archimedes, to be about $15\frac{2}{3}$ to 1 (that of gold is about 19, that of silver about $10\frac{1}{2}$). Boyle drew the conclusion that this powder was capable of altering the malleability, homogeneity, and specific gravity of "near a thousand times" its weight of gold.

The commercial use of such a powder is not apparent; but the experiment was certainly a very remarkable one. And Boyle closes his narrative with a dark hint of further wonders. "I have not (because I must not do it) as yet acquainted you with the strangest Effect of our admirable Powder".

It may be as well to point out that this experiment was made, and the account of it published, when Boyle was in the prime of life, or nearly so. I emphasize this, because some of his later writings indicate the gradual growth in him of a rather unscientific credulity. This is strongly marked in his last work,* published in the year of his death. In an appendix he gives, admittedly at second and remoter hands, a small collection of "Strange Reports", which he presumably published because he believed them. Strange they certainly are. We read of a piece of malleable red glass, owned by a "Monsieur P——r"; of a liquid (distilled from bismuth) that rises and falls in its vessel as the Moon waxes and wanes; of yet another "Stranger", believed to be an "Adeptus", who showed a very learned and experienced Physician "a runing (sic) Mercury of a lively Green"; and of a number of swallows dug out of the ice in Prussia and subsequently resuscitated. However, we must remember, in the last case, that even a sound naturalist like White of Selborne was doubtful whether swallows did not hibernate, while to Johnson this was quite an article of faith.†

Although occurring at widely different times and places,‡ the events narrated by Van Helmont, Helvetius, and Boyle are so closely similar that they could almost be reduced to a common formula. In each case the story is told by a man of reputation and authority, who has effected transmutation by means of a very small quantity of a substance (more or less uniformly described) given to him by a mysterious and vagrant stranger, who thereupon disappears. The transmuting agent is expended, and none therefore remains for analysis. The principal actor publishes a statement of the events.

As already remarked, it would be easy to adduce many similar narra-

* *Experimenta & Observationes Physicæ*, London, 1691.
† "He seemed pleased to talk of natural philosophy. . . . 'Swallows certainly sleep all the winter. A number of them conglobulate together by flying round and round, and then all in a heap throw themselves under water, and lie in the bed of a river.'" Boswell's *Life*, anno 1768.
‡ Brussels, 1618; Hague, 1666; London, about 1677.

tives. But those already instanced are sufficient, I think, to serve the purpose of an introduction to the very singular facts surrounding the tragic death of Dr. James Price of Guildford, commonly termed "The Last of the Alchemists".

Dr. James Price, F.R.S.*

Price's style and title may, perhaps, conjure up a mental picture of someone not unlike the Elizabethan Dr. Dee, or Sidrophel in *Hudibras*— an old man with a fur gown and a nanny-goat beard, sitting in a room full of cabalistic books and curious instruments, with a skeleton grinning in the corner and a stuffed crocodile slung overhead. Actually, he was a brilliant young man of independent fortune, a Fellow of the Royal Society and an honorary M.D. of Oxford. At the age of thirty he seemed to have the ball at his feet—to be one of fortune's favourites. He had something more than a competence; he had powerful friends; he had scientific tastes and the means of gratifying them; he had won honourable distinctions and he might reasonably hope to win more. He stood as high, in the early years of manhood, as many who count themselves fortunate in reaching such a position only at the close of their lives. And yet within a few months he was dead by his own hand, leaving his whilom friends and admirers to decide, if they could, whether he were an impostor or a madman. It is my own conviction that he was neither; but it must be remembered that no adequate biography of him is extant, and that the facts have to be put together piecemeal, after disentangling them as far as possible from a nexus of prejudice and exaggeration. Of contemporary information we have very little—and of first-hand evidence practically nothing except a pamphlet published by Price himself. These sources, with a certain amount of additional matter (chiefly obtained by re-working the authorities cited in the *D.N.B.* article on Price), have furnished the main outlines of the following sketch.

James Higginbottom,† afterwards James Price, was born in London in 1752.‡ Entering Magdalen Hall, Oxford, as a gentleman commoner, he matriculated there on April 15, 1772, and subsequently "proceeded M.A." (November 21, 1777). Early in 1781 his maternal uncle, James Price of London, died, leaving to his nephew a fortune of some £130 per

* See Plate IV.

† This name is so spelled in his certificate recommending him for admission to the Royal Society. The *D.N.B.* and Brayley's *History of Surrey* both have "Higginbotham". The point is not of fundamental importance.

‡ He was the son of James Higginbottom by Margaret his wife, sister of James Price.

annum from real estate, and £10,000 to £12,000 in the funds. Under the terms of the bequest, Higginbottom adopted his uncle's name, and became James Price; and, determining to devote his life to chemical research, he purchased a small estate at Stoke, near Guildford, where he fitted up a laboratory in a beautiful, rambling house* which had previously been inhabited by another "character", one Dr. Irish.

Price seems to have possessed a natural bent for chemistry; and this, coupled with the improvement in his circumstances, pointed him out as a very fit person to be proposed for election into the Royal Society. It may be noted that in the early years of George III's reign the portals of that august body were not so closely guarded as they are to-day. Under the energetic presidency of Sir Joseph Banks (who ruled over it from 1778 until his death in 1820) much, however, had been done to debar candidates of the entirely useless and unscientific type so cordially welcomed by his predecessor, the amiable numismatist Martin Folkes.† Banks set his face—which, judging by his portraits, was well adapted to express scorn and contempt—sternly against the dilettante, the "distinguished foreigner", and the sprig of nobility; and it is a testimony to Price's merits and accomplishments that so young a man (he was elected F.R.S. at twenty-nine), little known outside his own circle, and with nothing of his work yet published, should have made his way into the charmed circle which Banks had been at such pains to delineate.

The certificate recommending him for election runs as follows:

"James Price ~~Higginbottom~~ of Magdalen Hall Oxford M.A. A Gentleman well versed in various branches of Natural Philosophy & particularly in Chymistry being desirous of becoming a Member of this Society we whose names are here underwritten do from our personal knowledge recommend him as a person very worthy of that honour & likely to become a very Usefull Member

(*Endorsed*)		R. Kirwan
Read Feby 8. 1781		S. Hemming
1	15	Geo. Atwood
2	22	Rd. Hy. Alexr. Bennet
3 March	1	Richard Brocklesby
4	8	R. Barker

* Pulled down c. 1928.

† The Royal Society, in Folkes' time, once came within an ace of adding to their number a gentleman whose only claim to scientific honours lay in his invention of a new water-closet.

(*Endorsed*)

Read 5 March	15	Wm. Seward
6	22	Nevil Maskelyne
7	29	J. Lockman
8 April	5	Willm. Wright
9	26	Dan Solander "
10 May	3	

Ballotted for and Elected
May 10, 1781

One or two of his proposers were a little above the rank and file of the Society. Atwood is still remembered by "Atwood's Machine" for diluting and measuring the acceleration of falling bodies; Maskelyne was Astronomer Royal, and had not yet initiated that revolt against Banks' authority in which he was to be so signally worsted; and Solander had sailed round the world with Banks and Cook in the *Endeavour*, and was a close friend of the former.

During 1781, Price busied himself in experiments and preparations which gradually assumed a definitely alchemical trend. He left, so far as I can trace, no notes or MS. which were examined by competent chemists, and the sole source of information for his work is the pamphlet* which he published in 1782—a source whose reliability must stand or fall with the estimate which one forms of his whole character. If it be assumed that he was insane when he took his life, it is a fair inference that he was equally or nearly so when he wrote it, and when he made his public experiments: and if, on the other hand, it is considered that his experiments were deliberately fraudulent, his pamphlet will fall to be classed as a piece of propaganda directed to the same end. In what follows I have assumed that he did his best to set down an account of the truth—but, as will be seen, not the whole truth.

Here is his own account of the lines on which his work was planned.

"A frequent perusal of ancient chemical writers, and an early attachment to the metallurgic branches of Chemistry, inclined the author of the ensuing narrative to believe that the wonders related in books at present little read, though frequently exaggerated, had at least some foundation. The phænomena which he continually met with in the pursuit of his experimental enquiries contributed greatly to strengthen this opinion:

* An / Account / of some / Experiments / on / Mercury,/ Silver and Gold/, Made at Guildford in May, 1782. / In the Laboratory of / James Price, M.D. F.R.S. / to which is prefixed / An Abridgment of Boyle's Account / of a degradation of Gold./ . . .
Oxford: At the Clarendon Press. MDCCLXXXII.

He found also, that some discoveries supposed to be modern, were really recorded in very ancient writers; but in terms so obscure, that the fact must rather be applied to explain the description, than the description to illustrate the fact.

"The positions of the Spagyric Philosophers* respecting metals, seemed to be very easily reconciled with the notions of more modern chemists. . . .

". . . Of their Earths, most have allowed the diversity; but specific gravity being usually considered as the least dubious mark of real identity between two bodies otherwise dissimilar, it seemed probable that Mercury and Gold had a basis nearly alike. . . .†

"The remarkable analogies between the habitudes of Silver and Mercury, to chemical solvents and other agents, are known to every Chemist.

"These, and a thousand other analogies, too obvious as well as too minute to relate, occurred in a course of incessant experiment, in which an ardent curiosity involved the author at a very early period. . . . Among this matter of unformed matter, where opinion fought with opinion, and *Chaos judged the strife*, the specious glitter of some broken gems, allured him to prosecute his search, and, if possible, dive to the bottom; the turbid stream did not permit his view of its utmost depths, but he returns to shew that he has been below the surface, and not quite in vain.

"To the Chemist it is unnecessary to hint at more analogies; to others it would be useless. . . ."

In other words, Price, as the result of studying the writings of the old alchemists in the light of his own chemical knowledge, had come round to their doctrine that the heavier metals, such as gold, silver, and mercury, were really variant forms of the same substance; the doctrine enunciated, for example, by "Eirenaeus Philalethes":‡

". . . All metallic seed is the seed of gold; for gold is the intention of Nature with regard to all metals. If the base metals are not gold, it is only through some accidental hindrance; they are all potentially gold."

Some of the alchemists, indeed, went further, and regarded all the so-called "elements" as different disguises assumed by one elemental

* Believers in the transmutability of metals. The term was coined by Paracelsus.

† Their approximate specific gravities are: gold, 19·5; mercury, 13·6 (lead, 11·4; silver, 10·5). It is curious that Price does not mention lead, which is denser than silver. The modern atomic weights are still closer: gold, 197·2; mercury, 200·0; lead, 206·4.

‡ In *The Metamorphosis of Metals* (see *The Hermetic Museum*, Vol. II, p. 19). The identity of this writer is not known with certainty. It seems most probable that he was one George Starkey (*ob.* 1665).

substance; corresponding, in modern times, to the "urstoff" of Hinrichs or the "protyle" of Crookes.

Having accepted this theory Price proceeded, strictly following the alchemical tradition, to search for some ingredient which, if added in small quantity to certain of the "base metals" under favourable conditions of heat and fluidity, would convert them, wholly or in part, into the precious metals—gold and silver. That such an ingredient (the so-called "Philosopher's Stone") actually existed was a widely accepted belief; and if, as seems likely, he knew the narratives of Van Helmont, Helvetius, and Boyle, he must have had at least an inkling of its probable character and of the technique required for its employment. In his reading, moreover, he must have encountered a large number of alchemical recipes; which, by reason of their obscure language, could, by his plan of interpreting them in the light of his own knowledge, be made to square with almost any formula he might select for experiment.

In the spring of 1782, Price believed himself to be in possession of small quantities of two ingredients, one capable of transforming mercury into silver, and the other silver or mercury, indifferently, into gold. These took the form of powders, the former white and the latter red. As to their composition, apart from the fact that they contained arsenic, nothing is known. According to Price, their preparation involved "a process . . . tedious and operose", and, moreover, injurious to health. At the beginning of May 1782 he possessed about sixteen grains of the white powder and five of the red, all of which he expended in the once-celebrated experiments which he performed at Guildford between May 6th and 28th in that year.

I say "experiments", since that was what Price himself called them: but I am certain that he used the term as the conjurer does who tells you that he is about to perform "a few experiments in the art of legerdemain or sleight-of-hand".* It is simply unthinkable that a man with a reputation to lose would invite witnesses to see him perform an important and novel experiment which he had never attempted before. He must have first satisfied himself that his powders were capable of effecting transmutation; afterwards he expended what remained of them in repeating his results before some of his neighbours and a few persons of note who had come from farther afield.

Naturally, but somewhat unfortunately, he decided to give his demonstrations in his own laboratory. Naturally, because there he was working with familiar appliances and extensive resources; he avoided, for example,

* Most of the best modern illusionists, of course, have discarded this sort of traditional hocus-pocus.

handicapping himself by undertaking the management of a strange furnace. Unfortunately, because he thereby furnished his detractors with two excellent arguments. A man desirous of committing a fraud would naturally prefer to do so in a place under his sole control, and one whose distance from London militated against the attendance of witnesses possessing an inconvenient amount of expert knowledge. Price himself, as will be seen, thought that some explanation of the latter circumstance was necessary.

For the first experiment (made on May 6, 1782) he had only four witnesses, all neighbours; but rumours of his doings spread like wildfire, and he was soon able to command the attendance of as many selected persons as could be got into his laboratory. For example, the seventh experiment (May 25, 1782) was attended by:

> Lord King
> Lord Onslow
> Lord Palmerston, F.R.S.
> Sir R. Barker, Bart.
> Sir Philip N. Clarke, Bart.
> Rev. O. Manning, F.R.S.
> *Rev. B. Anderson
> Rev. G. Pollen
> Rev. J. Robinson
> Dr. Spence
> W. Mann Godschall, F.R.S.
> W. Godschall, Jun.
> Wm. Smith, Esq.
> — Gregory, Esq.
> †F. Russell, F.R.S.

Price's experiments were of three kinds:

(a) Fusing mercury, and transforming a small portion of it into silver (with the white powder) or gold (with the red powder).

(b) Fusing silver, and obtaining, by the red powder, an alloy of eight silver to one gold.

(c) Forming an amalgam of mercury with either powder, resulting in the production of a small quantity of silver or gold.

* An amateur chemist living near Guildford.

† This identification is not quite certain. Price speaks of him only as "Mr. Russell, a magistrate of the Place". Apparently, he knew enough of metallurgy to be able to make an assay.

The following account of the first experiment is quoted verbatim (stops included) as giving a fair example both of his results and methods, and of his style.

EXPERIMENT I

"Made May the 6th, 1782, before the Rev. Mr. Anderson, Capt. Francis Grose;* Mr. Russell, and Ensign D. Grose. The Gentlemen mentioned in the Introduction as the most proper witnesses of the process, then resident in the Town.

"Half an ounce of Mercury provided by Capt. Grose (bought at an apothecary's of the town) was placed in a small hessian crucible, brought by Mr. Russell on a flux composed of Borax, (also brought by him) a small piece of charcoal, taken out of a scuttle (fortuitously) by Mr. D. Grose and examined by the rest of the company, and a small piece of Nitre also taken out without selection, by the Rev. Mr. Anderson, from a quantity in common use, in the Laboratory; these being pounded together in a mortar which all the company had previously inspected, were pressed down into the crucible with a small pestle: on this flux the mercury was poured by Mr. Anderson, and upon it half a Grain, carefully weighed out by Mr. Russell, of a certain powder, of a deep red colour, furnished by Dr. P. was put on it by Mr. Anderson.

"The crucible was then placed in a fire of a moderate red heat by Dr. P. who from his greater facility in managing the fire from long habit, was thought most eligible to conduct the experiment. He repeatedly called the attention of the company to observe the stages of the process, and to remark that in every part of it that any voluntary deception on his part was impossible.

"In about a quarter of an hour, from the projection of the powder, and the placing the crucible in the fire, he observed to the Company, who on inspection found his observation true, that the mercury, though in a red hot crucible, showed no signs of evaporation, or even of boiling: the fire was then gradually raised, with attention on the part of the company, and repeated calls for that attention from Dr. P. that no undue addition might be made to the matter in the crucible; in a strong glowing red, or rather white-red, a small dip being taken on the point of a clean Iron Rod, and when cold, the *scoriae* so taken and knocked off, were shown to the company and found replete with small globules of a whitish coloured metal,

* A well-known antiquary, celebrated both for his learning and for his Falstaffian bulk and humour. His *Classical Dictionary of the Vulgar Tongue* (first edition, now rare) and his *Olio* may confidently be recommended to certain ultra-frank lady novelists— they have a fescennine flavour which even eighteenth-century readers found a little disquieting.

which Dr. P. observed to them could not be Mercury as being evidently fixed in that strong heat;* but as he represented to them an intermediate substance between ☿ and a more perfect metal.

"A small quantity of Borax (brought by Mr. R.) was then injected by him and the fire raised, but with the same precautions on the part of Dr. P. to subject every thing to the minute inspection of the persons present; and after continuing it in a strong red-white heat for about a quarter of an hour, the crucible was carefully taken out, gradually cooled: on breaking it, a globule of yellow metal was found at bottom, and in the scoriae smaller ones, which collected and placed in an accurate ballance by Mr. Russell, were found to weigh *fully* Ten Grains. This Metal was in the presence of the above mentioned Gentlemen sealed up in a phial, impressed with the Seal of Mr. Anderson, to be submitted to future examination, though every one present was persuaded that the metal was gold.

"This seal being broken the next morning, in the presence of the former company, and of Captain Austen,† and the metal hydrostatically examined, the weight of the larger globule (the others being too minute for this mode of examination) was found to be in air 9 Grains and a Quarter, and in distilled water of temp. Fahren. 50 plus, it lost, something more than $\frac{3}{8}$ (but not quite an half) of a grain: the difference was not appreciable, as no smaller weight than the eighth of a grain was at hand, but was judged by all the company to be nearly intermediate; i.e. $\frac{7}{16}$:—at half a grain the sp. gr. would be rather more than 18 : 1; if only $\frac{3}{8}$ were lost in water the sp. gr. would exceed 24 : 1. the intermediate would be 21 : $\frac{1}{7}$ nearly; but as the loss seemed rather more than the intermediate, though apparently and decided (*sic*) less than half a grain, the specific gravity must have been nearly as 20 : 1. and in this estimate all present acquiesced.‡

"After this hydrostatical examination, the globule was was (*sic*) flattened by percussion into a thin plate, and examined by Mr. Russell in the manner of artists for commercial purposes; on finishing his scrutiny he declared it to be as good gold as the grain gold of the *refiners*, and that he would readily purchase such gold as that which he had just examined at the highest price demanded for the purest gold.

"The plate being then divided, one half was before the company

* Mercury vaporizes at about 662° F.

† I have not been able to trace any particulars about this witness. In Banks' copy of Price's pamphlet (now in the British Museum) is a list in his handwriting of the witnesses who attended Price's experiments; but Austen's name does not appear in it.

‡ It must be remembered that in 1782 chemical balances were very far from modern standards of accuracy. The method here indicated is the usual plan of weighing the body in air and in water, from which data the sp. gr. is easily calculated. The figure obtained (20 : 1) pointed unequivocally to the metal being gold.

sealed up by Mr. A. to be submitted to a trial of its purity, which Dr. P. proposed, requesting his friend, Dr. Higgins, of Greek Street, to make; the remainder being put into Aq. Regia of Nit. acid and Sal. Ammon. afforded a solution sufficiently rich, before the company separated, to yield with sol. of Tin, a richly coloured crimson precipitate.

"Capt. G. was accidentally absent when the precipitate was made, but saw it next day. In about four hours the portion of metal employed was completely dissolved, and the next morning before Capt. and Mr. D. Grose, and Mr. Russell (Mr. A. being prevented from coming). The solution being divided into three portions the following experiments were made.

"To the first portion, diluted with water, was added a quantity of Caustic Vol. Alk. and the precipitate, which was copious, being duly separated and dried, about a grain of it,* placed on a tin plate, was heated and found to explode smartly; this experiment was repeated three times.

"To the second portion, diluted, was added a portion of Sol. of Tin, in Aq. Reg. A beautiful crimson coloured precipitate was immediately formed in considerable quantity: which when dried, was mixed with a soluble fritt, composed of flint-powder, and the fluxes proper for the Ruby Glass of Cassius, in the proportion of 5 grains of of (sic) the precipitate to ʒij [2 oz.] of the frit, and in a vitrifying heat afforded in about three hours a transparent glass, which by heating again, assumed an elegant crimson colour: and the remainder which continued in the fire also acquired a bright red colour.

"The third portion being mixed with vitriolic Ether, imparted to it the yellow colour given to this fluid by solutions of Gold: and the Ether being evaporated in a shallow vessel, a thin purplish pellicle adhered to the side, spotted in several places with yellow.

"Dr. Higgins soon after receiving the piece of Metal, favoured the Author with an answer, in which he notified that the packet came to him under the proper seal: That he was well satisfied of the *purity* of the gold he received; and that he considered the authors experiments as exclusively sufficient to have ascertained the nature and purity of the metal."

This extract brings out a number of points common to the whole series of experiments. One notes, first of all, the eagerness shown by Price to ensure that his ingredients and their manipulation should be free from all suspicion of trickery. Probably, his eagerness defeated its own end; had he stressed the point less, less would afterwards have been made of it.

---

* The process formed the well-known "fulminating gold", mentioned by Pepys in his diary as early as 1663 (November 11th).

Secondly, it will be seen that the yield of gold was exceedingly small—although it was well outside the limits of experimental error. He obtained enough gold for a series of convincing tests; on the other hand, not enough to remove the suspicion that it might have been present beforehand as an accidental impurity. The most singular feature of the experiment, as described, is the fact that the mercury "showed no signs of evaporation, or even of boiling".

The table on pages 162 and 163 gives a summary of all Price's public experiments.

Needless to say, such reports of the demonstrations as found their way into print created an enormous sensation; and, not unnaturally, a good deal of adverse comment, duly noticed by Price when he published, in the autumn of 1782, his *Account of Some Experiments on Mercury* . . ." In his Introduction he remarks:

"Previous to this publication the Author has had frequent opportunities of hearing the opinions of many concerning its subject. Some say that they cannot account for the Theory of the process, and *therefore* that the fact is not true. Others ask, if it be true, is it profitable?* Illeberal minds suggest that the whole was a trick, and without knowing or enquiring what evidence it rests on, modestly call the Author a knave and the Spectators fools: —And some Heroes of incredulity, declare that they would not believe it though they saw it with their own eyes and touched it with their own hands."†

He asks how, by any deceit, he could keep Mercury from boiling in a red heat (Exp. II) or, when boiling, fix it almost instantly by adding not more than $\frac{1}{480}$ of its weight (Exp. III).

He *might* (but not in front of twelve or fourteen spectators) have conveyed metal into the crucibles, but in Exps. IV and V the silver was enriched with about 8 times as much gold as the powder projected on to it.

". . . He may further ask (though this is not properly an argument with the public at large, but only with those who know his situation) what could induce him to take such laborious and indirect methods of acquiring sinister fame: possessed as he was of total independence, and of Chemical reputation."

* It was certainly not profitable. Price is believed to have computed that the powder expended in one of the experiments, which had afforded about £4 worth of gold, had cost him some £17 to prepare.

† Helmholtz, the great German physicist, was a super-Thomas of this kind. "I would not", he remarks, "accept any abnormal phenomena on the mere testimony of my eyes."

PLATE IV

DR. JAMES PRICE, F.R.S.
From a portrait in pastel by John Russell, R.A.

Reproduced by courtesy of
The National Portrait Gallery

Facing page 160

It will be noticed that on his title page he described himself as M.D. This was a complimentary degree, conferred on him by his university on July 2, 1782. It seems to have been generally assumed, then and afterwards, that this honour was paid him as the reputed discoverer of the Philosopher's Stone. He was at some pains to refute this in a second edition of his pamphlet, which appeared early in 1783:

"He also begs leave to remark, that the Gentlemen who in some of the public prints represented his late degree as confer'd in consequence of these experiments, must have been misinformed. There was not the least connection between them, as is well known to almost every member of the Convocation; nor, indeed, could there be, since the degree was given some time *before* the experiments were known in *Oxford*. It was conferred expressly on account of his *former* chemical labours. . . ."*

Oxford may be a mental backwater†; but it is a little difficult to believe that no one there had heard, by the end of June, of the experiments, made by an Oxford M.A., which had been the principal topic of conversation in London for some six weeks past. And, indeed, when the question was raised (some years after Price's death) in *The Gentleman's Magazine*, a member of Convocation, in defending the grant of the degree (which, he admits, was strongly opposed), could find no better reasons to justify it than that Price was a gentleman commoner, that he had behaved with sobriety, and that "he was going abroad, where the degree would be a recommendation to him."‡ He added, it is true, that he was reputed to be "the best chemist in the kingdom", but it is difficult to understand how Convocation could test this assertion, since Price had then published nothing whatever. In any case, it seems not improbable that, but for the interest attaching to his alchemical experiments, Price might have whistled for his "M.D.Oxon".

By the autumn of 1782, he had reached the peak of his career. His

---

* In the original, the text is in italics, and the words here italicized in ordinary type.

† "It is scarcely necessary to say that, in this hot competition of bigots and slaves, the University of Oxford had the unquestioned pre-eminence. The glory of being farther behind the age than any other portion of the British people, is one which that learned body acquired early, and has never lost" (Macaulay, *Sir James Mackintosh*).

‡ *Gentleman's Magazine*, 1791, p. 893, in a letter signed "R.C." His antagonist, "L.L.", in a rejoinder (p. 1009) pointed out that none of the reasons adduced could be taken seriously, and that the third, in particular, reminded him of the conscientious gun-makers, "who lay apart all barrels so faulty as to be likely to burst when once heated, that they may not be used in home consumption, but all exported together to furnish the African Negroes with musquetry. . . ."

No.	Witnesses.	Materials.	Powder.	Result.	Date.
I	Rev. B. Anderson Capt. F. Grose Mr. Russell Ens. D. Grose	Hg ($\frac{1}{2}$ oz.) Borax Charcoal Nitre	Red ($\frac{1}{2}$ gr.)	Gold (10 grs.)	6.5.1782
II	Sir P. Clarke Dr. Spence Rev. B. Anderson Capt. Grose Mr. Russell Ens. D. Grose	Hg ($\frac{1}{2}$ oz.) Charcoal (1 oz.) Borax (2 dr.) Nitre (1 scrp.)	White (1 gr.)	White metal (13 grs.) Partial failure owing to using too much charcoal	8.5.1782
III	Rev. B. Anderson Capt. Grose Ens. Grose Mr. Russell	Hg ($\frac{1}{2}$ oz.) Charcoal Borax	White ($\frac{1}{2}$ gr.)	Repetition of No. II White metal (4 grs.)	9.5.1782
IV	As for III	Silver (60 grs. = 1 dr.) Flux as above, more borax added during fusion	Red ($\frac{1}{2}$ gr.)	Crucible cracked. Flux escaped, but no silver. Remaining metal found to contain gold	9.5.1782
V	As for IV + J. D. Garthwaite (who was also present at finale of Experiment IV).	Silver (30 grs.) Borax Charcoal Some "glass of borax" (to avoid moisture of crude borax) added later	Red ($\frac{1}{2}$ gr.)	Metal of original weight, but containing gold NOTE.—Silver of Experiment V (30 grs.) did not contain so much gold as that of IV (60 grs.), but the proportion was the same = $\frac{1}{8}$	9.5.1782

	Names	Materials	Colour	Result	Date
VI	Sir P. N. Clarke, Rev. B. Anderson, Capt. Grose, Dr. Spence, Ens. Grose, Mr. Hallamby	Hg (2 oz.) Rubbed with a drop or two of Vitreous Ether	White (1 gr.) Rubbed into Hg for 3 minutes	Bead of silver (29 grs.), formed in Hg Experiment repeated 18.5.1782 before Manning, Rev. Dr. Fulham, Anderson, Robinson, and Spence. Result, 12 grs. silver in proportion of 28 : 1, as before	15.5.1782
		Hg (5 dr.) Rubbed with Vitreous Ether	Red ($\frac{1}{4}$ gr.)	Bead of $6\frac{1}{4}$ grs. gold obtained	
		Hg (ʒij, about)	Red ($\frac{1}{8}$ gr., about)	Rather more than 1 gr. of metal, containing gold	18.5.1782
VII	Lord Onslow, Lord King, Lord Palmerston, Sir R. Barker, Sir P. N. Clarke, Rev. O. Manning, Rev. B. Anderson, Rev. G. Pollen, Rev. J. Robinson, Dr. Spence, W. M. Godschall, W. Godschall, W. Smith, Mr. Gregory, Mr. Russell	Hg (ʒij) (rubbed up with a few drops of Vitreous Ether)	White (1 gr.)	10 gr. silver (about $\frac{1}{4}$ of total mass)	25.5.1782
		Hg ($\frac{1}{2}$ oz.) Charcoal Borax	Red ($\frac{1}{2}$ gr.)	About 10 grs. gold	
		Hg (30 oz.) Hg (1 oz.)	White (12 grs.) Red (2 grs.)	> 600 grs. "Fixed white metal" (Silver) 120 grs. "Fixed and tinged metal" (Gold)	28.5.1782 (Before *some* of the previous company)

---

pamphlet, for all its cautious title and sober style, had brought him acclamation and celebrity; "monarch of all he surveyed" at Guildford, he was also a social success in London. Majesty itself condescended, no doubt with turkey-like gobblings and much vain repetition, to inspect and approve specimens of his artificial gold and silver.* A baronetcy, at least, could scarcely be avoided; and who could say what further honours were in store?

Yet there is much ground for believing that Price knew, even before he sent his pamphlet to press, that his apparent success was purely ephemeral—a house of cards which a breath of adverse criticism would destroy. No amount of testimony could get over the facts that his experiments had not been made under strict test conditions; that he had not divulged the composition of his powders; and that he was not prepared either to submit them to analysis or to repeat the experiments. He was compelled, we must imagine, to adopt this attitude—and he struggled in vain to explain it away. Here are his own words:†

" . . . The whole of the materials producing the extraordinary change in the metal employed, was expended in performing the processes which are now to be related: nor can the Author furnish himself with a second portion, but by a process equally tedious and operose, whose effects he has recently experienced to be injurious to his health, and of which he must therefore avoid the repetition.—The repetition, indeed, would avail but little to establish the facts, or gain belief. That more would believe if more had been present, is indeed true; but as the Spectators of a fact must always be less numerous than those who heard it related, the majority must at last believe, if they believe at all, on the credit of attestation. . . ."

In other words, he invited the public to regard and tolerate him as a dog in the manger, possessed of a most valuable bone which he would neither share nor eat. If he had gone out of his way to devise a plan which would unite all shades of opinion in condemning and vilifying him, he could scarcely have acted differently. Peasants and politicians alike re-

* " . . . These last portions of Gold and Silver . . . have had the honour of being submitted to the inspection of His Majesty; who was pleased to express his royal approbation. This honour may be mentioned with the less impropriety, as it is conferred by a Sovereign equally revered for his patronage of Science and beloved for his amiable condescension."

One is reminded of the courtly French chemist who, giving a demonstration before Louis XVI, began: "I have here certain volumes of hydrogen and oxygen, gases which will shortly have the honour of combining before Your Majesty."

† Loc. cit., p. v

garded him as a man who could make the whole kingdom, impoverished by the loss of its American possessions, fabulously rich and powerful in the twinkling of an eye—and who would not; scientific men were shocked by his lack of candour and his unscientific secrecy; men of rank began to regard him as an adventurer; his personal friends felt their loyalty severely and unfairly tested. Kirwan and Higgins, for example—both chemists of standing, one of whom had signed his R.S. candidature certificate, while the other had analysed some of the artificial gold—both pleaded earnestly with him, for the sake of his reputation, either to admit that he had been deceived by some flaw in his operations, or to put his cards on the table and disclose the formula and manufacture of his powders. But he could not bring himself to do either.

Indeed, he never seems to have formed a clear judgment on this crucial point. At one time, he appears to have half admitted that he had deceived himself. Thus Priestley, writing to Wedgwood, remarks:*

(Birmingham, Oct. 10, 1782)

" . . . You have heard of a pretended transmutation of quicksilver into gold by Dr. Price. Yesterday I had a letter from Mr. Kirwan, who, after some account of it, adds: 'But I have lately seen him, and he has owned, that he believes that he was deceived, and that his mercury previously contained gold: that he bought it from the makers of *Or moulu*,† &c. I said so much to him, that he is now satisfied to pass only for a mere able extractor of gold, and says he uses a preparation of arsenic, of which I persuaded him to promise he would give a paper to the Royal Society. If you have not heard this before you will like to have the information. . . ."

But although such may, for a time, have been Price's conviction, he speedily altered it. To the 1783 edition of his pamphlet (now entitled only "An Account of Some Experiments on Mercury"—"Silver" and "Gold" being omitted)—he prefixed an "Advertisement", in which he says:

" . . . The Author avails himself of this opportunity to observe, that the reports circulated respecting a mistake in these processes from employing Mercury accidentally impregnated with Gold by having been used in the manufacture of *Ormolu*, &c., are entirely without foundation;

* *Scientific Correspondence*, New York, privately printed, 1892, p. 42.
† Ormolu—an alloy of copper and zinc, whose colour, closely approximating to that of gold, was generally enhanced by a wash of gold lacquer. In Price's time it was much used for furniture mounts and other pieces of cabinet-work.

as indeed is evident from Exp. IV and V, and Exp. VII, p. 26. l 5 (1st Edit.).*

"He has not on enquiry found any reason to believe that the Mercury employed in these Experiments had in it more precious Metal than is usually contained in all Mercury:† and, indeed, the notion of manufacturers suffering Mercury so richly impregnated to pass out of their hands, without extracting all the Gold separable by the *common* methods, is so very improbable as scarcely to require refutation."

Two other passages from the same "Advertisement" (which may be regarded as a final manifesto, flung out by Price as a gesture of defiance in the face of an ever-growing body of adverse opinion) are important enough to deserve quotation:

"The Author of the following account intends to publish an appendix, in which he will attempt to explain the principles of some of his processes, and to shew their analogy to experiments related by Chemists of reputation:—as the collecting these must require some reading and attention, he cannot assign precisely the time at which the appendix will appear, but it will be prepared with all convenient expedition. . . .

"Many other remarks which he has heard might be removed by an attentive perusal of the narrative. He has only to add, that he is sorry his account, to which he himself gave only the unassuming title of 'Experiments on Mercury,' should have been held out to the World as announcing the discovery of the Philosopher's Stone, which in the *usual* sense of the word, he perhaps as well as others, thinks merely chimerical."

It seems likely that this was written towards the end of 1782, when Price was still trying to temporize with the world—and with himself. But the toils were closing around him. What disclosures the appendix‡ was designed to contain—whether it was intended to be an honest account

---

* The passage referred to is: "half an ounce of Mercury revivified from Cinnabar, brought by the Rev. Mr. Anderson, was by him placed in a small round English crucible. . . ." In Experiments IV and V, grain silver, bought from a refiner, was used —not mercury. (Original text is in italics.)

† In view of this statement, a footnote added to this edition is decidedly ambiguous: "The Author, by the words *product, produced*, and the like, here and in other places, means only to express that a quantity of precious metal was really obtained; and neither to affirm or deny any speculative opinions relative to the action of the Matter projected on the Mercury, or concerning the *manner* in which the precious metal is contained in Mercury."

‡ Price announced that it would also embody his abstract of Boyle's narrative (omitted from the second edition of his pamphlet) and "some references to other writers".

of the preparation of his powders or only a chain of theoretical reasoning (fortified by quotations from the early alchemists, backed up by Van Helmont, Helvetius, and the like) which should supply, if possible, an avenue of retreat from a position which had become untenable—will never be known. It never appeared, and no MS. of it has been found.

The relations subsisting at this period between Price and the Royal Society are involved in a good deal of obscurity. Officially, the Society took no cognizance of his experiments or of his pamphlet. Under its rules, it could scarcely do so. No MS. account of the alleged transmutations had been sent in by Price; and although he may have sent a complimentary copy of his pamphlet to the R.S. Library,* this could not have been regarded as being on the same footing as a personal communication of his results designed for the official consideration of the Society's Council. Moreover, so long as Price clung to his "secret", and refused to disclose the composition of his powders, the Royal Society—which has never exhibited the slightest toleration of obscurantism—would most undoubtedly have refused to give the slightest attention to his results.

But, although definite proof is lacking, there can hardly be any doubt that it was widely felt—and by none more strongly than by Sir Joseph Banks, P.R.S.—that Price's doings were not such as were calculated to enhance the prestige of the Society as a body, or to increase the estimation in which its Fellows were held by the general public. "Here (we can imagine Banks growling to himself) is a youngster with more money than sense, pitchforked into our body on the understanding that he is going to do valuable work in experimental chemistry on sound lines. No sooner does he write F.R.S. after his name than he comes out with a fantastic story about the essential truth of alchemy, backed up by a few experiments made before credulous bumpkins and Town rakes—experiments in which he says that he used a secret powder which he can't or won't make again, and whose composition he won't disclose. He may have bubbled the King (God bless Him for a kindly fool), but he won't bubble Joseph Banks. I believe the whole story is a pack of lies, and damme, but I'll find out before I'm much older. He shall repeat his damned experiments before a committee of my nomination, or show me cause why I shouldn't lay his name before the Council, with a request that they will take into their consideration whether his conduct has been such as we have a right to expect from our members."†

* No trace of such a present is to be found in the Society's records.

† The outlines of Banks' character are pretty well known; and while the above outburst is, of course, purely imaginary, I think that it may be regarded as giving a fair picture of what Banks thought about Price and his doings. He was undoubtedly very

Let us say, at any rate, that Banks, in a Chucks-like manner, put pressure on Price, "in the most delicate manner in the world", to repeat his experiments, or take the consequences. And the consequences—expulsion from the Royal Society and from "Society", general infamy, the revocation of University honours and degrees, the open derision of the "public prints", and the public whose trough such papers fittingly supplied, the quiet scorn and sarcasm of some erstwhile friends, and the scarcely more bearable pity of others, the shame and the disgrace—must have presented a terrifying vista to the sensitive mind of a young man who had not lived long enough to discover that there are very few things in life that really matter, and that public applause and public blame are not among them.

Apart from any question of mere social infamy, there is some reason to think that, as matters stood, his life itself was not safe. The end of the eighteenth century was an era of considerable "violence to the person"; and it requires little imagination to see Price's house sacked and himself pursued by a raging mob (as happened to Priestley a few years later): or to visualize him being kidnapped by some precursor of Carl Petersen,* and tortured to extract his secret.

In January 1783 he left London and went down to Guildford, having (it appears) given an undertaking to his friends that he would use his utmost endeavours to prepare more of his powders and repeat his experiments. Previously, he had tried (and failed) to obtain information about some German alchemical recipes which, he thought, might prove more serviceable than his own. It is significant of his state of mind that, on his arrival, his first act seems to have been to draw up his will, beginning with the phrase "Believing that I am on the point of departing from this world. . . ."

What, exactly, was his state of mind? Apart from a conviction of imminent ruin (which, on almost any hypothesis, it is safe to assume had taken possession of him) nothing can certainly be deduced as to this, but it may be of interest to examine the alternatives.

much of an autocrat; and while he generally played the part of a benevolent despot (for which his presence and ample fortune well fitted him) those who had the misfortune to cross him usually emerged from the conflict with a confused impression that they had become involved with the business end of a mule. It may be added that he was a sciolist rather than a scientist, and that natural history was the only branch of science about which he knew more than the average squire.

* The reference is to the series of "Bulldog Drummond" novels written by "Sapper". He thought fit, alas, to terminate Petersen's existence in a manner which, unlike the demonstration of *ju-jitsu* given by Sherlock Holmes above the Reichenbach Fall, left us no hope of a resurrection.

In May 1782 Price performed, before selected witnesses, experiments which, *prima facie*, tended to show that he had actually performed the transmutation of mercury into silver and into gold. We have, as Mr. Gladstone was so fond of remarking, three courses open to us. We may conclude:

(*a*) That he was a deliberate impostor
(*b*) That he deceived himself, and in so doing also deceived others
(*c*) That he actually accomplished transmutation

There would be nothing remarkable in his being a deliberate impostor. Most of the mediæval alchemists were cut to that pattern: and, indeed, there is something in the very name of gold which infallibly brings out the mean and base side of human nature; just as association with that noble animal the horse tends to develop a human type—bookies, tipsters, tic-tac men, gangsters, and the like—of which the world would be well rid. It is true that he was of independent fortune, but there are many instances of men having stooped to do for fame, or pride, or enmity, what nothing on earth would have induced them to do for money.

To reasoning like this, Price's defenders—if, indeed, at this distance of time, any such hardy persons can be found—have no ready answer. Admittedly, if we assume that he was an impostor we have an immediate explanation of the marvellous element in the story: the pretended transmutations, the unvaporizable mercury, and so on.

But it is also to be noted that, by accepting a theory which gets over the main difficulties, we elevate the more reasonable parts of the story into mysteries of their own. If Price were honestly minded, it would be natural that, at all hazards to his fortune and peace of mind, he should strive to convince others of the reality of his discoveries. But, in the name of common sense, why should a man build a stone wall for the purpose of running his head against it? Why should he deliberately engage in a campaign of deception which, it was obvious, could not be long sustained, and in which he must ultimately perish? Why should he choose to go up like a sky-rocket, if he knew that he must come down like the stick? If he were unprincipled enough, and adroit enough, to make a good trickster, how could he have been, at the same time, fool enough to undertake anything of the kind? No sane man, one feels, could have been, at the same time, so much of a knave and so much of an ass.

It is, of course, tempting to suppose that Price was a monomaniac: that he had become so as the result of a long course of alchemical reading and experiment: and that, as in the parallel case of the modern "snowbird",* his obsession lent him cunning and plausibility enough to deceive all those around him, while it so blunted his moral sense that he saw no harm in what he was doing. Or we may more charitably suppose that his *idée fixe* had so subjugated his reasoning powers that—like the earnest believers in spiritualism whose faith in some particular "medium" survives the most crushing possible exposure in their own presence†—he drew unwarrantable deductions from his own data, and unconsciously selected only those points favouring his views, discarding the remainder. On the other hand, after a careful perusal of his pamphlet I confess to a strong impression that he was of sound mind when he wrote it; and therefore presumably so when he made his experiments.

As to the possibility of his having actually effected the transmutations which he claimed, it need only be remarked at this stage that, unless the statements of Van Helmont, Helvetius, Boyle, and the considerable body of similar extant testimony be rejected on *a priori* grounds, it would seem that this can scarcely be ruled out. On the other hand, the conditions under which his experiments were made were certainly not stringent enough to exclude the possibility of fraud (deliberate or unconscious) and the most charitable verdict which can be passed on them is "not proven". Once Price's honour and veracity are questioned—and the question cannot be avoided—one looks in vain for corroborative testimony. His pamphlet remains the sole record of his doings. It is true that he informs us:

" . . . The following succinct account [of the experiments] was read over to the respective witnesses of each experiment. He [the author] now requests publicly, as before privately, their confirmation, without the slightest fear of contradiction or dissent."

But, so far as I can trace, no particle‡ of any such confirmation was ever given by any one of the men to whom he so confidently and pathetically appeals—men who had once been proud to call him their friend.

Price spent the last months of his life at Guildford, in ever-growing seclusion and despair. He is believed to have attempted to prepare more of his powders, and to have failed. It may be that, like Dr. Jekyll,§ he came to believe that his former success had been due to accidental impurities in his materials; or that he turned again to his former theory that his mercury

* Female cocaine-addict.

† Although scarcely credible, this has repeatedly happened.

‡ Not even, to quote Lord Oxford's celebrated peroration at Cambridge, "one jit or one tottle".

§ "In the year 18—, Dr. J. purchased a somewhat large quantity from Messrs. M. He now begs them to search with the most sedulous care, and should any of the same

had not been free from gold at the outset: or that he simply lost whatever faith he had ever possessed in his own operations. What is certain is that he gradually was forced by circumstances into that black pit of despair whose edge most men have skirted at some period of their lives, and whose depths have seemed, to only too many tortured minds, the one way out of their miseries. The game—if it were a game—was up. The tragedy had reached its last act. His friends forsook him one by one; he dared not show his face in London and, indeed, hardly ever left his house.

Yet in the last days of July 1783 he seems to have shaken off his apathy, and to have made his way to London for the purpose of formally inviting the Royal Society, or such members of it as could conveniently attend, to witness a repetition of his experiments at Guildford on August 3rd. Three only attended. Price received them cordially, but his face showed how much he felt the silent stigma of receiving this tiny and sceptical band of inquisitors in the place which, a few months before, had been full to overflowing with a fashionable and admiring crowd. He led the way to his laboratory, and invited an examination of his apparatus. Before this had ended, he was lying on the floor insensible, having poisoned himself with prussic acid. A doctor was called in, but the case was hopeless from the first.

> Cut is the branch that might have grown full straight,
> And burnéd is Apollo's laurel-bough,
> That sometime grew within this learned man.
> Faustus is gone. . . .

According to the only report of the inquest which I can trace,* the verdict was "Lunacy, upon general evidence of his having, in many instances, acted like a man insane". "It was 'generally supposed', in the neighbourhood of Guildford, 'that his studies hurt his mind'. . . . His feelings also were nice, and he could not stand the ridicule of the news-papers about the gold business. . . . This, and other things together, 'overset him'."

His epitaph still stands, and lies, in Stoke Church, to the following effect:

"Near this place are deposited the remains of James Price, M.D., F.R.S., . . . who departed this life the 31st of July, 1783, aged 25 years. *Heu! qualis erat.*"

quality be left, to forward it to him at once. Expense is no consideration. The importance of this to Dr. J. can hardly be exaggerated."

So far the letter had run composedly enough; but here, with a sudden splutter of the pen, the writer's emotion had broken loose. "For God's sake", he had added, "find me some of the old!"—*The Strange Case of Dr. Jekyll and Mr. Hyde,* ch. viii.

* A letter written by one of Price's neighbours eight days after the event—quoted in *The Gentleman's Magazine,* 1791, p. 894.

There is little doubt that the true date is August 3,* 1783, and none at all that he was thirty-one.

Semler

Price's youth, affluence, and tragic end have combined to make him a romantic figure, and to win for him the title of "The Last of the Alchemists";† but the term is a complete misnomer. For example, a German rival and contemporary of Price attracted, for some time, a good deal of attention, and added to the gaiety of nations in no small degree.

Professor Semler, of the University of Halle, had made theology his life-study; but in his early days he had indulged a passion for alchemical research. He was of an engagingly simple turn of mind, and an astute Jew took advantage of this to fool him to the top of his bent by professing to be possessed of various wonderful alchemical secrets which he had picked up in Barbary. Disheartened, Semler abandoned his laboratory, and betook himself to the study of the Mishna.

However, *on revient toujours à ses premiers amours,* and in his later years he began again to dabble in chemistry at a time when one Baron Hirsch happened to be advocating the transcendent virtues of a patent medicine which he called the "Salt of Life". It seems to have been a lineal descendant of Berkeley's tar-water, and an ancestor of many a like nostrum of our own day.

Semler took a good deal of "Salt of Life" and, having survived this successfully, deduced therefrom that it must have done him a great deal of good; an opinion to which he devoted several treatises, no more readable than such matters generally are. He was then struck with the idea that if Hirsch's nostrum were a universal medicine it might be able to cure the base metals as well as the human frame, and to convert them into gold. He made a solution of the "Salt of Life", and put it in an earthenware jar near a stove.

In a few days he found that the solution had precipitated some thin flakes of metal, which proved to be gold. He repeated the experiment several times, always with the same surprising result; finally, he published an account of it—greatly to the delight of Hirsch, for in a short time it became *de rigueur* throughout Germany to ornament the fireplace with a

* It was certainly either the 3rd or the 8th of August. He was buried on the 9th.

† There is an unconsciously funny article of this title in *All the Year Round,* June 13, 1863. The writer makes Price perform his experiments in 1787 at Salisbury, of which he is Dean! A mysterious and hostile stranger proves to be the Secretary of the Royal Society, and his return to London is followed by an imperative summons from Banks, citing Price to repeat his operations before that body. He complies; and poisons himself, after an appeal for clemency, in the ante-room!

jar of dissolved "Salt of Life". These, however, remained purely orna-
mental, not at all to the satisfaction of their owners.

Worse was to come. An eminent German chemist, one Klaproth, analysed the "Salt of Life", and, caring nothing (like the B.M.A.)* for its
proprietor's fulminations, published the result; a mixture of Glauber's
salt† and sulphate of magnesia, which, in the nature of things, could not
contain the slightest particle of gold.

The known probity of Semler's character made it obvious that he
must have been deceived in some way; but he did not accept this view, and
a prolonged paper warfare followed, in which the chemists insinuated that
Semler, as a theologian, was bound to be a fool, while the theologians retorted that Klaproth, as a chemist, was not improbably a knave. Finally,
Klaproth agreed that if Semler would send him some of his gold-bearing
solution he would make a public analysis of it.

The result showed the presence of something which looked like gold,
but proved to be "Dutch metal", a kind of brass.‡ A legal inquiry was
ordered, and the solution soon appeared. Semler had an old man-servant,
much attached to him, who had thought it a pity that, if his master wanted
to find gold in the solution, this should not somehow occur. Accordingly,
he used to buy small quantities of gold-leaf, and surreptitiously introduce
them into the jar at intervals. Being compelled, however, to leave home
to draw his pension, he instructed his wife to carry on the good work,
giving her money for the purpose. The good lady, having little sympathy
with the Professor's experiments, and a better use for the windfall, spent
most of it at the local tavern on "Dutch courage", and used the balance to
purchase "Dutch metal".

Theodore Tiffereau

There existed in France at the end of the nineteenth century (and, for
all I know, still exists) a body terming itself "L'Association Alchimiste de
France".§ It was founded by Albert Poisson (d'Avril?), who died in
1894. It boasted a Secretary-General and seven Councillors, who met
annually. In July 1897 it also had two Honorary Members, Camille
Flammarion and (of all people) August Strindberg!‖ The latter, although
better known as dramatist, novelist, and woman-hater, seems to have

* In their *Secret Remedies*, London, 1909, and its sequel.
† Decahydrated sodium sulphate, Na_2SO_4 $10H_2O$.
‡ Also called "tombac".
§ My account of the French alchemists is based, in part, on H. C. Bolton's very
entertaining *Modern Alchemy*, New York, 1897.
‖ Dr. S. H. Emmens was subsequently added to this list.

dabbled, at least, in alchemy—of a rather futile kind. Here, for example, are some "correspondences" which he claimed to have discovered and which, to those who like that sort of thing and can shut their eyes to arithmetical discrepancies, are no doubt full, like Gilbert's "Basing-stoke",* of hidden meaning.

$$K_2MnO_4 \text{ (at. wt. } 197) = Cu_2Cl_3 \text{ (196)} = Fe_3S \text{ (197)}$$
$$= C_2H_5I + \tfrac{1}{2}Br. = Au.$$

It will be noticed that he uses 196 and 197 indifferently as the atomic weight of gold.† Incidentally, Fe_3S is a hypothetical compound, whose atomic weight would be 200.

And here, from the same source, is a nineteenth-century alchemical recipe:

"Put into a crucible layers of sheet tin and of powdered vitriol; place over it another crucible pierced with a hole for respiration. Heat in an in-tense fire. But a flux must be added to the crucible to prevent melting, viz. one kilo litharge, one kilo clean white sand—mix and add to the crucible at a red heat. Remove the yellow oil with an iron spoon, and put it aside. The two compounds have not lost weight. This oil is dry water, a fire, a salamander. . . .

"You obtain a metal of a golden yellow, having a density of 241, not capable of being minted. This is changed into ordinary gold."

The zoological aside, occurring at an important point in the process, is rather confusing. I understand that those who have attempted to make gold in this manner have concluded that some important step has been omitted from the recipe, or that the printer was not feeling quite at his best when he set it up.

But if the names of Flammarion and Strindberg lent a certain amount of éclat to "L'Association Alchimiste de France", the doyen of French alchemists in modern times is certainly Theodore Tifferau; who, after a long life of obscurity, attained a fleeting notoriety in 1899. No sooner had the *New York Herald* published its account of how Dr. Emmens was making gold—and not only making it, but selling it to the U.S. Mint (a perfectly correct statement, by the way)—than the French Press, after its manner, proclaimed *urbi et orbi* that Emmens was a base imitator of the illustrious French genius, Theodore Tiffereau!

Tiffereau was then an old man. His work, such as it was, had been done many years before. In 1854–55 he bombarded the Académie des Sciences

* See (or, better, hear) *Ruddigore*.   † It is actually 197·2.

with a series of six memoirs on transmutation, describing a process which he claimed to have discovered in 1849 at Guadalajara, Mexico, where he was earning a precarious livelihood as a photographer. Here is an extract from his third memoir, presented May 8, 1854:

"My first success was obtained at Guadalajara. The circumstances were as follows:

"After having for two days exposed pure nitric acid to the action of the solar rays, I placed in it some filings of pure silver alloyed with pure copper in the same proportions as those of the alloy used for making silver coins. A brisk reaction was manifested, accompanied by a very copious disengagement of nitrous gas, after which the liquid, on becoming quiet, allowed me to see an abundant deposit of the filings quite intact and agglomerated in a mass.

"The disengagement of nitrous gas still continuing, I left the liquid to itself for twelve days, and I remarked that the aggregated deposit became sensibly augmented in volume. I then added a little water to the solution without any precipitate being produced, and I again allowed the liquid to rest for five days. During the whole of the time there was no cessation of the vapours.

"At the end of the five days I heated the liquid to ebullition, and maintained it at that temperature until no more nitrous fumes were given off, after which I evaporated the solution to dryness.

"The substance thus obtained was dry, dull, and of a blackish-green colour; it presented no appearance of crystallization; *no saline matter was deposited.*

"This residue was then heated with pure boiling nitric acid for ten hours, and I noticed that it became of a clear green colour without any change as regards its aggregation in small masses. I added a further quantity of pure concentrated acid; I again boiled the liquid, and then I at length saw the substance become aggregated and take on the brilliancy of natural gold.

"I collected this product, and I consumed most of it in a series of tests as compared with pure natural gold, but I was unable to perceive even the least difference between natural gold and the gold I had succeeded in obtaining."

According to Emmens, who examined a specimen of this Guadalajara gold, it was a little redder than ordinary gold, and consisted of a number of irregular fragments showing what looked like file marks. He did not consider that it could be "parted" gold, obtained by merely dissolving an alloy of silver, copper and gold in nitric acid.

Tiffereau's process was tested at the Paris Mint by M. Levol, the chief assayer, "with little success". The result was communicated to the Académie on October 16, 1854. According to Emmens, M. Levol, who had furnished the silver for the experiment, and certified it as free from gold, became annoyed because in the course of the experiments small traces of gold kept making their appearance. He declared that the silver was obviously impure, and suspended the demonstration *sine die*.

Unfortunately, Tiffereau subsequently published a work in which he exposed his lack of chemical knowledge rather cruelly.* And in 1896† he sent another memoir to the Académie, in which he attempted to show that aluminium is a compound. His method of doing so was to leave aluminium and nitric acid in a sealed test-tube for two months. On opening it, he detected a smell "rather like" ether, and some crystals which "looked" like acetic acid. These being both carbon compounds, he concluded, somewhat hastily, that aluminium must be one also. Such are the mental aberrations of the aged.

Dr. S. H. Emmens

Tiffereau's claims can be dismissed without much difficulty as the product of defective knowledge crossed with imperfect technique. A similar case occurred, during his last years, in America. One Edward C. Brice, of Chicago, applied in 1896 for a patent on a process of making gold from antimony. The patent was refused, whereupon Brice demanded, as was his legal right (I believe), that the process should be officially tested at the United States Mint. Three assayers accordingly conducted a conclusive test under Brice's eyes and in accordance with his instructions. All that it showed was, that by Brice's method it was possible to recover part of the (very slight) trace of gold which is present in all commercial antimony. Even for this purpose, the process was comparatively inefficient. It may be added that its discoverer's record was not adapted to bear searching investigation.

But hard on the heels of "the great Brice joke" came a most singular event. It gradually became known that Dr. S. H. Emmens, of New York, claimed to have discovered a substance, intermediate between gold and silver, which he had named "argentaurum", and which was capable of being changed into gold. Not only so, but he was actively engaged in

---

* *Les Metaux sont des Corps Composés*, Paris, 1855. (New edition, Lermina, Paris, 1889). In this, Tiffereau enunciated his theory that transmutation is effected by the action of "the microbe of gold".

† At this period, according to Reverchon's *Petite Histoire de L'Horlogerie* (Besançon, *n.d.*), he was engaged in making sand-glasses for the French Navy, but still devoted all his spare time to alchemical experiments.

manufacturing gold from silver in this manner, and selling the product in moderate quantities to the United States Mint. The matter first attracted universal attention in 1899, when the *New York Herald* came out with a "scoop" article, containing such headings as

THIS MAN MAKES GOLD AND SELLS IT TO THE UNITED STATES MINT

IS DR. EMMENS A MODERN ROSICRUCIAN?

UNCLE SAM HAS BEEN BUYING HIS BRICKS FOR TWO YEARS

As the last of these indicates, the *New York Herald* was a little behind the times. It had not heard of Emmens before; but others had, both in connection with chemistry and with many other lines of research. He was the author of many books on a great variety of topics: a work on logic, another on explosives, several novels, and many papers on chemistry, electricity, and metallurgy—even a book of poems. English by birth, he was a member of several learned societies* and of the United States Board of Ordnance, and had invented a high-explosive, "Emmensite", which had been officially adopted by the United States Government. With regard to his alchemical doings, some account of these had been appearing at intervals in the United States Press since 1897.† It may be added that he published an outline of his work and methods, together with his correspondence on the subject with Sir William Crookes, in a book issued in 1899,‡ and that the following account is chiefly based upon this.

It appears to be a pamphlet written for sale at the Greater Britain Exhibition, at which Emmens was invited to exhibit his process of making "argentaurum"—which he did. It is ably and temperately written. If we are to regard Emmens as a crank, he is a very favourable specimen of the breed; and, after all, cranks keep the wheels turning.

He is convinced of the truth of the old theory that all forms of matter are ultimately one. He defends his "argentaurum" theory as follows:

"We find gold wherever we find matter (e.g. greenstone) that has made its way from the interior of the earth to regions within our reach, under conditions that have admitted of very slow cooling. We do not find it in

---

* Am. Inst. of Mining Engineers, Am. Chemical Society, Soc. Intern. des Electricians, U.S. Naval Inst., U.S. Military Service Inst. (and sometime Fellow of the Inst. of Actuaries, Gt. Brit. & Ireland).

† An article entitled "Changing Silver into Gold", by Herbert C. Fyfe, and based on information communicated by Emmens, appeared in *Pearson's Magazine* for March 1898.

‡ *Argentaurana, or some Contributions to the History of Science*, Stephen H. Emmens, Bristol, 1899.

ordinary lava streams where thermal energy has been rapidly dissipated.
Yet lava and greenstone are composed of similar material from a terrestrial
point of view; whence it becomes reasonable to infer that a non-auriferous
limestone, subjected to the same natural laboratory treatment as an
auriferous greenstone, is capable of producing gold by the transmutation
of some of its own constituent particles.

"Also when, as a matter of fact, we find that natural gold *in situ* is
invariably associated with silver, we cannot avoid the conclusion that such
association is not portentous (*sic*).* We are forced to admit that some kin-
ship, as it were, exists between gold and silver—e.g. that in the course of
natural chemical evolution silver becomes transmuted into gold, or gold
into silver, or that some third substance exists which changes partly into
gold and partly into silver."

Emmens claimed to have produced this third substance in his laboratory, by a method which he kept secret—but which apparently consisted
largely of the mechanical treatment of silver by hammering it incessantly
under conditions which allowed of the heat generated by the blows being
rapidly conducted away. By his own account, the process was composed of
five principal stages:

(*a*) Mechanical treatment
(*b*) Fluxing and granulation
(*c*) Mechanical treatment
(*d*) Treatment with modified nitric acid
(*e*) Refining

"I regard", he remarks, "the mechanical treatment as the *causa causans*.
The fluxing and granulation serve, I think, merely to render the mole-
cular aggregates susceptible of displacement and rearrangement". In
producing his "argentaurum gold", Emmens used as his material Mexican
silver dollars, certified by the United States Mint as containing "less than
a trace" (i.e. less than one part in ten thousand) of gold. These he proceeded to change by his process, the mechanical treatment being applied
by means of a "force-engine"—which seems, so far as one can follow the
vague hints which he gives of its powers, to have been a cross between a
pneumatic riveter and a hydraulic press. The product, consisting of ingots
containing an alloy of silver and gold in varying proportions (with
occasional traces of other metals) he disposed of, after an official assay, to
the United States Mint.

    * I imagine that the "not" is redundant, or else that "portentous" is a misprint for
"fortuitous".

Here are the official figures for the amounts of "argentaurum gold" purchased by the United States Assay Office between April and December 1897.

Month	Weight in oz.	Net value (£ sterling)
April	16·65	43
May	23·05	64
June	16·60	40
July	31·10	88
August	71·64	190
September	79·42	215
October	194·75	379
November	164·14	329
December (half month)	63·66	180

The results of the process were not very consistent, for the ingots sold in 1897 varied in fineness of gold from 305/1000 to 751/1000, and those sold in 1898 from 313/1000 to 997/1000—this last, of course, being practically pure gold.

The boom given to the subject by the *New York Herald* did not last long. The proprietor of that paper, James Gordon Bennett, printed a public challenge to Emmens to give a demonstration of his process before a committee. This was at once accepted. There only remained the question of paying the necessary expenses and selecting the witnesses. Both proved insoluble problems.

Emmens estimated that it would cost about £2,000 to equip a new laboratory for the demonstration; on the other hand, if this were given in his own, the cost might amount to £3,000, since if the committee suspected fraud they could not satisfy themselves on the point without taking up the floors, and so on. On the face of it, this seems reasonable; but Gordon Bennett began to think that the gold bricks in question were of a kind with which the public was already familiar.

It was next found that it would be no easy matter to get any scientist who valued his reputation to sit on the proposed committee. Mason (of the United States Assay Office) and Nikola Tesla, for example, flatly refused, and many others followed their example—one which, on the face of things, showed commendable prudence. They could scarcely gain reputation by taking part in such a proceeding; on the other hand, they were by no means unlikely to lose it. It is fairly safe to say that journalists and scientists have somewhat different conceptions of the nature of truth, and of the best methods of arriving at it.

In the end the *Herald* withdrew its offer (March 5, 1899); alleging, *more suo*, that Emmens' conditions were impossible to satisfy, and retreating, under cover of a great many ill-chosen words, with all the honours of defeat. I have the impression that, if it could have proved Emmens an impostor, it might possibly have brought itself to publish this fact.

In his correspondence with Sir William Crookes, F.R.S., which lasted a year (May 1897 to May 1898), Emmens afforded a good deal of information as to his personality, but much less as to his operations, and practically none as to the details of his process—which, it must be admitted, he had a perfect right to keep secret so long as he did not seek to make converts. And he did not—witness the following, in reply to an inquiry from Crookes:

"The gold-producing work in our Argentaurum laboratory is a case of sheer Mammon-seeking. It is not being carried on for the sake of science or in a proselytizing spirit. No disciples are desired, and no believers are asked for."

Later, when the correspondence was becoming acrimonious, Crookes made use of this statement:

(Crookes to Emmens, 23.5.1898)
"On the one hand you take very high ground, and affect to despise the opinions of scientific men. 'No disciples are desired and no believers are asked for.' . . . I am at a loss to reconcile this disdainful attitude with the eager way at (*sic*) which you snatch at every word that is said in your favour by men of the despised sect, and insist on giving to an unsuccessful experiment I was rash enough to describe to you in confidence, an importance it does not deserve and an interpretation absolutely against my explicit declaration. . . ."

The "unsuccessful experiment"* came about in this way. Emmens, in a letter to Crookes dated May 21, 1897, indicated an experiment having a bearing on the making of "argentaurum gold". He writes:

" . . . Take a Mexican dollar, and dispose it in an apparatus which will prevent expansion or flow. Then subject it to heavy, rapid, and continuous beatings under conditions of cold such as to prevent even a

---

* Actually, it is illogical to call any experiment "unsuccessful". As an American professor once remarked: "Every experiment proves something. If it doesn't prove what you wanted it to prove, it proves something else."

temporary rise of temperature when the blows are struck. Test the material from hour to hour, and at length you will find more than the *trace* (less than one part in ten thousand) of gold which the dollar originally contained."

This, after making some further inquiries as to details, Crookes proceeded to do; and here is his account of the result:

(*Crookes to Emmens, 22.2.1898*)
"I put about half an ounce of cuttings from a Mexican dollar into a steel mortar with a close-fitting piston, and screwed it firmly on a strong base. Over the piston I have a steel bar, 1·5 inches square, and sufficiently long to weigh twenty-eight pounds. This was provided with a collar, and was raised and allowed to drop one foot by means of a cam on a rotating shaft. It made sixty blows a minute.

The steel mortar was enclosed in a coil of pipes immersed in a water-bath, and ice was put in the bath; and through the coil of pipes a slow current of liquid carbonic acid flowed. This kept the temperature down considerably below zero F. the whole of the time. The water was hard frozen all the time of the operation. It went on for forty hours, stoppings being allowed at night (say, five hours at eight hours a day).

The results are as follows:

Hammered Mexican silver taken for assay	100·258 grains
Weight of gold bead	0·075 grain
Equal to	0·075 per cent
Some of the same silver before treatment	96·837 grains
Weight of gold bead	0·060 grain
Equal to	0·062 per cent

The difference is 0·013 per cent., which I consider is not enough to enable me to form an opinion on, as it is within the errors of experiment."

Such was Crookes's first attempt to repeat Emmens's production of gold from silver. He regarded it as "merely a preliminary canter", for the machinery was not working smoothly. Having overcome the defects, Crookes made a second attempt, which resulted in total failure. The reason for this, as given by Emmens, is rather curious.

Emmens was of opinion that, for his process to work at all, the silver which he used should have a suspicion of gold in it; say, 1/20,000. Crookes, who had been informed of this, but had either forgotten it or regarded it as unimportant, made his second trial with chemically-pure silver, which remained entirely unaffected by the "force-engine".

By this time the friendly tone of the Emmens-Crookes correspondence had been replaced by a pronounced subacid flavour. Crookes' experiments must have cost him a good deal, and he had, I think, come to suspect Emmens' candour. The latter, on his side, was beginning to be irritated by Crookes' apparent ineptitude and his incontestable vagueness of language. Then again, the interpretation put on the first experiment by Emmens differed widely from that of its maker. Emmens considered that, if Crookes' assays were worth anything, they demonstrated a rise of 20·9 per cent in the gold content of the silver—from 0·062 to 0·075. He regarded this as valuable independent testimony to the soundness of his theories, and was at some pains to make the experiment generally known.

Another incident which did nothing to heal the growing breach was the publication by Crookes in the *Chemical News* (which he controlled) of what professed to be an analysis of a piece of "argentaurum" sent to him by Emmens. It ran as follows:

"A specimen of argentaurum sent me by Dr. Emmens has been examined in the spectrograph. It consists of gold with a fair proportion of silver and a little copper. No lines belonging to any other known element, and no unknown lines, were detected."*

This was an unfortunate slip on Crookes' part. What he had asked from Emmens, and what Emmens had sent him, was "a small piece of the *gold* you have made". What he had examined was a sample of the product sold to the United States Mint, of which a specimen analysis is:

	Parts
	Parts
Gold	528·80
Silver	383·82
Copper	86·06
Platinum	0·65
Lead	0·05
Zinc	0·23
Iron	0·39
	1000·00

It may be added that a much more unfortunate remark occurred in the report of an assay made for Emmens by Preston, of the United States Mint. Argentaurum gold was stated to contain impurities of a kind "constantly present in old jewellery". I have often speculated whether the *New York Herald* ever heard of this; and, if so, what they said about

* *Chemical News*, 3. ix. 1897.

it. It was as neat a way of calling Emmens a "fence" as could well be imagined.

On March 31, 1898, Emmens wrote to Crookes in a strain of dignified reproof slightly marred by a split infinitive:

" . . . You have made *two* experiments. In one you employed metal from a normal Mexican dollar and obtained an increase of nearly 21 per cent. in the contained gold. In the other you employed *abnormal* Mexican dollars, and obtained no gold. It seems to me that your duty is to dispassionately announce both experiments. . . ."

Crookes replied on April 30th declining further correspondence, on the ground that Emmens had violated his (implied) confidence by publishing portions of his private letters. And Emmens rejoined (May 12, 1898):

" . . . really, don't you think it poor sport to ride the horse of grievance? You and I are growing old, and we may surely turn our time to better account than in exchanging complaint and repartee over such a trifling matter as to whether an experiment with a bit of metal should or should not be treated as a weighty secret? . . ."

It is fair to recall that Crookes began the correspondence. On the other hand, it was chiefly Emmens who sustained it, and I have the impression that before it ended Crookes would not have been sorry if it had never started.

In a letter to Mr. H. C. Fyfe,* Emmens gave some details of the financial side of his process. By his own account, he would be prepared to convert 1,000,000 ounces of silver into 600,000 ounces of gold,† for the sum of about £900,000. In other words, he could profitably charge 18s. for converting an ounce of silver, costing some 2s., into three-fifths of an ounce of gold, worth about £2 6s. In the same letter he gave some remarkable particulars of other wonders which he claimed to have accomplished:

" . . . we have produced some remarkable allotropic forms of gold and a very singular growth of silver. We have dissolved an alloy by a mechanical method. We have rendered arsenious anhydride readily soluble in pure water. In light and radiant energy generally we are also obtaining some surprising results. And the list could be greatly extended.

"I hardly know why I tell you of these things. I think it is because you

* Published in *Pearson's Magazine*, March, 1898.

† This is over-optimistic. A million ounces of silver, even if completely transmuted, could only produce about 540,000 oz. of gold.

have been broad-minded enough and bold enough to acknowledge the existence of my Argentaurum Paper, No. 1, which is regarded with fear, anger, and horror by the Gravity-cum-Ether-cum-Contraction worshippers. . . ."

The paper to which he refers is entitled *Some Remarks Concerning Gravitation,** but it might equally well have been called *Astronomical Hiccups, with Some Remarks on the Partition of Poland,* or any other name of a mixed character. Mixed it certainly is. It deals chiefly with the misdeeds of Sir Isaac Newton and his followers (why is it that the average crank generally starts by picking a quarrel with Newton?) and thence passes to the old, old question of whether the Moon rotates. The reader will, no doubt, thank me for sparing him extracts from Emmens' views on this point: they are as wildly wrong-headed as those of the veriest flat-earther. As an indication of its author's mental ability, the book is immeasurably below *Argentaurana.*

Still, crank or not, Emmens' feat of persuading the United States Mint to buy a considerable quantity of what he assured them was artificial gold has never, I think, been duplicated. Nor can I form any theory of fraud which would make such a proceeding either practical or necessary. As to the facts of the sale, there is no doubt.

Miethe. Nagaoka

On July 21, 1924, it was announced in the Press† that Dr. A. Miethe, Professor of photo-chemistry and astronomy in the Technical High School, Charlottenburg, had obtained gold from mercury by the prolonged action of a high-tension electric current on it. The discovery was more or less accidental, and arose from an examination of the black deposit found inside mercury-vapour electric lamps in which too high a voltage had been used. This deposit was found to contain traces of gold, although the mercury had been twice distilled before being used for the lamps. Dr. Miethe made special experiments with a view to producing an appreciable quantity of the deposit under conditions precluding the accidental presence of any gold, and obtained results which satisfied him that a very minute quantity of the mercury had been actually transmuted into gold. It may be added that he held out no prospect of the operation ever becoming commercially profitable. The potential used was about 170 volts, the current being passed through the lamp (which consumed some 400–2,000 watts) for periods varying from 20 to 200 hours.

* The Argentaurum Papers, No. 1, Some Remarks Concerning Gravitation, etc. (New York, 1897).

† See, for example, the *Morning Post* for that date.

In *Die Naturwissenschaften* for July 17, 1925, Dr. Miethe gave a considered summary of his results. He claimed to have found that, in a mercury vapour lamp operated under suitable conditions, gold does make its appearance in minute but appreciable quantities. The yield, apparently, is proportional to the strength and duration of the current. Below a definite minimum voltage no gold is produced: *in vacuo* the process fails. Gold, and in some cases a metal resembling silver, can also be produced by discharges between two mercury electrodes dipping into a bath of paraffin wax.

Confirmation of these latter results was afforded by some experiments made in September 1924–May 1925 by Professor H. Nagaoka, of Tokyo. He used exceedingly high voltages, discharging through paraffin oil across a narrow gap, one electrode being iron and the other mercury. Like Miethe, he obtained minute quantities of gold, and believed that he had eliminated the possibility of accidental errors.

It has to be recorded, however, that the results of Miethe and Nagaoka are not universally accepted. The principal objection is of a most curious nature, and demands a short digression.

Believers in the possibility of transmutation, when asked to give reason for their belief, have always relied, as their sheet-anchor, upon the phenomenon of "allotropy"—the curious property which enables various of the "elements" to appear indifferently in two or more forms, possessed of widely varying properties and appearance. There are, for example, two kinds of phosphorus, yellow and red. Yellow phosphorus is highly inflammable, easily soluble in various fluids, and extremely poisonous. Red phosphorus is not inflammable, almost insoluble, and not poisonous. Yet yellow and red phosphorus are, literally, one and the same substance; and either can be changed into the other at will. Similarly, charcoal, graphite (the core of a "lead" pencil), and diamond are all allotropic forms of one and the same element—carbon. Again, many compounds are known which, although composed of exactly the same elements in exactly the same proportions, differ widely in certain physical characteristics. This phenomenon is covered by the general term "isomerism", which, for the convenience of chemists and the bewilderment of the man-in-the-street, is divided into four branches, "polymerism", "metamerism", "stereoisomerism", and "polymorphism". Lastly, it was discovered by Soddy in 1923 that various of the elements have "isotopes"; that is to say, that there are groups of substances which answer to all the recognized tests of a given element, but differ slightly, among themselves, in their atomic weights. It is this last discovery which, some consider, stands in the way of our accepting the transmutations reported by Miethe and Nagaoka.

It was pointed out by F. W. Aston in 1925 that from the known iso-topes of mercury one can deduce that gold obtained from mercury by a process of transmutation would have an atomic weight of 198 or over. Analysis of the gold obtained by Miethe, on the other hand, gave an atomic weight of 197·2, which is exactly that of ordinary gold. Hence, it is concluded, the gold which he produced could not have been the result of transmutation.

To the plain man this appears simply paradoxical. It amounts, in effect, to saying that a thing is so obviously and demonstrably itself that it cannot be what it is. But it must be remembered that the last word has not by any means been said on the subject. The atomic theory has already undergone such transmogrifications that its originator, Dalton, would certainly fail to recognize it in its present electronic form. Every year brings fresh emend-ations of last year's "epoch-making investigations", and at the present rate it may not be long before all our present notions seem, and are publicly proclaimed, as out-of-date as the "phlogiston" theory which delighted Boyle and Cavendish. For, after all, theories are nothing but efforts of the imagination, devised to help the mind to grasp the meaning of various related phenomena. They are not demonstrably or even necessarily true, and the proper way to regard them is as newspapers, to be thrown away when out of date—not as family Bibles.

One day, perhaps, we shall scrap the theory of the immutability of the elements and come, like the old alchemists, to regard them as varying forms of the same essential substance. There is nothing particularly im-probable in conceiving that out of the millions of possible forms of matter some hundred or so should, by virtue of their particular structure, possess such great comparative stability that they give the impression of distinct "elements". Opinion has been veering in that direction since the dis-covery of radium in 1906, and "transmutation", on the electronic hypo-thesis, is now regarded as depending mainly upon our ability to alter the charge of energy possessed by a given atom. It would seem, however, that until some cheap source of enormous power be discovered (in which case gold would lose most of its value) the cost of the requisite energy would vastly outweigh the value of the gold or other precious metal which it produced.*

It would almost seem, then, that we must admit the possibility of trans-mutation. But it is still a far cry to such transmutations as Van Helmont, Helvetius, and Price claimed to effect. It seems almost incredible that with their limited resources and empirical knowledge they should have

* The same applies to the many schemes which have been put forward for extracting the millions of tons of gold which the sea holds in solution.

performed feats which are still beyond us. But it is not altogether impossible. Many processes have been discovered by accident; some entirely depend upon the presence of small quantities of ingredients—catalytic agents—which remain unaltered at the end of the operation; some demand, for their success, tricks of manipulation which may easily become forgotten. What is done to-day with great difficulty and expense in a well-equipped laboratory may be a schoolboy's hobby fifty years hence—so much, most will grant. But the converse is also true: that things may have been done long ago, with very imperfect appliances, which may present, if the method of doing them has been lost, a difficult problem to the resources of the present day.

The "Philosopher's Stone" seen and handled by Van Helmont and the others, and Price's "transmuting powders", may have been vulgar tricks practised on the credulity of honest and unsuspecting men. They may also have been catalytic agents, whose nature might perhaps be rediscovered—either by direct experiment or by patient examination and sifting of the enormous extant mass of alchemical literature. The only man of modern times who explored both these avenues paid, in the end, for his temerity with his life. "Whence comes such another?"

ABRAHAM THORNTON
OFFERS BATTLE

" . . . *And if the said Abraham Thornton will deny the felony* and murder aforesaid, as aforesaid charged upon him, then the said William Ashford, who was the eldest brother, and is the heir of the said Mary Ashford, deceased, is ready to prove the said felony and murder against him, the said Abraham Thornton, according as the Court here shall consider thereof, and hath found pledges to prosecute his Appeal*".

MR. LE BLANC, Clerk in the Crown Office, paused for a moment, and looked round the crowded Court of King's Bench. Then, turning to the prisoner—a stout, strongly-built, round-faced young bricklayer—he put the usual question:—

"*Abraham Thornton, are you guilty or not guilty of the said felony and murder whereof you stand so appealed?*"

The answer, if not entirely unexpected—hence the crowded court— was in the highest degree unusual: it had not been heard in an English court of law for more than two centuries—and, as after-events showed, it was fated never to be heard again. Yet at the time (November 17, 1817) that answer, with all that it connoted, was strictly in accordance with the law of England.

Thornton produced a large pair of leather gauntlets,† and drew one on to his left hand. Then, reading from a slip of paper handed to him by his counsel, he declaimed:—

"*Not Guilty: and I am ready to defend the same with my body!*" at the same time flinging down the other gauntlet on the floor of the Court. He had "offered Battle"—in other words, he had claimed his *legal right* to have the question of his guilt or innocence determined by the issue of a mortal combat between his accuser and himself. And, as the event showed, it *was* his right—one of which, if he stood out for it, no one could deprive him.

Furthermore, the conditions governing the "battle" were clearly de-fined by ancient precedent. The combat must be staged upon the worst

---

* Rape.

† Fingerless bags of white sheepskin, with a drawstring at the wrist. One of them, presented by Thornton to his counsel William Reader, was long preserved in tha family, but is now lost. The other, I believe, is in private hands near Birmingham.

plot of ground, sixty feet square, that could be found within the limits of the King's Bench; and in the presence of that Bench's Judges. The two parties—Appellant and Appellee—would be clothed in leather, and armed with staves. Before fighting, they must make oath on the Bible that they had used no *sorcery* or *witchcraft* which might give them an unfair advantage. They would then fight, if need be, until sunset.* If either man killed the other, he went scot-free. If the Appellee, Thornton, could hold out until sunset, again he went scot-free. But if he gave in—if he confessed himself "Craven"—before sunset, he would be hanged then and there: while if Ashford, the Appellant, did so, he would lose all his rights as a free man and become, in effect, outlaw. All of this, be it noted, not in the Middle Ages, but in 1817—two years after Waterloo, and when parts of London were already lit by gas!

The death of Mary Ashford

That dramatic scene in the Court of King's Bench was the culminating point of a long, tangled and sordid tale—at its worst, one of rape followed by murder; and, even at best, one of seduction and premature death. The persons of the tale are a young couple, Thornton (*æt.* 24) and Mary Ashford (*æt.* 20); and its scene is laid in and around Erdington—then an isolated village, now a suburb of Birmingham.

A little more than two miles from Erdington along the London–Chester road is another village, Castle Bromwich (also a suburb, nowadays). Here Thornton lived with his father, a well-to-do builder; and here he had acquired—or at least liked people to think he had—something of a reputation as the local Don Juan. One of the most damaging stories told against him when on his trial was, that on first seeing Mary Ashford he remarked to a bystander (I quote the Bowdlerised language of a contemporary report), "I have been intimate with her sister three times, and I will with her too, if I die for it!"

Thornton and Mary met, *for the first and only time,* on the evening of Whit-Monday, May 26, 1817, at the Tyburn House,† a main-road inn between Castle Bromwich and Erdington which boasted a good-sized dancing-room—patronised, on such holiday occasions as this, by the local

* It is a fact that, in order to decide a Wager of Battle at Leicester long ago, two men once fought for their lives for *nine hours*! As it happened, the issue remained undecided. When both were all but spent, one man was saved from measuring his length over a hillock by his adversary, who lowered his club and remarked, "Take heed where you're going". This very sporting action so moved the spectators that they stopped the fight, and insisted that it should be drawn.

† It always went by this rather ominous title locally—"Tyburn" being the name of the surrounding district. Actually, the inn was "The Three Tuns".

workpeople's club. Dancing (and drinking) had already started when
Mary arrived at about 7.30—unchaperoned, but accompanied by a girl-
friend, one Hannah Cox, who lived at Erdington with her mother, Mrs.
Butler. To judge by portraits, Mary was an attractive girl—and that she
was strong and active may be inferred from the fact that, as a preliminary

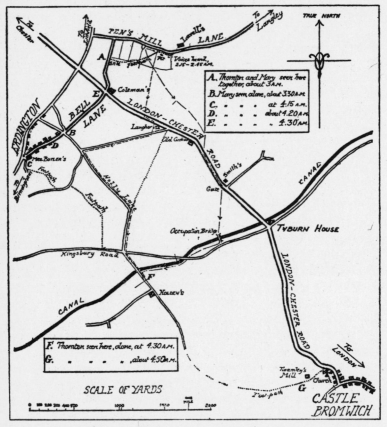

FIG. 16 —Tyburn House, and vicinity, in 1817

to an evening's dancing, she had already covered some 14 miles on foot
that day: walking from Langley Heath, where she kept house for her
uncle, to Birmingham, back to Mrs. Butler's at Erdington, and thence on
with her friend to the Tyburn House.

Certainly she attracted Thornton; as, also, he did her—less, one
imagines, by his physical beauty than by his reputation, and his prospects;
plus, no doubt, that elusive something which it is fashionable to term

"sex-appeal". They danced together frequently; and when, at eleven o'clock, the prudent Hannah decided that it was high time for them to go, Mary—who was enjoying herself—did not exactly agree with her. Hannah agreed to wait outside, on the bridge—where she was joined by a neighbour, one Benjamin Carter, who was going to see her home. As Mary had not shown up twenty minutes later, Hannah asked Carter to go to the dance-room and fetch her. He came back with the news that she was dancing with Thornton, but would be with them very shortly. Presently she and Thornton appeared, and the two couples took the Chester road for Erdington, Mary and Thornton leading. But Carter— not wishing, apparently, to play either gooseberry or second-fiddle—soon left them and went back to the dance—while Thornton, on the other hand, made himself so agreeable to Mary that when the trio, after passing the "Old Cuckoo" beershop, reached the Erdington road, Mary told Hannah that she was not going further with her, but would stay the night with her grandfather at "Coleman's" (corner of Bell Lane and the Chester road) so as to be nearer home in the morning. Her friend prob- ably saw that this was a polite excuse—Mary had left some of her clothes at Mrs. Butler's house at Erdington, and would have to fetch them in the morning before starting for home. However, Miss Cox accepted the position, and went on alone.

Mary and Thornton took their way *past* (not unnaturally) the grand- father's cottage, and into the fields on the south side of Pen's Mill Lane. It was a fine, warm night, with a bright moon.* A man named Umpage,† who had also been at the dance, and had gone on to court his sweetheart at Lavell's cottage in the lane, heard two persons talking together from about 2.15 to 2.45 a.m. in what is still called the "Fatal Field": and there is no doubt that these two were Mary and Thornton. A little later, Umpage, on his way to work, saw them together by the stile at point A (fig. 16). Thornton, whom he knew, wished him "good morning"—but the girl hung her head down as if she did not want to be recognised. That would be at about 3 a.m.—but one of the most irritating features of this puzzling case, in which the time-factor, as will appear, is all-impor- tant, is that the local timekeeping was very vague: there were not many clocks in the district, and such as there were differed widely from the local standard—which appears to have been Birmingham time. As will appear, efforts were made during the day to reduce the estimated or re- corded times of various material events to that of Birmingham, and the

---

* Full Moon was on May 30—four days later.

† So in the contemporary report. The late Sir John Hall, in his *Trial of Abraham Thornton* (London, Wm. Hodge & Co., 1926) speaks of him as "Hompidge".

results are the times here given—but it must be borne in mind that their accuracy is probably indifferent.

No one saw Mary and Thornton together again; but at 4 a.m. Mary arrived at Mrs. Butler's house, knocked up Hannah Cox (who was in bed) and said that she wanted to pack her things then and there, as she must get back to Langley before her uncle departed for Tamworth market. She certainly seemed anxious to waste no time, for she did not change completely into her working-clothes, but started on her long walk still wearing her white dancing-shoes, and carrying her walking-boots in a bundle along with her dance-frock. Hannah, although sleepy, was naturally curious as to Thornton, and Mary said that he had been with her for some time, but was now gone home. She seemed perfectly calm, and in excellent spirits.

On leaving the house at about 4.15 a.m. Mary was seen by a carter, John Kesterton, who knew her well. She was then walking hurriedly towards Bell Lane. A labourer named Dawson exchanged "how do you do's" with her a minute or so later: and at about 4.30 one Broadhurst, walking from Tyburn towards Chester, saw her cross the road in front of him, heading for Pen's Mills Lane, walking fast and carrying a bundle. She was never seen again alive.

About half-past six a workman named Jackson took the short cut from the stile at A across the fields into Pen's Mill Lane. The path ran by three flooded pits (since filled in) and he was surprised to see, at the top of the sloping bank of the middle pit, a bonnet, a bundle, and a pair of white shoes. One shoe was bloodstained, and he at once suspected foul play—a year before, a girl had been raped and murdered at Over Whitaker, some twelve miles away, and her body thrown into a pond. So he started for Pen's Mill* to get help—observing, on the way, some bloodstains about thirty yards from the pit, and a small pool of blood beside a bush a little further on. Turning into the lane, he saw Lavell coming out of his cottage door, told him the news, and sent him back to stand sentry over the clothing. He then raised the alarm at Pen's Mill and—apparently satisfied that he had done all that could be expected of him in a matter which was no concern of his—plodded stolidly on to his work.

Within a few minutes about a dozen men—workmen from the mill and labourers from the neighbouring fields—had gathered round the "Fatal Pit". All suspected that it contained a body; so, after some delay, a drag was improvised from a hayrake and some long reins. The first two casts drew blank—at the third, the drag took hold, and brought to the

---

* It was what would now be called a factory—a wire-drawing mill.

surface the body of Mary Ashford. It had, apparently, been lying sub-
merged not far from the water's edge.

Meanwhile Lavell and a fellow wire-drawer, one Bird, had been
casting round in quest of footmarks. In the "Fatal Field", which was
under grass, they found *one* only—that of a left foot, turned sideways, at
the top of the pit-bank; but the nearby field, on the other side of the stile,
had recently been harrowed—and here (see fig. 17) they found plenty—

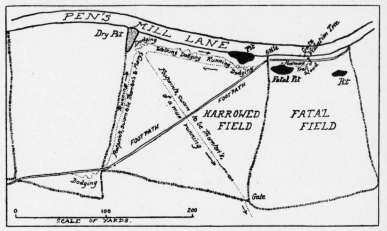

FIG. 17 —Tracks found in the "harrowed field"

those of a man and a woman, sometimes walking, sometimes running,
and sometimes "dodging about" as though one were chasing the other
along two sides of the field while heading towards the Pit. A little further
from the hedge was another distinct track—that of a man, alone, and
running away from the Pit. When he had nearly reached the "Dry Pit",
he had turned sharply back, and run diagonally across the field to the gate
at the opposite corner. At the other side of the gate his track was lost in
the grass. Lavell and Bird returned, and investigated the appearances
in the "Fatal Field". There was a spread-eagled impression—well, there
is no need to go into all the details; but these indicated that a couple had
had intercourse (attended, probably, by a certain amount of laceration)
near the "Violation Tree". From this point, a trail of blood-drops extended half-way to the pit.

Just as the body was being taken out of the water Mr. Webster, the
owner of Pen's Mill, arrived to take temporary charge of the proceedings;
and to him Lavell and Bird reported the footmarks. Webster satisfied himself that the woman's prints were made by Mary's shoes: so did Mr. Bedford, the local J.P., who reached the scene about 11 a.m. and went over

the ground with Webster, Lavell and Bird. By now rain was falling, and hundreds of "rubbernecks" were trampling here, there and everywhere; so Bedford had *a few* of the footmarks covered with boards. But, unfortunately, the most important of all—those of the man running diagonally across the field—were not protected in any way: and although, when Thornton's shoes were applied to the various marks (about 1 p.m.) it was confidently sworn by both Lavell and Bird that these had made both the (male) "dodging" and the "diagonal" imprints, the identification of the latter cannot be regarded as satisfactory. And it is a very curious fact, that the *unique* footmark in the "Fatal Field"—the deep left-footed one at the brow of the pit, which strongly suggested that its maker had turned sideways in order to throw in a heavy burden—was never compared with Thornton's shoe at all!*

Meanwhile, as soon as the news of the tragedy reached Tyburn House the landlord, one Daniel Clarke, rode over to Castle Bromwich, where he met Thornton on his pony.† Told that Mary Ashford had been "murdered and thrown into a pit", Thornton at once ejaculated, "Why, I was with her till four this morning!" He returned with Clarke to Tyburn House, where they were joined by a constable, Thomas Dale, who had been sent out from Birmingham. Dale at once interrogated Thornton, and then took him into custody. He made no objection to being searched; and when bloodstains were found on his shirt he at once admitted having had intercourse with the girl, but stoutly denied having either outraged or murdered her. About an hour later Mr. Bedford arrived, and had Thornton brought before him, subsequently taking down a deposition which the accused man signed. Its terms are important, for it covered Thornton's movements at all material times; it outlined every detail of the alibi which was successfully put forward on his behalf at the Assizes; and it was made within a few hours of the event, when he could scarcely have had much opportunity of consulting with his witnesses. Unfortunately, its exact text has not been preserved‡—but, as reported at the time, it stated in substance:—

* Hall suggests that Lavell and Bird, strongly imbued with the idea of Thornton's guilt, omitted this comparison "because they anticipated that it would yield a negative result". Thornton, by the way, wore right- and left-footed shoes—not the "straights", then still common, which fitted either foot indifferently.

† At the Assizes, the Crown counsel emphasised this point—the suggestion, no doubt, being that Thornton had made use of the pony to get quickly away from the neighbourhood of the pit.

‡ It was read in Court during the trial at Warwick. Thornton's counsel were not (officially) furnished with a copy, and were not allowed to allude to it in cross-examination.

"That he (ABRAHAM THORNTON) was by trade a bricklayer—that he lived with his father, at Castle Bromwich—that he had been at a dance at Tyburn House, on the night of the 26th of May last—that he danced with the deceased (MARY ASHFORD), and came away from the house with her, early the next morning,—that Hannah Cox, and a young man of the name of Carter, went part of the way with them—that after Examinant and Deceased were left by the other two, they walked on by themselves till they came to a stile, and then they went over four or five fields,—that they afterwards came back to the stile again, and sat on it, talking about a quarter of an hour,—while they sat there, a man came by, who wished them a good morning; Examinant wished him a good morning,—that they soon afterwards went on towards Erdington; he went to the Green at Erdington, with Mary Ashford, and then she went on by herself; she said she was going to Mrs. Butler's,—that he waited on the Green some time for the Deceased, but as she did not come back, he then went towards home.—In his road home, he saw young Mr. Holden near to his father's house;* he also saw a man and woman in the road there, at the same time,—that after he had passed Mr. Holden's house, he saw John Haydon, Mr. Rotton's gamekeeper, taking up some nets at the flood-gates, near Mr. Twamley's† Mill, and spoke to him; he stopped to talk with him about a quarter of an hour,—that he also saw John Woodcock, Mr. Twamley's miller, while he stood talking to Haydon, but he did not speak to him,—that he afterwards passed James White, who was at work at Mr. Wheelwright's bank;‡ and then he went straight home.— Examinant further said, that when he got home, it wanted twenty minutes to five, by his father's clock,—he took off a black coat which he had on, and put on another,—he also took off his hat and hung it up in the house,—that he did not pull off his shoes, though they were very wet, from walking through the grass,—he said that he had been drinking the whole evening, but that he was not much intoxicated."

Thornton was taken to Bordesley Gaol, Birmingham; and, the inquest (held at Pen's Mill on May 30–31) having returned a verdict of "Wilful Murder" against him, was transferred thence to Warwick for trial at the forthcoming Assize. The trial took place there on August 8, 1817, before Mr. Justice Holroyd. He had been raised to the Bench not long before,

* *I.e.* the elder Holden's house.

† The words "floodgates" and "Twamley" irresistibly recall the pompous ass who introduced himself (according to Dr. Johnson) as "the *great* Twalmley, who invented the New Floodgate Iron" (a form of box-iron).

‡ A grassy slope—not a banking establishment.

and this was his first murder trial. Mr. Nathaniel Clarke, K.C., led for
the Crown, assisted by Sergt. Copley (afterwards Lord Chancellor Lynd-
hurst). For the defence were Mr. William Reader and Mr. H. R. Rey-
nolds. The indictment was twofold, a second count—rape—being added
to that of murder.

The case for the Crown, as opened by Clarke, seemed a very strong
one. He undertook to show that Thornton, having failed to seduce the
girl when they were in the fields together after the dance, had lain in wait
near the stile in Bell Lane, knowing that Mary, on her way home,
would take the short-cut across the fields to Pen's Mill Lane. He had then
pursued her, quieted her cries, outraged her and—rape being then a
hanging matter—finally thrown her, stunned or fainted, into the pit,
afterwards making off towards Castle Bromwich at a run. On the whole,
Clarke concluded, the chain of circumstances which he had laid before the
Jury, and would proceed to substantiate by evidence, was so strong that it
could leave no doubt of the Prisoner's guilt.

I have already summarised the facts, now sworn in evidence, as to the
finding of the body and the footmarks, etc., and as to Mary Ashford's
movements. The medical testimony (given by Mr. Freer, a Birmingham
surgeon who examined the body on the evening of the tragedy) and also
that relating to the condition of the clothes found on the body* and in the
bundle, was indecisive as to the main question at issue—had the intercourse taken place *before* Mary's return to Erdington (which indicated
consent) or *after* (which implied rape and murder)? Freer deposed that
prior to the dance the girl had undoubtedly been a virgin. She was at one
of her monthly periods—but he considered that the blood found in the
"Fatal Field" was not menstrual, but the result of intercourse. An important point in Thornton's favour was that the black woollen stockings into
which she had changed at Erdington showed no signs of blood, while the
white cotton ones she wore at the dance (found in her bundle) were
plentifully spattered with it, as were her dancing shoes—which, also, she
had worn in the fields. Thornton's remark about having Mary if he died
for it was not clearly established. A farmer named Cooke, who was at the
dance, attested that he had overheard Thornton make it to one Cottrell—

* In summarising the Crown's case, Hall has loaded the dice in its favour by a most
curious slip. He contends that the white spencer (short over-jacket) which Mary wore
at the dance, and afterwards in the fields, was perfectly clean—indicating that intercourse could not have taken place until after her return to Erdington. In support of
this, he reprints the contemporary account of the trial as saying "The white spencer
was quite clean". But actually, what that account says is "The white spencer was not
were quite clean"—an obvious misprint for " . . . *nowhere* quite clean": valuable
evidence in Thornton's favour, instead of against him!

but he had to admit that he had kept it entirely to himself, and had not come forward with it at the inquest. Cottrell—who, Reader suggested in his cross-examination, had denied hearing Thornton say anything of the kind—was not called by either side. *Cadit quæstio.*

The defence, as already remarked, was an alibi. In advancing it, Reader, as the law then stood, was gravely handicapped by being debarred from either putting his client into the witness-box or addressing the Jury. Thornton, by the way, had the right to do so, but wisely declined to exercise it. In those days, counsel could only conduct a defence to a criminal charge by examination, or cross-examination, of witnesses. But Reader managed to establish the main features of the alibi, as foreshadowed in Thornton's deposition, without difficulty. He put into the box the four witnesses who had seen him walking "quite slowly" past Holden's farm, towards Castle Bromwich, at 4.30 a.m. by the farm clock. All four swore to Thornton's identity (one of them, John Holden Jr., knew him well by sight) and two agreed that if, as the Crown suggested, he had come down the tow-path from the "Occupation Bridge", they could scarcely have failed to observe this, the path being in plain view for some 300–400 yards. Reader also called the three men* who had met and talked to Thornton on his way from Holden's farm to Castle Bromwich: and he brought forward two local gentlemen—Mr. W. Twamley and Mr. J. W. Crompton—who had had the sense to make some comparisons between various of the clocks involved.

Here a short digression is necessary. Throughout the British Isles, in those days, accurate time was hard to find and equally hard to keep: furthermore, and in consequence, little importance was generally attached to it. It is curious, nowadays, to look back to a nineteenth-century era when there was no such thing as Greenwich Mean Time available; yet in 1817 that was the case everywhere save at Greenwich Observatory itself. Time could only be *found* at a few scattered observatories, or from sundials whose very rough indications could, even then, only be reduced to a common standard by correcting them for "equation of time", and for longitude;† it could only be *kept* by un-compensated pendulum-clocks

---

* John Haydon (gamekeeper), John Woodcock (miller) and James White (labourer). The first two, going by the striking of a stable-clock at Castle Bromwich, estimated that Thornton met Haydon (at point G) about 5.5—in which case he had taken quite half an hour to cover the mile from Holden's. White, going by Castle Bromwich Church clock (he believed) saw Thornton, a little over half a mile further on, at about 5.20. Note that, after Thornton had walked yet another half-mile after passing White, he reached his father's house, *by the latter's clock*, at 4.40!

† I am assuming that the gnomons of such dials were correctly cut for their particular latitude.

(church clocks and long-case* house-clocks) liable to change their rate of going by a minute a day if the average daily temperature should alter only 10°, also much affected by any lack of oil; and it could only be *distributed* by watches which were, in general, extremely defective. Here and there, one might find some wealthy man who took an interest in astronomy, and who possessed, in addition to a small private observatory (boasting a transit-instrument and a "regulator" clock) a really good watch—duplex, lever, or pocket-chronometer—which he could trust to a few seconds a week. But, in general, the watch of the period was the silver "turnip"—the uncompensated verge-watch, seriously affected by the slightest change of temperature, by any lack of oil, by any motion (such as walking or riding) and by its position in the wearer's pocket—while even such watches were far beyond the means of all but a very few of the working-classes. These either went by the sun, or by some local house-clock; this was occasionally set to the time of the nearest church-clock; that, in turn, would be referred, for time, to some main-road town; and the last-named would probably take time from the "Post-Office watches" carried, in locked padded boxes, by the guards of the mail-coaches and set at St. Martins-le-Grand before the coach took the road. In such circumstances, if two independent observers agreed as to the time they assigned to some particular event, this was probably by sheer accident.

Twamley, in his evidence, attested that he and Webster, of Pen's Mill, "agreed to ascertain the state of the clocks. I went to Mr. Holden's and Mr. Webster to Castle Bromwich". Twamley found Holden's clock to agree with his own watch; and, repairing to Birmingham, found his watch right by St. Martin's Church clock, and a minute and a half slow by the Tower clock. We can take it, then, that Holden's clock was just about right by Birmingham time—and Twamley, having performed his share of the joint agreement, disappears out of the story.

Unfortunately, Webster's comparisons are not so trustworthy—and, owing (I presume) to some peculiarity of the law of evidence then obtaining, such testimony as we have relating to the Castle Bromwich clocks was given by Crompton, who rode there with him "for company", and not by Webster himself. His direct evidence is only available for Mrs. Butler's clock, and was given during the case for the Crown. Apparently, he did not compare his watch with Twamley's: he took his time from Crompton's watch, which its owner believed to be keeping Birmingham time "very accurately", and then, comparing his own with Mrs. Butler's clock, ascertained that the latter was 41 minutes fast.

* The term "grandfather clock" is quite modern, dating only from the eighteen-eighties.

Crompton testified that "the Castle Bromwich clock"—by which it appears, though he does not directly state, that he meant the stable-clock whose striking was mentioned by Haydon, the keeper who met Thornton near Twamley's Mill—was fifteen minutes fast by Birmingham time. This agrees, as far as it goes, with the evidence of Haydon, Woodcock and White. But Crompton does not seem to have tested Thornton *pere's* house-clock, which must, by his son's evidence, have been nearly as much slow as Mrs. Butler's was fast!*

In all this tangle, what we chiefly look for—and, unfortunately, in vain—is a direct comparison between Holden's clock and Mrs. Butler's: for, essentially, Thornton's alibi stands or falls by the difference of their times. Holden's clock is, undoubtedly, pretty well tied to Birmingham for time by the transport of Twamley's watch from one to the other; but the best that can be said for Mrs. Butler's is, that it was compared with Webster's watch, which in turn was compared with Crompton's, which was *believed* to be keeping Birmingham time! Personally, I find it difficult to suppose that Webster and Twamley could have failed to compare watches when they made their initial agreement, although this was not brought out in evidence.† If they did, then Mrs. Butler's clock probably was, as stated, some 41 minutes fast on Holden's clock—from which it results that, simultaneously with Mary being seen (by Broadhurst) walking hurriedly up Bell Lane to her death, Thornton was walking slowly past Holden's farm—a mile and a quarter away from her as the crow flies; and, by the shortest practicable route, at least two miles from the pit!

William Coleman, Mary's grandfather, who was the final witness for the defence, merely testified that she had not spent the night, after the dance was over, at his cottage. The trial had now lasted for some ten hours—yet, after a short recess, Holroyd began to charge the Jury.‡ He summed-up the evidence temperately and fairly—on balance, in Thornton's favour§—but his address is marked by a singular oversight; and (if correctly reported) he also seems, in the course of his speech, to have misled first himself and then his hearers.

---

* Thornton can scarcely have got home before 5.15 Birmingham time. The house-clock showed 4.40!

† I imagine that Webster, having given evidence for the prosecution, was estopped from testifying for the defence.

‡ The Crown Counsel forewent their right of a final address to the Jury at the close of the defence.

§ He is alleged to have held a strong conviction of the prisoner's innocence; and, after the trial, to have made no secret of this opinion. In the circumstances, it is a little surprising that he was one of the judges who heard the subsequent Appeal.

He entirely omitted to indicate—what, I am certain, Reader would have promptly pointed out had he been free to address the Jury—that there was *no evidence that any murder had been committed*. Nor, for that matter, was there any to support the charge of rape—Freer, the surgeon, had admitted that the appearances presented by the body were all consistent with Thornton's assertion that the girl had been a consenting party. There was nothing against the supposition that she might have committed suicide; or, which was much more likely, that she had met her end by accident. She had left Mrs. Butler's in a great hurry—probably to avoid awkward questions. No doubt she intended to finish changing at the nearest convenient spot. What spot could be more convenient than the path by the pit, secluded from observation and with water handy? Depositing her belongings at the top of the bank, she might have gone to the water's edge to wash, or to drink—and, while standing on the steep slope, been overcome with sudden faintness. She had—as the medical evidence showed—been without food for many hours; she had been up all night; she had tired herself, first with walking and next with dancing, and had then undergone an exhausting physical and emotional experience; and, in addition, she was for the moment physically below par. If she had fainted —as she might well have done—she would unquestionably have fallen in and been drowned. This might happen even without her fainting; for some unexplained reason, she was in her stocking-feet, and the slope was steep and muddy. She may have found herself in the water before realising that she had slipped—in all likelihood she could not swim—and any cry for help she managed to utter* may have gone unheard.

But on this point Sir George Holroyd was completely silent. Like everyone else at the time, he seems to have tacitly assumed that murder *must* have been committed.† On the other hand, when dealing with Thornton's alibi he made, at intervals, a sequence of three statements of a progressively misleading character. Here they are, with a few words of comment:—

1. "It was very material to see at what time the Deceased came to Mrs. Butler's house, and what time she left; and, therefore, what space of time there was for the transactions to take place, between that time and the time when the Prisoner was seen *three and a half miles*‡ from that place".

* About half a pint of water was found in her lungs.
† On the other hand, when giving judgment on the Appeal he stressed the fact that there was no evidence of any murder.
‡ My italics.

The actual distance from Mrs. Butler's house to Holden's farm—where Thornton was first seen after the "transactions"—was 2000 yards in an air-line, or about 2100 by the footpath: and the discrepancy between this 1¼ miles and the judge's 3½ is the more surprising when we learn that he had a map of the district in his hand, and referred to it frequently while charging the jury. Clearly, what he meant to impress on them was, that the distance from Mrs. Butler's to Holden's, *via the pit*, was 3½ miles; and that the two portions, "Butler's-pit" and "pit-Holden's", must have been covered *successively*, by two different persons.

2. " . . . the Prisoner might have come down by the canal towing-path, through the meadows. . . . But then, he must have gone the distance of *three miles and a half*,* from a quarter past four o'clock, and all this pursuit and the transactions which followed, must have taken place within the period of time within which he was afterwards seen. It would have taken up no inconsiderable space of time, including the running and pursuit; and he thought it could not be done in a quarter of an hour."

Here again, the "three miles and a half" is actually the distance successively covered by Mary and by Thornton. The "quarter of an hour" runs from 4.15, when Mary was seen outside Mrs. Butler's, to 4.30, when Thornton was seen at Holden's.

3. " . . . it was their duty well to consider, whether it was possible for the pursuit to have taken place, and all the circumstances connected with it, and for the prisoner to have reached Holden's house, a distance of nearly *three miles and a half*,* in so short a time—a period of not more than 20 minutes".

I suggest that any intelligent person, taking this passage as it stands, and not having grasped Holroyd's peculiar manner of expounding the time-factor, would most undoubtedly conclude that, *after* the pursuit and the murder, Thornton must *next* be assumed to have run 3½ miles—and that this distance, consequently, intervened between the pit and Holden's house. Actually the distance, as the crow flies, is just under a mile and three furlongs—and, by either of two practicable routes† along lanes, etc., it is exactly two miles. If the trial had been held at Birmingham, instead of at Warwick, the apparent overstatement would probably have been

* My italics.

† From the pit, straight for the main road, and along this to Laugher's (see Fig. 16). Thereafter, either sharp right and so to Holly Lane and Holden's; or else along the main road to "Smith's", and thence "on trespass" to Occupation Bridge and down the towpath.

queried at once—but the Warwick jury seems to have accepted it (and it made the hypothesis of Thornton's guilt look absolutely ridiculous) without question.

The conclusion of the trial was sudden, unexpected, and ill-received by the public. The jury, who had been sitting for twelve hours, did not retire. They conferred in the box—and, after only *six minutes*, returned a verdict of "Not guilty" (of murder—the Crown withdrew the charge of rape).

Actually, it was a most reasonable verdict—in fact, the only possible one on the evidence; though a Scottish jury might well have found "Not proven". As already remarked, there was no evidence either of murder or rape—and all the appearances seen in the two fields might just as well have been made at 2.30, when the pair were overheard talking together, as at 4.30. The only one which cast suspicion on Thornton was the track crossing the "Harrowed Field" diagonally—but this was not definitely proved to be his. Against the murder theory, too, was the fact of the girl's belongings being found deposited at the brink of the pit. If she had been chased to the "Fatal Field", outraged, and thrown in, she could not have placed them as they were found; and it is improbable that Thornton would have taken pains to put them where they were bound to catch the eye of the first passer-by. Still, if he were a quick-witted man, that is exactly what he would have done—confidently assuming that no one would ever believe it was his doing.

On the other hand, while his defence has the merit of being put forward immediately and supported by entirely independent evidence,* it is far from perfect. If he had faced trial in a French court, and consequently had to prove his innocence, his alibi would have been of little service. Prosecuting counsel, enlarging the obvious holes in it, and twisting the defective comparisons to suit his own view, could easily have contended that, say, an hour had elapsed between Mary leaving Mrs. Butler's and Thornton being seen at Holden's; and he would no doubt have suggested that Thornton, in his flight, had run "on trespass" along the dotted line (fig. 16) from "Laugher's" to the elbow of Holly Lane, reducing the total distance between the pit and Holden's to less than one mile and six furlongs. From this point of view, one might say that there was *some* evidence that Thornton *might possibly* have murdered Mary Ashford: but, in this country, we should not hang a dog on such evidence and no more.

* Thornton was not acquainted, it should seem, either with the four witnesses who saw him at Holden's or with Twamley, Webster and Crompton—who made their comparisons spontaneously, and at a time when Thornton was already under arrest.

Although the theory of accidental death leaves one or two points unexplained—the "diagonal" track, and the fact that the victim was in her stocking feet—it is most improbable that any murder was done in the "fatal field". But to those who obstinately remain convinced that it *must* have been, I commend the following extremely far-fetched theory on two grounds—it can never be tested now, and it covers *all* the facts.

Imagine that Mary had an undeclared lover—a young man of nerve, courage and intelligence, with a passionate (or even unbalanced) mind. He goes to the dance, and sees the pair flirting. He follows them into the fields; and his love is turned to hatred when he sees the girl he once adored give herself to the local Lothario. He must be revenged on both— and he sees how. He watches them as far as the stile into Bell Lane—perhaps hears Umpage wish them "good morning". They start for Erdington. Thornton, no doubt, will go on from there to Castle Bromwich— Mary, before long, will be returning *alone*. He lies in wait, and accosts her. He is known to her, so she does not scream; but his manner alarms her, and she evades him until, breathless, she faints. Violence, for which he had prepared, is unnecessary. Thrown into the flooded pit, she will drown—he will see that she does. But, thereafter, the body must be found as soon as possible; so he first removes the bloodstained shoes and the straw bonnet with its bright yellow ribbons. Next he throws his victim in, and while a few gasping bubbles rise he disposes the finery and the bundle prominently on the bank. Then he climbs the stile to the "harrowed field", runs along the hedge to the angle, and diagonally from there to the gate at the lower end—leaving a track which no one can possibly miss, since it crosses the footpath at right angles, and which *heads straight for Castle Bromwich*.* Once through the gate, he makes off over the grass, which will show no footmarks. His revenge is accomplished. He is safe. Mary is dead. Thornton will hang.

But the people living near the scene of the tragedy wasted no time in speculations such as these. As soon as the verdict became known, they received this with intense dissatisfaction. It was generally felt—the feeling was not merely local—that the trial was a miscarriage of justice, and that the verdict had been brought about through perjury, subsidised by the elder Thornton. No one held this view more strongly than Mr. Bedford, the magistrate who had taken Thornton's deposition; and, as a beginning, Bedford vented his indignation on Dale, the Birmingham constable who had made the arrest, and whom he suspected of favouring

---

* I am morally certain that Lavell and Bird, who swore to this track as being Thornton's, would have done the same in respect of any track made by a foot of anywhere near the right size.

Thornton.* The unfortunate Dale was speedily dismissed the force; and Bedford then took counsel's opinion as to whether further proceedings might not still be taken against Thornton, in the form of the obsolete (but still legal) "Appeal of Murder".

The Appeal of Murder

So far as the law of England is concerned, the "Appeal of Murder", and its concomitant, "Wager of Battle"—trial by judicial combat—are of Norman origin, and gradually ousted the Saxon "trial by ordeal". They were an alternative form of proceeding in a limited class of actions— charges of treason, or of murder, and Writs of Right (the most solemn method of trying title to land). This form was that of an Appeal—an action not brought in the King's name, but by a private party known as the Appellant, against whom the Appellee might claim to "offer battle"— to prove his innocence by combat. If battle were waged, the victor went scot-free—the vanquished, if still alive, was hanged forthwith. The Appellant could "oust the battle", and compel the Appellee to face a jury, if the latter had been caught red-handed; failing this he must, in general, accept the defiance. There were, however, certain recognised exceptions. A man of over sixty, or one maimed by wound, was exempt from waging battle, by reason of his infirmity—a woman, or a child, for the same reason—a citizen of London, and some other towns,† by charter-privilege as not being trained to arms—a clergyman, by reason of his cloth. All of these, however, might and often did nominate a champion to fight for them.

An Act passed in the reign of Henry VII‡ removed certain abuses which had crept into the system of Appeals. The "false peler"—the criminal turned King's evidence who fought, for an extremely hazardous living, with his former comrades: or, in default of such, with anyone handy—found his occupation gone. At the same time, the procedure relating to Appeals of Murder (and Treason) was revised. Formerly, the heir-at-law of a murdered person had a year and a day,§ from the date of the crime, in which to bring his Appeal—and the Crown could not

* He was the sole witness to the fact—on which Holroyd had particularly remarked, as being much in the Prisoner's favour—that Thornton had never attempted to conceal the nature of his relations with Mary.

† Winchester, Lincoln, Northampton, and Leicester (the last, in consequence of the nine-hours fight already mentioned).

An Appellee had no such privilege—if he offered battle, he must fight in person.

‡ Henry VII, cap. 1.

§ This links up with the accepted usage that a man can only be charged with murder if the person he has injured die within a year and a day of receiving the injury.

prosecute until this period was over. Henceforth, the Crown was to have priority—but it was enacted that a man acquitted at the suit of the Crown and subsequently appealed (within the year and day) by the heir-at-law could not bar such an Appeal by pleading "autrefois acquit" or "autrefois attaint". Moreover, he must give bail for his appearance, so long as the possibility of such an Appeal existed. Lastly, if he were convicted on the Appeal, the Crown had no power to pardon him—though the Appellant might, on his own terms.

It gradually became accepted practice for the Appellee to forego his right of offering battle, and to face a second jury.* When Thornton threw his glove down, battle had not been offered in this country for more than a century and a half.† Indeed, a hundred years earlier the right of offering battle (and, also, the Appeal of Treason) had passed out of living memory. The Writ of Right was still occasionally used; but its nature—an action to establish a title to land—did not attract much public attention. In pursuing the history of the subject, therefore, one is more or less restricted to such scanty records as survive of an occasional Appeal of Murder.

A very interesting case—that of Spencer Cowper, grandfather of the poet—occurred in 1699. Four barristers, of whom Cowper was one, were tried at the Hertford Assizes for the murder of a Quaker girl, one Sarah Stout. It was proved by overwhelming evidence, including the girl's own letters to Cowper, that she had committed suicide as the result of an unrequited passion, concerning which his three companions had been overheard chaffing him. But the motto of the Stout family seems to have been, "So much the worse for the facts"‡—as Cowper bitterly said, they would rather send four innocent men to the gallows than admit that a member of their sect could possibly take her own life. After all four men had been acquitted at the Assize, Sarah's heir-at-law accordingly brought an Appeal of Murder against Cowper—but the Under-Sheriff of Herts (designedly, I think) omitted to serve the writ within the prescribed year and day; and an attempt to secure an extension of this period failed, the King's Bench very properly holding that the prosecution was merely malicious.

---

* Even, curiously enough, if he were a Peer of the Realm. In 1689 the Upper House ruled that its members, if appealed of murder, could not demand to be tried by their own Chamber.

† Not since 1638, so far as I can discover; in a Writ of Right, Claxton v. Lilburn, heard at Durham. It had not been offered, in an Appeal of Murder, since Egerton v. Morgan, in 1612.

‡ In fairness, it must be admitted that Macaulay's account of the matter goes almost as far in the other direction. As Paget pointed out in his New Examen, Cowper's behaviour to the girl was extremely indiscreet, and he had himself largely to thank for being brought to trial.

Cowper afterwards rose high in his profession—he holds the distinction of being, so far, the only British Judge who once stood trial for his life.*

Another Judge has the equally rare distinction of having instigated an Appeal of Murder from the Bench. In 1709 a man named Christopher Slaughterford, tried for the murder of a girl whom he had seduced,† was acquitted for lack of evidence. But Holt, J., took the unusual, though not illegal, course of detaining him in custody, holding that the case was one in which the interests of justice demanded that an Appeal of Murder should be brought. This was accordingly done—and Slaughterford, convicted at the second trial, was duly hanged. There seems no doubt that he only got his deserts; yet one has an uneasy suspicion that the second jury may have prejudged the issue, holding themselves morally bound to reverse their predecessors' verdict. This was, in fact, one of the three principal objections, in practice, to the Appeal of Murder; the second being that the power of pardon, on terms, which it conferred on the successful Appellant was an incitement, and cover, to extortion and/or blackmail; while the third—by very far the most vitally important—was that it conflicted flatly with the long-established principle of English law, that "a man shall not be tried twice for the same offence".‡ But until Thornton's "wager of battle" directed renewed attention to the subject these glaring defects were overlooked, or even praised—in 1774 Mr. Dunning, afterwards Lord Ashburton, referred to the Appeal of Murder, during a debate in the House of Commons, as "That great pillar of the Constitution".

The Ashford-Thornton Appeal, 1817–18

I return to the acquittal of Thornton at Warwick Assizes, and to the incensed Mr. Bedford, thirsting for further action against him by way of an Appeal of Murder. The first counsel to whom he submitted the "grounds of action" (Mr. Const; 3 gs.) was dubious, and said so. The Judge should have held Thornton to bail, in case an Appeal might afterwards be brought (this *was* the law, in fact, but it had long been disregarded in practice). Had this been done, it would have been easy enough to re-arrest Thornton; but as matters stood, great difficulty would be experienced in doing so. Moreover, in default of fresh evidence it was very doubtful whether a second jury would find a different verdict.

* Two bygone Archbishops *might* have undergone the same chastening experience: Abbot (Canterbury) for manslaughter, and Blackburne (York) for piracy.
† It is a coincidence that her body, like Mary Ashford's, was found in a pond.
‡ Except, of course, if the Jury disagree on the first trial.

Mr. Bedford cut his losses, and took a second opinion (5 gs.) from Mr. Joseph Chitty, who was justly regarded as *facile princeps* in all matters of obsolete or antiquated law. To his delight, Chitty pointed out that, provided security were given for the prosecution of the Appeal, the Court of King's Bench would readily issue a warrant (returnable there) for Thornton's re-arrest. As rumour had it that the bricklayer, finding himself cold-shouldered locally, was intending to emigrate, Bedford lost no time in following Chitty's advice. Mary's brother William, a meek young labourer, was induced, as the heir-at-law, to bring his Appeal of Murder against Thornton; £100 was put up as security;* the warrant was duly issued, the arrest effected (at Castle Bromwich), and the prisoner brought to London.

After some preliminaries, the Appeal proper came on for hearing in Westminster Hall on Monday, Nov. 17, 1817. The Judges were Lord Ellenborough (Lord Chief Justice), Mr. Justice Bayley, Mr. Justice Abbott, and Mr. Justice Holroyd—who had presided at the Warwick trial. The counsel were unchanged, Clarke leading for Ashford, and Reader for Thornton. The Appeal was read by the Clerk, Mr. Le Blanc —and this, patient reader, is where you came in. But please stay for a little—I shall not keep you much longer, and you missed the finish last time.

Ashford made no attempt to pick up Thornton's gauntlet (which had cannoned off his head on its way to the floor)†, so Reader asked that Mr. Le Blanc should retain it. Then came a pause—broken by Clarke observing that he was much surprised‡ that "this sort of demand" should have been made. Trial by Battle was an obsolete practice. He went on:—

" . : . it would appear to me extraordinary indeed, if the person who has murdered the sister should, as the law exists in these enlightened times, be allowed to prove his innocence by murdering the brother also, or, at least, by an attempt to do so."

Lord Ellenborough—"It is the law of England, Mr. Clarke, we must not call it murder."

* By William Ashford and his two uncles; John Coleman of Langley Heath (Mary's employer) and Charles Coleman of Erdington. Funds for the actual prosecution seem also to have been raised locally.

† I think this was accidental.

‡ This, of course, was one of those deliberate lies which the exigencies, and the curious ethics, of their profession compel barristers, in the course of their duty, to tell occasionally. Clarke, having attended two consultations on this very point, knew perfectly well that Thornton would, in all probability, offer battle.

After apologising for "too strong an expression", Clarke hoped that the Court would take into account the very different physique of the two men, and not allow a combat. Here Reader interposed that Clarke's proper course was to counterplead, and not to waste the time of the Court by offering such arguments. He added, that he had advised his client to offer battle "in consequence of the extraordinary and unprecedented prejudice which has been disseminated against him throughout the country". Clarke then asked for time to counterplead—and this was granted, Thornton remaining in custody.*

The Counterplea, of course, was entrusted to Chitty. His main object was to "oust the battle"—to deprive Thornton of the right of meeting Ashford in mortal combat, and to compel him to put himself, for a second time, upon his country. The reason for this course of action was clear and cogent—if the two men were to meet in battle, William Ashford would most assuredly go home on a stretcher, if one were available. He was a timid weakling of 21; Thornton was a powerfully-built man of 24 who, as his demeanour at the Warwick trial and later had sufficiently shown, was an entire stranger to fear.

Chitty, accordingly, devoted every weapon in his armoury to a legal contest which occupied the time of the King's Bench, at intervals, for the next five months. His opening broadside—the Counterplea—was a most singular production. As afterwards appeared, the gist of the case which he put forward for Ashford was this. He started with the admitted fact that a man could not offer battle who was "taken with the mainour"—caught red-handed (or, in U.S.A. parlance, "with the goods on him"). That was because his guilt in such circumstances was so manifest that he ought not to have even the uncertain chance of acquittal which a combat would give him. Chitty went on to argue—which was much less warranted—that this principle also applied in cases where a man was not actually caught red-handed, but against whom there was, nevertheless, a strong presumption of guilt. Consequently, his Counterplea took the form of an affidavit, sworn by William Ashford, which set out, as the ground for such presumption, practically the whole of the evidence for the Crown at the Warwick trial—much of which evidence did not, and could not, lie within the Appellant's own knowledge!

Reader countered this, in his "Replication"—a similar, but much longer, affidavit sworn by Thornton, and containing the evidence given at Warwick for the defence. But Chitty then brought up his heaviest

---

* He was confined in that part of the Marshalsea usually reserved for political offenders, and was allowed visitors and special food. He travelled to and from Westminster Hall, when necessary, in a hackney coach—at Ashford's expense.

PLATE V

ABRAHAM THORNTON.

ABRAHAM THORNTON, the last man to offer battle in an English
Court of Law

From the Cooper report
(Warwick, 1818)

Facing page 208

artillery, and in his "General Demurrer"*—which was of enormous length—came out with a mass of citations from byegone authorities such as Glanville, Bracton, Fleta, Horne, Staundforde, Hearn, Pulton, Finch, Hawkins and Blackstone, together with extracts from every English chronicler and historian who ever touched upon the subject of Trial by Battle.†

On such matters Chitty carried rather too many guns for the ordinary barrister; so Reader co-opted Chitty's great rival, Nicholas Tindal, afterwards Chief Justice of the Common Pleas. Tindal's answer to Chitty was comparatively short, but crushing. He began by showing that the option of battle lay, *as of right*, with the Appellee; and if, battle having been offered, the Appellant declined it without sufficient reason, the Court should at once order the Appellee to be discharged "without a day" (i.e. permanently). ‡Even if Ashford's affidavit were a valid Counterplea—which he did not admit, since it was so vague—Thornton's was an equal valid Replication to it. And how could it be contended, with any semblance of truth, that a "strong and pregnant suspicion" of guilt existed against the Appellee? Chitty had brought forward no new evidence —and that on which he relied to prove his "suspicion" had already been attentively considered by the Warwick jury; which had then acquitted Thornton in six minutes! Presumably, therefore, he was innocent—and, if so, he had a perfect right to wage battle; or, if his gage were not accepted, to be at once discharged by the Court.

The Ashford party had, of course, done their best to find new evidence against Thornton, and also to upset his alibi—in both cases unsuccessfully. They had, however, once been visited by a gleam of hope—the statement of Homer Hall.§

Hall was a Staffordshire banker who had fallen low, and was now a convict in the prison-hulk *Justitia* at Woolwich, awaiting transportation for the petty offence of stealing a parcel of fowls. In the summer of 1817 he had shared a cell in Warwick gaol with Thornton, then awaiting trial.

---

* In such proceedings, the Counterplea and Replication concerned themselves with the facts of the case—the Demurrer, and the reply to it, with the legal construction of those facts in accordance with precedent and argument.

† At least, such is my impression—he may have missed out a few.

‡ Before making these points, I fancy that Tindal must have read with profit *Appeal of Murder*, by E. A. Kendall, which had appeared about a month earlier and rapidly went through at least three editions. It is a little difficult to discover how the author escaped being committed for contempt of court.

§ Some accounts call him "Omar Hall". As, at the time, the *Iliad* was still widely read in the original, while the *Rubá'iyát* was unheard of even in a translation, I have followed the Greek form of the name rather than the Persian.

Hall swore that Thornton had confessed to him that he had chased and outraged Mary Ashford—that she had then and there died of shock—and that to avoid being hanged for rape and/or murder he had thrown the body into the pit. He added that he was at ease as to the result of the trial, for his father had taken care of the evidence, particularly that of Dale, the constable. On at least two occasions Dale visited Thornton in the prison, and chatted earnestly with him.

So far Homer Hall. One part of his story, at least, was true—he *had* shared a cell with Thornton, and Dale *had* visited the latter. But all the rest of it was suspect from the word "go"; for Hall, as a convicted felon, could not testify in a court of law *unless he first received a free pardon.* This the Home Secretary, not being exactly a born fool, did not see his way to granting; and Hall left his country for his country's good.

Chitty's last chance of obtaining fresh evidence against Thornton having vanished, he made a final effort on his client's behalf—a reply, on the same historical lines, to Tindal's criticisms of the Counterplea. But he found himself compelled to give ground on various points—and frequent interruptions by the Bench indicated that the Court was keenly critical of his arguments. When he sat down, it was clear that he had lost his case.

After fifteen minutes for deliberation, all four Judges found in Thornton's favour: Holroyd making amends for his former oversight at Warwick by emphasising that there was no clear evidence of any murder—nothing in the Counterplea inconsistent with the supposition that Mary Ashford had met her death by accident, and when alone. The Lord Chief Justice required only two sentences to put the whole matter in a very clear light:—

"The general law of the land is in favour of the Wager of Battle, and it is our duty to pronounce the law as it is, and not as we may wish it to be. Whatever prejudice, therefore, may exist against this mode of trial, still, as it is the law of the land, the Court must pronounce judgment for it".

He reserved for argument, if necessary, the question whether Ashford, by declining to pick up Thornton's glove, and instead counterpleading, had already—in effect—declined battle. Personally, I think that Reader would undoubtedly have raised this point sooner or later—and that if he had omitted to do so the King's Bench would, of its own mere motion, have taken advantage of it to prevent the public scandal which a judicial combat in the nineteenth century would undoubtedly have given. But actually the point was never raised. During the next four days, rumours circulated that Ashford had determined to accept the challenge to combat: but on April 20, when the case came up for the last time, Clarke informed the Court that his client prayed no further judgment. Before doing so, he had obtained Reader's assurance, in open court, that Thornton had no intention of praying anything against Ashford.*

Reader thereupon asked that his client might be discharged "without a day". The Lord Chief Justice, however, reminded him that the Crown could take no cognisance of an arrangement arrived at between two private persons. Thornton must therefore be formally arraigned, at the suit of the Crown, for the crime with which the Appellant had charged him—to which, however, he could plead "autrefois acquit". This he did —and the Attorney-General, who had been summoned and was in court, admitted the plea. Thereupon Thornton walked out of Westminster Hall a free man—Lord Ellenborough tactfully suggesting that he should leave by the back-entrance, and thus escape the attentions of a large and ferocious mob which had gathered at the front of the building to give him a warm reception. On the same day the Attorney-General gave notice, in the House of Commons, that he would introduce a Bill to abolish the Wager of Battle and the Appeal of Murder.

Thornton went back to Castle Bromwich, and tried to live down the past. But, rightly or wrongly, the brand of Cain was on him, and he found himself feared and shunned on all sides. So he carried out his original intention, and emigrated to the U.S.A. Efforts to trace his career there have been largely unsuccessful—but it is believed that he prospered (under another name) and married, dying at Baltimore in 1860. William Ashford, his opponent, died at Birmingham in 1867—his prudence in declining battle having, in all probability, prolonged his life by fifty years.

Meanwhile, 59 Geo. III, cap. XLVI had forever made an end, in this country, of the strange law which he had once so lightly invoked, and of which he had had such mortifying experience. The title of this short Act is:—

"An Act to abolish Appeals of Murder, Treason, Felony, or other Offences, and Wager of Battel, or joining Issue and Trial by Battel, in Writs of Right." (22nd. June 1819).

and its preamble runs:—

"Whereas Appeals of Murder, Treason, Felony, and other Offences, and the Manner of proceeding therein, have been found to be oppressive; and the Trial by Battel in any Suit, is a Mode of Trial unfit to be used; and it is expedient that the same should be wholly abolished; Be it therefore enacted . . ."

* Precedents existed under which, on the Appeal being abandoned, the Appellee could have obtained damages for "infamy and imprisonment" from the Appellant.

(that, after the passing of the Act, all such Appeals shall cease, and it shall no longer be lawful to bring them; nor shall Battle be offered in any Writ of Right). In such manner were Wager of Battle and Appeal of Murder removed, "unwept, unhonoured, and unsung", from that majestic, if often incomprehensible, labyrinth which constitutes the Statute Law of England.

Yet they lingered for many years in the last place where one would look for them—the U.S.A. In 1857, they were undoubtedly lawful in Kentucky; and, many years later,* battle was offered (and declined) in Pennsylvania—it being found, to the general astonishment, still legal in that state. Possibly, though improbably, one or two of the less progressive states may yet find a place for them in their codes—although "imagination boggles at" the thought of two grim, bespectacled American citizens, probably chewing gum, making oath that they have used no "sorcery or witchcraft" as a preliminary to committing mayhem on each other with wooden clubs. But the film-rights would certainly be worth a fortune.

Exeunt ambo. No tears are likely to be shed, on either side of the Atlantic, for the Appeal of Murder; but I feel that there was, and is, something to be urged in favour of the Wager of Battle when forming, as it originally did, the standard method of deciding all such Appeals. It could not then be used—as the Appeal of Murder afterwards was—to further oppression or extortion: whoever invoked it must be prepared to stake his life on the truth of his charge and the courage which that knowledge gave him. And it was the private citizen's last chance of getting justice in a matter which affected him far more intimately than it did the State. Since its abolition, the balance has tipped the other way. The convicted murderer may now go to the Court of Criminal Appeal; the heir-at-law of a murdered person has no redress whatever in the event of an unwarranted or perverse acquital. And there have been many such— even in recent years one can, without difficulty, call to mind murder trials in which the accused have been, to put it mildly, extremely fortunate.

In these days, if I were the near relation of a murdered person, and if I were to sit through the trial and see a man whom I *knew* to be guilty acquitted through the histrionics of some highly-paid advocate, or through the scrupulosity of some juryman's over-tender conscience, I should wish most heartily that the Act which made an end of the Wager of Battle had never reached the Statute Book: because I should feel that the Law, which I had always respected, and to which I had always looked for protection—or, failing protection, for vengeance—had played me false when I had most need of it. And, if I felt this strongly enough, I should

* I believe, in 1890.

be tempted to take the matter into my own hands, and to do with them what the Law could not do for me. In these enlightened days, such feelings will no doubt be stigmatised as very retrograde, and very anti-social: I can only plead that they are not entirely unnatural, not entirely cruel, not entirely ignoble—that, in a word, they are human.

NOTE: In describing the proceedings against Thornton, I have followed the report of them by John Cooper (Warwick, 1818), which I believe to be the most accurate. This was the one adopted by the late Sir John Hall in the Thornton volume of the "Notable British Trials" series. I have also re-worked most of the sources indicated in his bibliography, while adding a little information obtained from private sources.

The contemporary maps, in spite of asseverations to the contrary at the Warwick trial, are not trustworthy either for orientation or for distances. Fig. 16 is based on the modern Ordnance map of the district and is, I believe, accurate—but it must be borne in mind that the topography has changed almost beyond recognition in the past century. Much of what was then open country is now bricks and mortar—and the joint activities of a railway company and a golf-club have played havoc with the remainder. Almost the only identifiable landmarks remaining are the London–Chester road, the Birmingham-Fazeley Canal, Pen's Mill Lane, and Castle Bromwich church.

THE CANALS OF MARS

> ... But who shall dwell in those worlds, if they be inhabited? Are we, or they, Lords of the World? ... And how are all things made for Man?

To these questions, asked long ago by Kepler, there is no ready answer. Nor, indeed, is the need of an answer very apparent; they bear a family likeness to the irritating conundrums of which the Book of Job is full. With most of us, the living of our own lives gives us more than enough to worry about—and if we take an interest in the lives of others (outside our own immediate circle), it is fairly safe to assume that they are persons of some notoriety; and, at the very least, that they are, or have been, co-inhabitants of our own little planet.

Some, indeed (chiefly eminent persons of advancing years, duly impressed with a proper sense of their own importance), have stoutly denied the possibility of there being any form of life in any other world than this. Thus in the 'fifties of last century William Whewell, Master of Trinity, published a work entitled *Of the Plurality of Worlds*,* for which a better title would have been *"The Creator's Power Limited to this Earth, and the Reasons. By One on the Steps of the Throne"*. As has been said, it seemed planned to demonstrate that

> ... throughout all Infinity
> There is no one so great as the Master of Trinity.

It stung Sir David Brewster into the composition of an almost equally bizarre reply,† *More Worlds than One, The Creed of the Philosopher and the Hope of the Christian.* The antagonists were well matched; it is difficult, even after reading their works with close and painful attention, to discover which should be awarded the palm of ignorance in matters astronomical. Whewell was the more dogmatic; on the other hand, Brewster laboured under the handicap of possessing a firm belief in the literal inspiration of Holy Writ. Peace to their ashes!

In much more recent times the late Dr. Alfred Russel Wallace published a work‡ in which he attempted to show that "the earth is the only inhabited planet, not only in the Solar System, but in the whole stellar

---

* *Of the Plurality of Worlds: An Essay.* (Anonymous.) 1853.
† Published in 1854.
‡ *Man's Place in the Universe*, Alfred R. Wallace, LL.D., D.C.L., F.R.S., etc.; London, 1903.

214

universe". It is fair to add that he was eighty when he wrote it. His preface breathes a spirit of serene and inextinguishable self-satisfaction:

"Having long been acquainted with most of the works dealing with the question of the supposed *Plurality of Worlds,* I was quite aware of the very superficial treatment the subject had received, even in the hands of the most able writers, and this made me the more willing to set forth the whole of the available evidence—astronomical, physical, and biological —in such a way as to show both what was proved and what suggested by it.

"The present work is the result, and I venture to think that those who will read it carefully will admit that it is a book that was worth writing. It is founded almost entirely on the marvellous body of facts and conclusions of the New Astronomy together with those reached by modern physicists, chemists, and biologists. Its novelty consists in combining the various results of these different branches of science into a connected whole, so as to show their bearing upon a single problem—a problem which is of very great interest to ourselves."

Actually, the problem raised by Wallace's unfortunate book was this. When an eminent scientist, in his dotage, rushes into print upon a complicated subject which he is no better qualified to discuss than thousands of other people, and endeavours to prove a universal negative by a jumbled mass of theories and opinions selected (according to his preconceived notions) from various conflicting authorities, what inference are we entitled to draw as to the probable value of his work upon his own special subjects?

Moreover, the question of whether any form of life as we know it exists in other worlds is not merely complicated—it is one which cannot be solved by any amount of *a priori* reasoning. The conclusions reached in this way are conditioned entirely by the assumptions which one chooses to make.

If one adopts the attitude that life can only exist under conditions closely analogous to those which obtain on the earth, then it is not difficult to make out a strongly-reasoned case for supposing that such conditions are not exactly paralleled anywhere else in the Solar System—or, for that matter, outside it. Such is the method of Whewell, Wallace, and others.

On the other hand, if we can bring ourselves to believe that life is still possible in conditions—such, for example, as a total absence of air, or of water; or temperatures ranging from (say) red-heat to something approaching the absolute zero—which would be immediately fatal to anything which we should regard here as "living", then there is no difficulty in concluding that

> . . . there's not the smallest orb which thou beholdest

which is not densely populated. Such was the method of Brewster, and by
its aid he concluded that not only the stars and planets but also the airless
moon, and even the sun, were to be regarded as the abode of life. It is only
fair to add that a very great astronomer indeed, Sir William Herschel, held
the same view with regard to the sun.

On such a subject, then, theory is an entirely untrustworthy guide.
But direct observation is scarcely better off. The largest and most powerful telescope in operation, the Mount Wilson 100-inch reflector,* working
under the most favourable atmospheric conditions, would scarcely enable
an observer actually to see living beings (of any ordinary dimensions) in a
body so near to us as our own moon. Such feats are reserved for instruments such as the telescope (apparently of the Rosse type) erected by the
Gun Club of Philadelphia on the summit of Long's Peak, Rocky Mountains:† or that alleged to have been set up by Sir John Herschel at the
Cape in 1836,‡ whose powers were so miraculously assisted, in flat defiance
of all principles of optics, by a "transfusion of light through the focal
object of vision", and whose reported disclosures of lunar sheep, bat-
winged savages of amorous inclination, and tropical vegetation were, for
some time, greedily swallowed by many people who ought to have known
better.

If, then, analogy gives no sound basis and direct observation fails, must
we conclude that there is no way by which we can come to any conclusion
as to whether life exists in other worlds? By no means. We may, if we
wish, inquire of "the spirits". Here are some "revelations" upon the subject, supposed to have been communicated by Sir Walter Scott§ (of

---

* A 200-inch telescope of this type is at present under construction. For planetary
observations, however, a large reflecting telescope is not greatly superior to a smaller
achromatic, definition in such cases being more important than light-gathering
capacity.

† According to Jules Verne (*Hail, friend of my youth!*) in his *From the Earth to the
Moon.*

‡ The reference is to the once-famous *Lunar Hoax,* published, as serious truth, by
R. A. Locke in 1836. It was cleverly put together and, up to a point, convincingly
written. The book is very scarce, but a fairly full discussion of it may be found in any
copy of Poe's complete works, as an appendix to his *Journey of Hans Pfaall.*

§ One wonders why they did not call up Brewster; or, for that matter, Newton, or
Herschel, or somebody who might be expected to have better qualifications. In the
spirit world, apparently, celebrities, although obviously suffering from softening of the
brain, are always ready on tap.

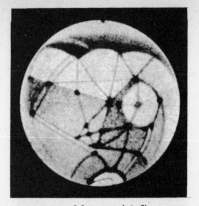

1920. MAGGINI (181°)   1920. PHILLIPS (182°)

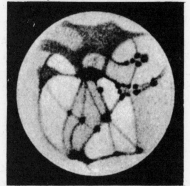

1922. MAGGINI (58°)   1922. PICKERING (58°)

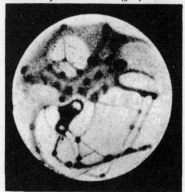
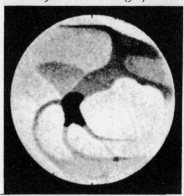

1922. MAGGINI (300°)   1922. PICKERING (299°)

DRAWINGS OF MARS, 1920–1922

By Dr. M. Maggini, the Rev. T. E. R. Phillips, and Dr. W. H. Pickering

The figures in brackets show the meridian longitude of the centre of the disc, which,
it will be noticed, is practically the same for each horizontal pair

The 1922 Maggini drawings were made with slightly higher powers, and better conditions of visibility, than the remaining four

Reproduced by courtesy of
Dr. W. H. Pickering

course, he would know) at a séance held in London on June 27, 1895. The medium was the celebrated Mrs. Piper, who professed to call up Scott at the request of Professor W. R. Newbold. Sir Walter is describing the sun.

"Well, now we move on towards this fire, now reach its borders, and notwithstanding the extreme heat we pass through it, and we find ourselves upon a solid bed of hot clay or mud. This is caused by gravity. Understand where we are; we have now reached the limit;* we find it very warm and deserted, like a deserted island. . . . Now we see what we term monkeys, dreadful-looking creatures, black, extremely black, very wild. We find they live in caves which are made in the sand or mud, clay, etc. Now, sir, for that I will be obliged to discontinue our journey until some future time."

At a sitting next day the medium, who may have tried to learn a little astronomy in the interval, had another shot, and attempted to explain that the scene described had been on the earth, not the sun. However, worse was to come.

"Prof. Newbold. What are the sun spots?

"Scott. This is the shadow of the earth, Sir.

"Prof. Newbold. You are thinking of eclipses. I understand this, but I mean the black spots sometimes seen on the sun?

"Scott. Oh, I beg your pardon, Sir; I did not understand your question-thoughts.

"Prof. Newbold. I beg your pardon.

"Scott. No, Sir; I understand now: the spots on the sun are . . . yes, Sir . . . are the so-called satellites which surround it; this produces a dark mass of spots."

On being asked about the climate of Mars, he replied, "Very fair: it is in the torrid zone!"

But, apart from these imbecilities, there is certainly one way in which we might be able to obtain evidence pointing to the conclusion that another heavenly body was inhabited. Our present instrumental resources are sufficient to let us scrutinize the nearer planets fairly closely; and if we

---

* So one would suppose: but the credulity of "spiritualists", unfortunately, is infinite.

detected on them any structures of an unmistakably artificial character, it
would be obvious that life existed, or had existed, there. By "structures",
I do not mean ordinary houses. But if, say, H.M.S. *Nelson* were suddenly
transported to the surface of the moon, she would probably be detected by
the Mount Wilson Observatory, to the great surprise of its Director and
the extreme consternation of Their Lordships the Lords Commissioners
of the Admiralty. *And if the Panama Canal were transferred there, and
filled with water (there is none in the moon), the same telescope would
probably show it in its whole length, and would certainly pick up the
Culebra Cut and the Gatun Locks. Indeed, it was suggested many years
ago, by (not unnaturally) a German mathematician, Von Littrow, that
we should attempt to communicate with the planets by outlining with
lights, in some such place as the Sahara or the Russian steppes,†
geometrical figures (such as Euclid I. 5 or I. 47)‡ of colossal size.
The proposal, however, met with no response. Its utility was highly
questionable, while its probable cost was sufficient to appal the most
stout-hearted member of the I.L.P. (which, however, was not then in
existence).

Now it so happens that on one of the nearer planets, and the one whose
surface can be most easily observed,§ many observers believe that they
have detected structures of an artificial character—the celebrated Martian
"canals". If we accept their observations and deductions, we must conclude that Mars is covered by a fine network of artificial canals, the work
of creatures of a very high order of intelligence and possessed of engineering abilities and resources much in advance of our own. These resources
they have devoted to what must be the greatest engineering work ever
accomplished—an irrigation system designed to conserve and distribute
their ever-dwindling water supply; a standing monument of a magnificent
resistance offered by intelligence to the cruel fate which must, ultimately,

* We must, however, remember the saying: "There is nothing the Navy cannot do".
I do not think that the Admiralty have ever contemplated operations in the Moon;
but it is a fact that in 1812 they proposed to send a frigate up the Falls of Niagara for
the purpose of reinforcing our squadron on the Great Lakes.

† With the same end in view, the Soviet Government has recently planted, "somewhere in Siberia", an equilateral triangle of trees, with sides 5 miles long.

‡ The famous "Asses' Bridge", and the equally famous theorem that the square on
the hypotenuse equals the sum of the squares on the other two sides. I am not sure
which of the eighty-odd known proofs of this proposition it was intended to employ.

§ The only nearer planet at any time (excepting one or two asteroids) is Venus, with
a cloudy atmosphere, and never well-placed for detailed observation. It is fairly certain
that the giant planets—Jupiter, Saturn, Uranus, and Neptune—are worlds in the
making, which are gradually cooling and consolidating. Mercury is subject to the
same observational obstacles as Venus.

overtake life in our own planet, and which has pressed more insistently upon the Martians because, so far as we can judge, their planet is both smaller and older than ours.

It is a fascinating theory, which admits of being worked out in great detail. For example Mr. C. E. Housden, in a work published in 1914,* has gravely discussed the hydraulic problems of the hypothetical Martian canal system. His monograph would, no doubt, be of considerable assistance to an engineer who contemplated applying for a post in this undertaking. But it is open to one objection of a rather formidable character. No clear and unquestionable proof has yet been given that the Martian canals—understanding by that word artificial structures of any kind—really exist.

It may be as well to recall a few facts about Mars itself. It is much smaller than our earth, having a diameter of a little over 4,000 miles.† Like ourselves, it revolves around the sun, but further off—some 50,000,000 miles further—and takes nearly two of our years to complete its circuit. About every two years and fifty days, on the average, Mars and the earth are in opposition—that is to say, in line, or practically so, viewed from the sun: but Mars' orbit is so eccentric‡ that the actual dates of these oppositions—which are the most favourable opportunities for examining the surface of Mars—and the distance between the planets on such occasions, vary considerably. In the most favourable circumstances, Mars' distance when in opposition is about 35,000,000 miles.

Now, as astronomical measures go, 35 million miles is not very much: it is, for example, less than half the distance from the earth to the sun, while in comparison with the distance of some of the nearest stars it is, as Sir Boyle Roche once said (or did not say), "a mere flea-bite in the ocean". But, at the same time, it militates very seriously against our examining the surface of Mars in detail. There are comparatively few astronomical telescopes now in existence which give as good a view of Mars, even when in opposition, as can be obtained of the full moon with the naked eye:§ and quite an ordinary single-draw hand telescope will give a better view of the latter than can be got of Mars with any telescope yet constructed.

---

* *The Riddle of Mars the Planet*, C. E. Housden, London, 1914.

† About 4,250 miles.

‡ It was this eccentricity—greater than that of any other planet except Mercury—which induced Kepler to discard the old theory that the planets revolved in circles: a step which led him to discover his famous three "Laws".

§ In other words, the apparent disc of the planet looks considerably smaller than a silver threepenny-bit held at arm's length.

The earliest telescopic observations of Mars (made with telescopes of small power) revealed, so far as can be judged by the drawings which have survived, very little real detail;* and Sir William Herschel's sketches, made with a large reflector not very well adapted for planetary work, have been described as caricatures. Beer and Madler (1830–37) produced the first reasonably accurate chart of the planet's principal features.

By the middle of the nineteenth century, it was generally agreed that Mars exhibited snow-caps at its poles which almost entirely disappeared, alternately, during the Martian summer of their respective hemispheres; that it had seasons resembling our own; and that on its disc could be traced large areas of fluctuating outlines, some being of a reddish-yellow colour, while others were darker, appearing of a neutral tint to some observers and a greenish to others. It was assumed that the former portions were land and the latter (which seemed to be united in various places by narrow straits) seas. Such, in general, was the state of areography (the mapping of Mars) at the time of the memorable opposition of 1877.

It was memorable for two reasons. Mars had for long been regarded as possessing no satellites,† except in the imagination of Swift‡ and Voltaire§ (both of whom had stated, long ago, that it had two). But on August 11–17, 1877, Asaph Hall, working with the Washington 26-inch refractor, succeeded in detecting two tiny attendants of Mars, which he very aptly named Deimos and Phobos.‖ They are absurdly small, Phobos being about a dozen miles in diameter, and Deimos about half as much: but, if small, they move quickly. Deimos makes his circuit in about thirty hours, and (the Martian day being much the same length as ours) stays in the sky for days at a time; while Phobos presents the unique spectacle of a satellite revolving round its primary more than three times as fast as the latter rotates, so that it rises in the west and sets in the east.¶

---

* It should be gratefully remembered, however, that drawings made by Hooke (1666) and Huygens (1672) have proved most serviceable in determining Mars' rotation-period, which is practically the same as that of the earth (actually, 24h. 37m. 22·67 secs.).

† Tennyson, for example, sang of " . . . the snowy poles of moonless Mars". He altered this, later, to " . . . the snowy poles and moons of Mars".

‡ In *Gulliver's Travels*. His (quite imaginary) details are curiously near the truth: in particular, he gives his inner satellite's period as 10 hours—it is actually 7½.

§ In *Micromegas*.

‖ Fright and Panic—the Homeric names of Mars' chariot-horses.

¶ During Scott's second Antarctic expedition, one of his parties had the curious experience of seeing the sun set in the morning and rise the same afternoon. They were a little west of 180°, and kept G.M.T.

It was during the same opposition that G. V. Schiaparelli,* of Milan, discovered a number of fine streaks on the Martian disc which had not been charted by any previous areographer. These he termed *"canali"*†— "channels"; a perfectly suitable term, not implying any artificial origin. That other observers, with better instruments than Schiaparelli's 8¼-inch refractor, should have failed to notice these "canals", as they rather unfortunately came to be called, seemed a little surprising, but it is now known that, whatever the nature of the phenomenon, most of the canals are best seen at oppositions when Mars is not very favourably placed for observers in the higher northern latitudes.

A few of Schiaparelli's canals were confirmed by old drawings made by such observers as Dawes and Green, on which indications of them could be traced; but most of them had to wait for even a limited acceptance until 1886, when they were independently‡ observed by Perrotin and Thollon with the Nice 15-inch telescope. In the interim, it was generally supposed that Schiaparelli had been the victim of an optical illusion or of an unusually vivid imagination; and support seemed to be lent to this view when he announced that at the opposition of December 1881 he had observed that as many as thirty of the canals which he had previously observed as single streaks had now proved to be *double*, the two streaks running parallel. In certain cases a canal was seen as single one night, and as double the following night; while the distance apart of the pairs amounted, in extreme cases, to as much as 500 miles.

However inexplicable, this duplication was also confirmed by Perrotin and Thollon, and it gradually came to be accepted that the canals were not figments of Schiaparelli's imagination, and that the failure of observers in general to see them was due simply to the fact that they lacked one or more of three essential requisites which the Italian astronomer possessed —a good telescope, great skill in observation, and favourable atmospheric conditions. Opinion swung round, and before very long observers were competing as to the number, size, and extent of the single and double canals which they could find, and make room for on their Martian charts (see Fig. 18).

Easily the most prominent of these observers was the late Dr. Percival Lowell. Before he erected his famous observatory at Flagstaff

---

* Born 1835; Director of the Milan Observatory 1862–1900; died 1910. During the last years of his life he was totally blind.

† The term had been used, in like manner, by Secchi in 1859.

‡ So we must believe: but the canal-chart produced by the Nice observers is almost indistinguishable from Schiaparelli's own (which was available to them) and differs widely from more recent observations.

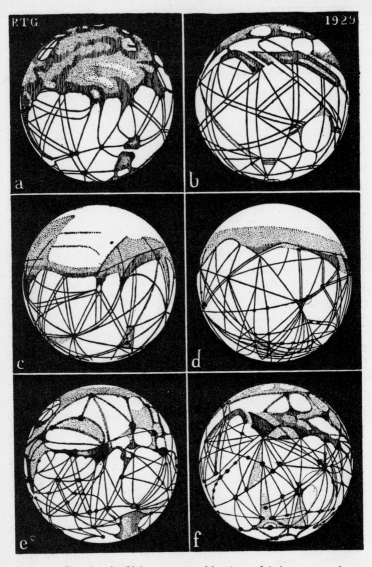

FIG. 18 —The Canals of Mars, as mapped by three of their most prominent
exponents

a, b, after Schiaparelli   c, d, after Lowell   e, f, after Maggini

NOTE.—a, c, and e show exactly the same aspect of Mars (merid.
longitude 0°): so do b, d, and f (merid. longitude 180°). It will be noted
that the members of each triplet differ very widely in detail.

(Arizona), Lowell visited France, Algeria, and various American sites, always looking for clear conditions of atmosphere. As he himself remarked:

"A steady atmosphere is essential to the study of planetary detail, size of instrument being a very secondary matter. A large instrument in poor air will not begin to show what a smaller one in good air will; when this is recognized, as it eventually will be, it will become the fashion to put up observatories where they may see rather than be seen."

He began his life-work at Flagstaff with an 18-inch refractor, to which a 24-inch refractor and a 40-inch reflector were afterwards added. Certainly, as regards instrumental equipment and favourable conditions for observation, his observatory had, and has, few rivals.

Lowell's results, which he embodied in a large number of scientific papers issued as periodical *Lowell Observatory Bulletins*, and also in three popular works,* were of a very remarkable kind, and it is not surprising that few were found who could accept them in their entirety. As depicted by him, the disc of Mars was covered with a perfect spider's web of canals, some 700 in all, of an almost rigidly geometrical character.† Many of the canals were duplicated (the components, in general, being strictly parallel), and at many places where one canal intersected another appeared a large dark spot (termed an oasis) usually of a strictly circular shape. Upon his charting of Mars Lowell erected and defended an elaborate argument, almost as ingenious and complicated as his canal system itself, demonstrating that the canals were unquestionably planned to serve as an irrigation system, and that they could be nothing else but the work of living and intelligent beings.

Granting the premises, his conclusion seems eminently reasonable. Many of his opponents wasted a lot of ink and paper in laborious attempts to show, as Whewell might have done, that there was no water on Mars; or, at least, not enough to fill the canals; or that the mean temperature on Mars was such that the water would always be frozen, and so on. To my mind such reasonings, even if sound in themselves, are beside the point. If the canals, as drawn, exist, they are almost certainly artificial. If they are artificial, then, whatever their purpose, they prove that there is intelligent life on Mars.

---

* *Mars*, 1895; *Mars and its Canals*, 1906; *Mars as the Abode of Life*, 1909.

† It has been suggested that Lowell's rendering of the canals was influenced by the fact that in early youth he was taught to draw in a manner which reduced free-hand curves to a series of short straight lines.

Actually, many of the *a priori* arguments have now been abandoned. Dr. W. H. Pickering, of Jamaica, who has devoted many years to the study of Mars, and who has organized a systematic and continuous examination of its details by various observers in different countries, has summed up the position thus:*

"I believe it is now time for planetary astronomers to change their views with regard to surface conditions on that planet, and adopt the position that not merely its temperature, but also its atmospheric pressure, closely resembles that found on the earth.† Heretofore we have doubtless all felt that it was possible that it supported animal as well as vegetable life, and even that intelligent life, if not proved, was not impossible. Now, however, we may perhaps say that with similar conditions to those found on the earth, and vegetable life assured, animal life is almost certain. Furthermore, if it, and if intelligent life exist there, as the straight and narrow canals seem to imply, then the evidence now adduced indicates that it need not be so very unlike ourselves as we have heretofore been led to surmise."

But Lowell's opponents—and a man of such outstanding personality and novel views was bound to make opponents—were (and, for that matter, are), on much stronger ground in questioning the objective reality of the canals *as drawn by him*.

We see with the brain, not the eye. The eye is only an instrument, and not a very perfect instrument at that; in fact, Helmholtz once said that if his instrument-maker were to send him a mechanism as badly designed as the human eye he would send it back, and decline to pay the carriage. The function of the brain is to put the right interpretation on the messages which it receives from the eye: and interpreters, however competent, are never infallible. It is often very difficult to determine exactly how much we see, and how much of what we think we see is supplied by our imagination; and that is the crucial difficulty in deciding as to the reality of the Martian canals.

The expert can see more with half an eye than the novice with two. Agassiz, the American naturalist, used to give a student some quite simple fossil to study, and ask him to say when he thought he had seen all he could in it. This usually happened in about ten minutes, after which Agassiz would show him something quite obvious and important which

* *Report on Mars*, No. 30, W. H. Pickering (Mandeville, Jamaica, December 20, 1924).

† This view has since found further support in observations made with thermo-couple apparatus in 1926 by various observers.

he had overlooked. The process would be repeated until (in about two days) the student had learned to appreciate the difference between seeing and observing.

Similarly, the campanologist can at once detect all sorts of overtones and partial tones in the note of a bell; refinements which the ordinary man fails to appreciate simply because he does not know what he should listen for. And the same, *mutatis mutandis*, holds good of all our senses— the right use of them no more "comes by nature" than, as Dogberry imagined, do reading and writing.

On the other hand it is possible to be over-subtle, and to get into a state of "expectant attention" in which the brain outruns the senses and reads into their messages more than these contain. And, in consequence, while it is true that a novice at areography might fail to see canals on the Martian disc which, to the eye of a trained observer, were staring him in the face, it is no less true that the latter might persuade himself that he saw canals where he actually saw disconnected marks which, he was convinced, formed a continuous line.

There is a well-defined limit, for any person, as to what he can see clearly enough to appreciate its shape correctly. Below that limit one tends to see objects, whatever their real shape, in one of two forms— lines or spots. And it must be remembered that in straining one's vision— as, even in the best conditions, one must—to make out the Martian canals one is putting a considerable tax upon both the eye which receives the impression and on the brain which interprets it. It is not surprising, therefore, if the result is to some extent, an illusion.

Perhaps I may be allowed, in this connection, to mention an experience of my own. The drawing of Fig. 18 necessitated a good deal of work under conditions somewhat resembling the actual mapping of Mars through the telescope. The original maps which I used had to be redrawn on the orthographic projection,* which entailed tracing the path of each canal through a set of some four hundred squares occupying an area of about four square inches. Each tracing was then reduced and inked-in, viewing it through the paper by transmitted light, in a darkened room. The work occupied about a fortnight, and at the end of this period I found that I was beginning to "see canals" in all sorts of places—in the foliage of trees, in the shadows dappling a garden path and, most curious of all, on the smooth and well-lit surface of a billiard table. After a few days' rest, this illusion—undoubtedly a product of eye-strain—disappeared.

* Schiaparelli's map was on the stereographic projection; Lowell's and Maggini's on Mercator's.

The late E. W. Maunder, in his *Are the Planets Inhabited?** has put
the case for the illusory nature of the canals very clearly:

"It is sufficient, then, for us to suppose that the surface of Mars is
dotted over with minute irregular markings, with a tendency to aggregate
in certain directions, such as would naturally arise in the process of the
cooling of a planet when the outer crust was contracting above an un-
yielding nucleus. If these markings are fairly near each other it is not
necessary, in order to produce the effect of 'canals', that they should be
individually large enough to be seen. They may be of any conceivable
shape, provided that they are separately below the limit of defined vision,
and are sufficiently sparsely scattered. In this case the eye inevitably sums
up the details (which it recognizes but cannot resolve) into lines essentially
'canal-like' in character. Wherever there is a small aggregation of these
minute markings, an impression will be given of a circular spot, or, to
use Prof. Lowell's nomenclature, an 'oasis.' . . .

"The above remarks apply to observation with the unaided eye, but the
same principle applies yet more strongly to telescopic vision."

Maunder, with Mr. J. E. Evans,† carried out a rather striking experiment in support of his views. A number of boys at Greenwich Hospital
School were set to copy what they could see of a design, similar to a map
of Mars, pinned to a blackboard. The design was tinted to correspond
with the general outlines of the Martian "seas" and "continents", but had
no definite lines of any kind on it. The drawings produced by the class
varied in a very peculiar manner. The boys sitting nearest the board
reproduced the design practically in facsimile. Those at the back of the
room did much the same, but of course less accurately. In neither case was
anything extraneous introduced. But some of the boys at intermediate
distances also thought that they saw (and accordingly drew) lines which
resembled the Martian "canals". It should be added that none of them
had any knowledge of the question at issue, nor was anything hinted as to
what they ought to see. But it must be admitted that, while suggestive in
its result, the conditions of the experiment were so different from actual
observation that, as Lowell pointed out, the fact that some of the boys
were mistaken in what they thought they saw did not prove that he had
been.‡

Still, it is difficult to escape the conclusion that Lowell's drawings, and

* London, 1913, pp. 102, 103.
† E. W. Maunder and J. E. Evans, *Monthly Notices, R.A.S.*, lxiii. 488, June 1930.
‡ He afterwards claimed to have proved, by a very similar experiment, that his
canals were undoubtedly no illusion!

those of his assistants and disciples, owe their peculiar and distinctive look to a convention which he adopted (consciously or otherwise); that, in short, he founded a "Lowell School of Areography". I have not seen any of the drawings produced at Flagstaff since Lowell's death in 1916, but much of his influence is undoubtedly to be traced in the Martian drawings of Dr. Maggini, Director of the Royal Observatory, Catania (see Fig. 18).* The "spiritual home" of a Maggini drawing is as distinctly Flagstaff as that of a Maggini violin is Brescia. In this connection a remark of Pickering's, as to the Maggini drawings published by him, is very interesting:

"He [Dr. Maggini] says for instance that he could make drawings of Mars closely resembling those of the other observers if he chose to do so. That is to say, their drawings resemble the planet as he sees it. He prefers however to add to the general outlines and canals that he readily sees, certain other features which are extremely faint and difficult, so difficult in fact that in order to show them at all on paper their intensity must be greatly exaggerated—exaggerated out of all proportion to the other detail. This of course destroys the resemblance of the drawings to the planet. This statement at once explains a good deal, and I believe really solves the question."†

It certainly explains a good deal, but it must be remembered that Lowell never made any admission of the kind. Yet the history of areography has many instances of structures—at first drawn in all good faith, as Schiaparelli and Lowell drew the canals and oases, as simple, regular, geometrical lines and circles—gradually becoming resolved, by patient examination, into finer and more complex detail. With the gradual advance of telescopic power, it seems not unlikely that even the larger canals, whose existence is possible, may be found to present a very different appearance, and that the smaller may be resolved, as Maunder suggested, into irregular markings. E. M. Antoniadi, whose work on Mars with the great 32·7-inch refractor of the Meudon Observatory near Paris is well known, has gone so far as to say:

"The conclusion is that if, by the canals on Mars, we mean straight lines, then they certainly have no existence; but if, by canals, we mean irregular lines of complex structure which have been produced by natural causes, then their existence is undoubted."

* It is fair to say, however, that Dr. Maggini has distinctly stated that he does not accept "the Lowellian theories of Mars".
† Report on Mars, No. 25, 1922.

And it may be recalled that while Lowell claimed, in 1897,* to have observed similar canal-like streaks on Venus, "perfectly distinct" markings, whose contours "had the look of a steel engraving", he spoke of the same streaks in 1906† as "hazy, ill-defined and non-uniform", while later he gave them up as an optical illusion—although, later still, he once more asserted that they were objective! Again, Dr. A. E. Douglass, who was Lowell's chief assistant at Flagstaff from 1894 to 1901, stated in an article published in 1907‡ that he considered many of the faint canals mapped at Flagstaff to be illusory. It may be added that Pickering has shown that, by using a very low power, it is quite easy to "see" canals on the surface of the moon.§

One might think that if, as shown by Fig. 18, there is so much difference in the drawings made of Mars, under exactly the same aspect, by different observers, and if there is, in consequence, so much variation in the maps of Mars based on those drawings, the obvious course would be to have recourse to photography. This has been done, but unfortunately the results (or, at least, such results as are generally accessible) are almost as difficult to interpret as the Martian disc which they depict.

The first photographs claiming to show the canals were, appropriately enough, taken at Flagstaff. After various unsuccessful attempts, Mr. C. O. Lampland, using a colour screen and with the aperture of the telescope reduced by a diaphragm, succeeded in obtaining a number of photographs, of which six were published in the *Lowell Observatory Bulletin*, No. 21.

To judge by Lowell's accompanying remarks, headed

"THE CANALS OF MARS—PHOTOGRAPHED"

the existence of the canals had been triumphantly vindicated. He says:

". . . The negatives thoroughly confirm the eye in showing not only the existence of the canals but the fact that they are continuous lines and not a synthesis of other markings. Beyond a certain magnification, if a magnifier be used to examine them, the grain of the plate will show. This must not be taken for discontinuity in the image.

Two points are worthy of notice:

1. The corroboration of the fact of the canals by the photographs.
2. The corroboration of the methods found most efficient to their detection visually.

PERCIVAL LOWELL "

* *R.A.S. Monthly Notices*, March 1897.   † *Mars and its Canals*, pp. 178f.
‡ *Popular Science Monthly*, May, 1907.   § *Report on Mars*, No. 6.

But at first sight it is difficult, on examining the photographs, to take them seriously.

To begin with, they are quite minute. The disc of Mars is just a quarter of an inch across. Three such discs, arranged clover-leaf fashion, could be covered by a silver threepenny-bit.

Secondly, they are not at all sharp in definition, and four of the six so dark that it is difficult to make anything of them.*

Thirdly, while on the other two it is certainly possible to detect the main outlines of some of the larger Martian continents—if such they be—it is utterly impossible to detect anything remotely resembling a canal. In view of the scale, no one of ordinary intelligence would dream of looking for such a thing. And yet Lowell claimed, quite seriously, that eight canals and an oasis ought to be recognized with the aid of a map of Mars. What was really needed was a pair of very rose-coloured spectacles.†

Larger and better photographs have since been taken at Mount Wilson, and at the Yerkes and Lick Observatories; but on those which I have been able to examine there is no vestige of any canals.‡ One could not expect to see them, for on the largest photograph the Martian disc is less than an inch in diameter; and, of course, they will not stand much enlargement. Lowell's, by the way, were enlarged $1 \cdot 4$ times, so that on the plate the diameter of Mars would have been $0 \cdot 18$ inches only.

It is fair to say, though, that photographs which appear to show at least some of the canals have since been taken at Flagstaff, although I have not been able to scrutinise any. I had some correspondence on this point in 1928 with an American friend, and subjoin a few extracts.

(*J. S. to R. T. G.*, 24.11.1928)

"I have seen these photographs,§ and there is no doubt that the canals (when I say 'canals' I really mean 'the markings that we call "canals"')

---

* It should be noted that they are actual positives, and not reproductions by any mechanical process.

† I think I ought to say that I have examined these photographs carefully, both with and without a Coddington lens. I do not need glasses (1929), and I will back myself at any time to write the Lord's Prayer in capitals, without a magnifier, on a disc considerably smaller than a threepenny-bit. [I took to glasses in 1941. Since then, I have repeatedly written the prayer three times over (in Latin, English and Greek), in capitals, within the disc of a silver threepenny-bit.]

‡ There are certainly one or two streak-like markings, possibly 3–400 miles wide or so—but nothing which in the least resembles the straight, narrow spider-lines depicted by Lowell.

§ The Lick photographs.

are there. But the best photographs of them are those made at the Lowell
Observatory, in Arizona. I have been there several times, the latest being
but a few months ago, and Dr. Slipher and his colleagues have shown me
their actual negatives. . . . I think that my experience is especially significant because I firmly believed them to be due to optical illusions until I
made my first visit to Flagstaff in 1923, and was not convinced of their
objective existence until I saw the negatives.

"So far as Lowell's interpretation of them goes I am still quite sceptical,
for I think it quite likely that these markings have some natural origin.
. . ."

(R. T. G. to J. S., 19.12.1928)
"Did the negatives you saw show any duplication? I ask this, because
to my mind the duplication is the *experimentum crucis*. And, if you could
identify any particular canal in different positions on two or more negatives, did it always appear straight, or did it curve, as a natural marking
should do, to an amount varying with its distance from the centre of the
disc?"

(J. S. to R. T. G., 18.1.1929)
"As regards the 'gemination' of the canals, I must say that I have not
seen this on any negatives. I have seen the statement that they have been
photographed in this condition, but I am unable to verify this from my
own experience. Nor could I say that the photographs of the canals show
them curved at the side and straight in the centre as a real marking on the
planet should be. However, the canals can only be photographed well, it
appears, when they are in the centre of the disc. The greater thickness of
the planet's atmosphere seems to obscure them when they are near the edge,
so that I doubt if this test could be applied very conclusively. Of course,
the drawings show them curved at the side as they should be, and I, for
one, am willing to accept as accurate these drawings by experienced
observers."

No doubt, many others will say the same, and quite justifiably so. But,
as previously explained, the trouble is that against such drawings can be
set a very large number of others whose provenance is equally unassailable
—and which, while they depict the planet under precisely the same aspect,
show no canals at all. The existing body of evidence from drawings, while
it is insufficient to settle the existence of the canals, speaks with no uncertain voice on at least one point. And that is, that such evidence is entirely
unreliable. The drawings, pro and con, cancel each other out, and any

conclusion based upon them is really determined by the selection of the mappings on which one decides to pin one's faith. It is this regrettable, but not incomprehensible, fact which makes it so vitally necessary to obtain, if possible, clear photographs of at least a good many of the canals.

It is not, as a matter of fact, absolutely certain that, with our present photographic methods, we should be able to say with confidence that if a canal appeared as such on the plate it was so in reality. It seems possible that, when dealing with faint detail not far from the limit of visibility, detached spots may run together, so to speak, in the lens as they do in the eye; and there is, moreover, the grain of the emulsion to consider. It might be thought that we could avoid this by taking our photographs on silver, after the manner of the old daguerreotype; but, unfortunately, a long exposure (such, for example, as is used for photographing faint stars) is out of the question by reason of Mars' rotation. However, the problem is one which we may legitimately hope to see solved in a comparatively short time; and, whether the famous canals are proved to be real, or partly real and partly illusory, or wholly illusion, there can, I think, be only one opinion as to the skill and devotion shown by the many astronomers who have already done so much towards the solution of one of the most fascinating of the many astronomical enigmas.

POSTSCRIPT

A novel and interesting theory respecting the origin—wholly, or in part—of Schiaparelli's "canals" was communicated to me in November, 1944, by Dr. G. S. Brock, F.R.S.E. He draws attention to the possibility that some or all of the appearances which the Italian astronomer believed that he had discovered on the Martian disc were actually situated *in the lens of his own eye*, and were symptomatic of incipient cataract.

It is undoubtedly true that in certain conditions of lighting an image of the lens of the eye (together with any defects which this may have) can be projected on to the object which its owner is observing. Dr. Brock informs me that this fact was first announced by an Austrian scientist c.1842, but was afterwards lost sight of in consequence of Helmholtz' invention of the ophthalmoscope some ten years later. He considers it quite possible that some, at least, of Schiaparelli's "canals" were caused by light from Mars, reflected from his retina, causing defects in the lens of his eye to be apparently projected on to the planet's disc—and, not improbably, blended with markings actually existing there.

INDEX

Aarhus, Denmark, 60
Abbot, Archbishop, 206n
Abbott, Judge, 207
Abnormality: in life span, 63, 64-65; in height, 63
Abominable snow-men (Migues), 23; possibly snow-bears, 23n
"Abraham Thornton Offers Battle," 188-213
"Abstract of Experiments to determine the Velocity of Sound" (Fisher), quoted, 37-38
Acland, Captain, on divisional signals of Tryon, 117
Acklin Island, 84
"Admirals" (sister-ships), 109
Admiralty: review of *Victoria* court-martial, 127-28; proposal to send frigate up Niagara Falls, 218n
Admiralty charts: identification of Watling Island as landfall of Columbus, 68; error concerning Santa Maria de la Concepcion Island, 84
Aelius Gallus, visits statue of Memnon, 30
Agassiz, Louis, 224-25
Agency, human, in mysterious disturbances, 104; *see also* "Poltergeist"
Agha, Zaro, Centenarian, 63
Ahasuerus, *see* Buttadeus, John
Air, occluded, as source of sound similar to that made by statue of Memnon, 34-35
Airy, Sir George B., on phenomenon observed by Parry, 39
Alberbury, England, 50
Albert, Jan van, 64
Alcester, Lord, *see* Seymour, Frederick Beauchamp Paget, 1st Baron Alcester
Alchemists, 137-87
Aldrich, Pelham, 124
Alert (ship), 118
Alexander the Great, 16n
Allotropy, and transmutation of metals, 185

All the Year Round, 172n
Amenhotep, *see* Amenophis III
Amenhotep, son of Hapu, erects statues of Memnon, 26-27, 35
Amenophis III (Amenhotep): statues of, at Thebes, erection of, 26-27; drawing of, 27; description of, 27-28; sounds emitted by eastern statue, 26, 28 ff.; reconstruction of, eastern statue, 28, 32, 34, 35-36; disappearance of original upper half of eastern statue, 36
Amphion (ship); at anchor off Beyrout, 109; remains at scene of tragedy, 123
Anatomy, comparative, ignorance of, until recent times, 15
Anchoring signal, of the *Victoria,* 110 ff.
Annual Register, quoted, 21
Annelids, marine, as source of mysterious light seen by Columbus, 90-91
Anson (ship), 109n, 133
Anthony, Charles, 50
Antoniadi, E. M., on Martian "canals," 227
Anyhow (ship), 109n
Apparition, of man on horseback, 96
"Appeal of Murder," 204-5; brought against Spencer Cowper, 205-6; brought against Christopher Slaughterford, 206; John Dunning on, 206; bill to abolish, 211-12
Appendix to Captain Parry's Journal of a Second Voyage, 36 and *n*
Arawak, as possible source of mysterious light seen by Columbus, 82
Are the Planets Inhabited? (Maunder), quoted, 226
Arithmetic, ignorance of, until recent times, 15
Armas, Juan Ignacio de, identifies Watling Island as landfall of Columbus, 69
Armour, outsized, found with bones at St. Bees, Cumberland, 16

"Last of the Alchemists, The," 137-87
Lavell, Mr., 192; finds footprints near
scene of Mary Ashford's death, 193;
swears that footprints were made by
Thornton's shoes, 194
Lavengro (Borrow), quoted, 46
Law, Edward, 1st Baron Ellenborough,
207-11 *passim*
Le Blanc, Mr., 188, 207
Leibnitz, Baron Gottfried Wilhelm von,
142
Le Maire, Jacob, said to have found
giant skeletons at Port Desire, 18
Letronne, J. A.: makes copies of inscriptions on statue of Memnon, 29*n;*
finds no Egyptian inscriptions on
statue, 33
Letters of Junius, Sir Philip Francis probable author of, 92-93
Lewis, Sir George Cornewall, refuses to
believe in existence of centenarians,
47
Lewis, Meriwether, on Barisal guns
heard at Great Falls, Montana, 42-43
Lewis and Clark expedition, 42-43
Lick Observatory, photographs of Mars,
229
Light, mysterious, seen by Columbus,
82; Markham's explanation of, 82;
Murdock denies existence of, 82;
Crawshay's explanation of, 90-91;
establishes landfall of Columbus as
either Cat Island or Conception Island, 91
Lightning, globular, as source of Barisal
guns, 43
Lincoln & Bennett (ship), 109*n*
Little Inagua Island, 80
Littrow, Joseph Johann von, suggestion
concerning method of communication
with planets, 218
Lloyd (or Flood), Jane, 2d wife of
Thomas Parr, 54
Lobachevski, N., 139
Locke, R. A., 216*n*
Lockhart, J. G., 132*n*
Lockman, J., 153
"Lombard-shot," as measurement, 73
Longevity, 46-65
Long Island (Bahamas), 83, 84, 85, 87,
88
Longitude, Parry's researches on, 36
Long's Peak, 216
Lough Neagh, Barisal guns heard at, 41
Lowell, Percival: seeks for ideal atmosphere, 222-23; Flagstaff observatory
of, 223; observations of Mars, 223;
opponents of, 224, 226; and "Lowell
School of Areography," 227; descriptions of "canals" on Mars, 228
Lunar Hoax (Locke), 216*n*
Luning, J. W., centenarian, 48, 49*n*

Macaulay, Thomas Babington; on science, 138; fails in mathematics, 138;
on Oxford University, 161*n*
McCarthy, Sheela, 1st wife of Thomas,
12th Earl of Desmond, 57
Machel MSS., 16*n*
Machnov, Fedor, 25, 64; drawing of, 24
Mackarny, Susan, centenarian, 48
Mackenzie, Alexander S.: identifies Cat
Island as landfall of Columbus, 67,
80, 81, 82; charts track of Columbus,
80-82, 81 (chart)
Madler (astronomer), 220
Magellan, Ferdinand: discovers Patagonia, 16-17; discovers gigantic Patagonians, 17; strangles Quesada, 17*n;*
gives name of "Patagones" to giant
natives, 18, captures two natives, 18
Magellan Strait, 17, 18, 19
Maggini, M., drawings of Mars, 227
Magrath, Cornelius, and Bishop Berkeley, 24*n*
Majestics, 109
Major, R. H.: identifies Grand Turk Island as landfall of Columbus, 67;
retracts opinion and accepts Watling
Island as landfall, 68
Mammoth, 25
Maneuvres, proposed, at Tripoli roadstead, 108 (map).
Man in the Iron Mask, 92
Man's Place in the Universe (Wallace),
214-15
Manuega Island, 92
Maps, early post-Columbian, scarcity
of, 71
Marius, 14
Markham, Albert Hastings: present on
the *Camperdown,* 109-10; on divisional signals of Tryon, 117-18; on
Tryon's maneuvres, 118*n;* message
to Tryon, delivered late, 120; anomalous position of, at *Victory* courtmartial, 124 ff.; opinion of courtmartial on, 126; opinion of Admiralty on, 127

Rickard, H. H., 124

Riemann, G. B. F., 139

Riolan, Jean, exposes "Teutobochtus" hoax, 14

Rivers, William, 101; on mysterious bell-ringings at Greenwich Hospital, 102

Robinson, C. G., 124

Roche, Sir Boyle, 219

Rodney (ship), 109*n*

Roquette, de la (translator of Navarrete's *Colecion de los Viages ...*), identifies Cat Island as landfall of Columbus, 67

Ros, Amanda McKittrick, 142

Royal Navy, The (Clowes), 129

Royal Society, 152

Royal Sovereigns, 109

Rum Island (or Rum Cay), 83-84, 88-89, 91*n*

Rupert (ship), 109*n*

R.U.R. (Kapek), quoted, 25

Russia, baseless reports of longevity in, 55

Sabina, consort of Emperor Hadrian, fails to hear sound made by statue of Memnon, 34

Saccheri (mathematician), 139*n*

St. Antoine, 13

St. Germain, Comte de, 147

"Salt of Life," 172-73

Salverte, explanation of sound made by statue of Memnon, 31 and *n*

Samana Island: considered by G. V. Fox to be landfall of Columbus, 68, 85, distinguished from Guanahani, 74; topography compared with Columbus' description of Guanahani, 76, 77; other island visible from, 78

Samaot, *see* Isabela Island

Sampford Rectory, mysterious bell-ringing at, 101

Samsoe, Count Danneskiold: becomes patron of Drakenberg, 60

Sand, Mr., 16

Sandstone, used in statue of Memnon, 28

San Salvador (island): discovered by Columbus, 66; confusion as to true identity of, 71-72; possible methods of identification, 72 ff.; visited by Ponce de Leon, 92

Sans Pareil (ship), at anchor off Beyrout, 109

Santa Maria (ship), 66-91 *passim*

Santa Maria de la Concepcion (island), 78

Saometo, *see* Isabela Island

Sarmiento, Pedro, sees giant Patagonians, 18

Satellites, of Mars, discovery of, 220

Saturr. (planet), 218*n*

Schiaparelli, G. V.: discovers *canali* (channels) on Mars, 221; Brock's theory concerning, 231

Schott, C. A., investigates probable variation in Bahamas in 1492, 73

Schouten, Wilhelm, said to have found giant skeletons at Port Desire, 18

Schurr, H. S.: on Barisal guns, 43-44

Schweikart (mathematician), 139

Scotland, Barisal guns heard in, 41

Scott, G. B.: on Barisal guns heard in Sundarbans, 40; on Barisal guns heard at Chilmari, 40-41

Scott, Sir Walter, séance with, 216-17

Sea, Barisal guns heard, 43

Semler, Johann Salomo: alchemical experiments of, 172-73; deception of, 172, 173

Septimius Severus, Emperor, fails to hear sound made by statue of Memnon, 34, 35

Serpent (ship), 135

Setebos (Patagonian deity), 18

Seward, Wm., 153

Seymour, Frederick Beauchamp Paget, 1st Baron Alcester, 110*n*

Sharphy, William, centenarian, 48

Shakespeare, William, quoted, 49*n*

Shawe, Mrs., 103

Shelley, Percy Bysshe, 36*n*

Short View of the State of Ireland (Harrington), quoted, 56

Signal Guns of Gungapore, The (Drury), 44

Size, physical, structural limit of, 25

Skeleton(s): found at Willisau, 13; found near castle of Chaumont, 13-14; found at Gloucester, 15; found at St. Bees, Cumberland, 16; found at Port Desire, 18

Sloth, giant (Mylodon), thought to survive in Patagonia, 23

Smith, A. (English traveler), claims to have heard sound made by statue of Memnon, 29-30

Smith, "Rainy-day," records instances of longevity, 48